To Betty
The best .....
Bill Turner
November 7, 2001

William W. Turner

REARVIEW MIRROR
Looking Back at the FBI, the CIA and Other Tails

PENMARIN BOOKS

Granite Bay, California

Parts of this book have appeared in different forms in *The Nation, Playboy, Penthouse, New West, The Progressive, Ramparts, Scanlon's Monthly* and *Pageant.*

Editorial Offices:	*Sales and Customer Service Offices:*
Penmarin Books	Midpoint Trade Books
2011 Ashridge Way	27 W. 20th Street, Suite 1102
Granite Bay, CA 95746	New York, NY 10011
	(212) 727-0190

Penmarin Books are available at special discounts for bulk purchases for premiums, sales promotions, or education. For details, contact the Publisher. On your letterhead, include information concerning the intended use of the books and how many you wish to purchase.

Visit our Website at **www.penmarin.com** for more information about this and other exciting titles.

Printed in Canada
1 2 3 4 5 6 7 8 9 10   05 04 03 02 01

Library of Congress Cataloging-in-Publication Data
Turner, William W.
       Rearview mirror : looking back at the FBI, the CIA, and other tails / by William W. Turner.
           p. cm.
       Includes index.
       ISBN 1-883955-21-1
       1. Turner, William W. 2. United States. Federal Bureau of Investigation—Officials and employees—Biography. 3. United States. Federal Bureau of Investigation—Corrupt practices. 4. United States. Central Intelligence Agency—Corrupt practices. 5. Subversive activities—United States—History. 6. Espionage, American—History. I. Title
HV7911.T89 A3 2001
327.1273—dc21   2001021225

To

MARGARET

who put up with all this

Contents

CONTENTS

Acknowledgments

It would be impossible to list the names of all those who have overtly or covertly helped over the span of a long career, although many have been singled out in previous books. There are a number who are specific to *Rearview Mirrow*.

The idea of writing the book in the first place was not mine but was suggested by lecture audiences who felt that a full memoir was in order. Early encouragement came from Steve Wasserman, a former journalistic colleague who now is editor of the *Los Angeles Times Book Review*, and Al Navis and Andrew Winiarczyk, booksellers specializing in the intelligence community.

Thanks, Oliver Stone, for your generous words in the foreword, and Studs Terkel for spurring me on over the years to speak out about the FBI. It is with gratitude that I remember the late Jim Rose, a rehabilitated CIA aviator whose prodigious memory refreshed my own on incidents that take up many pages of the book. Many thanks to Joan Mellen, author of *Hellman and Hammett*, for her kind comments on the first draft, particularly as it refers to Jim Garrison and his investigation into JFK's death.

Kudos to the estimable Ron Bryant and Cuban exile historian Gordon Winslow for their expert assistance with the photographs.

An emphatic *merci* to my literary agent, Rosalie Siegel, without whose enthusiastic boostering *Rearview Mirror* would still be a manuscript in a drawer. And my appreciation to publisher Hal Lockwood of Penmarin Books, a small press giant who believed in it.

Foreword

As a filmmaker and a student of history, I am indebted to Bill Turner's collected writings. His series of articles for *Ramparts* on the Jim Garrison investigation—rich with insight and details—were invaluable to my film, *JFK*. While the national media pilloried Garrison both personally and professionally, Turner gave Garrison and his case a fair hearing, checking out Garrison's leads, reexamining the case against Oswald and, most of all, taking the time to understand the political intricacies of New Orleans in the 1960s.

Turner's stories, like movies, work in three dimensions. A complex bureaucratic paper chase becomes a tale of human foibles and agendas. Names, dates and places are imbued with personalities, back stories and, most of all, Turner's marvelous eye for humor and the human condition. The most simple questions, often ignored or obscured, are brought to the forefront: What really happened? Who is responsible? What can we do about it? And despite the relative lack of happy endings in Turner's pieces, the reader comes away empowered, with renewed understanding that history and politics belong not to some select few but to all of us.

At a time when journalism is a profession increasingly dominated by self-interested egos and armchair critics, Bill Turner's writing remains exemplary of his craft's most vital qualities: truth, compassion and humor.

OLIVER STONE

Introduction

When I reported for duty as an FBI special agent on February 5, 1951, I had not the faintest notion that I was beginning a long day's journey into night. The journey would take me through the dark alleys of the intelligence agency underworld, baring its bastardized power. It would culminate in FBI publicist Thomas Bishop labeling me "that son of a bitch," while playwright Donald Freed called me "the Daniel Ellsberg of the anti-police state movement."

All I knew on that Monday morning was that I had been accepted by the paramount law enforcement agency under the vaunted J. Edgar Hoover, and was proud of it. The Eisenhower years were about to start, the Cold War was in full frigidity, people were buying backyard bomb shelters, there was a hot war in Korea, and the demagogic Senator Joseph McCarthy was throwing his warm-up pitches. But I quickly found out that the FBI was a hermetic society of which the Director was the sole authority, and that the only way to get along was to go along. For ten years I went along, performing criminal and counterespionage investigations, pulling off illegal burglaries, and becoming a junior executive, and in doing so earned personal accolades from the chief. But I had grown weary of the cult of personality surrounding Hoover, his exaggeration of the communist menace, and his strange reluctance to tackle organized crime, which, in contrast with the FBI's usual suspects, such as a car thief wandering across a state line, was corroding the very fabric of American society. Since the Director didn't signal any intent to retire, I decided to decamp. But I did so on my terms, petitioning for a congressional probe of Hoover's administration and priorities. As the first agent to poke the tiger from inside the cage, my name was, according to former Assistant Director William C. Sullivan, on Hoover's "enemies" short list. The Bureau kept an eye on my every move, hoping for a slip. In time my FBI file accreted to seventeen volumes of some two hundred pages each.

Many of those pages were internal reviews of books and articles I had written, for I had turned in my revolver for a trusty Underwood upright typewriter to chronicle how the intelligence agencies were the tail wagging the dog of foreign and domestic policy. The deceit, obfuscation, bad intent and downright bungling in the intelligence swamp all were bubbling to the surface. The turbulent 1960s were prime time for investigative reporting. I covered the 1963 assassination of President John F. Kennedy in Dallas, focusing on the breakdown in security. Trained by the Bureau in bugging, wiretapping and breaking-in, I wrote about the rampant illegalities unjustified by any emergency need. With the Vietnam War in full swing, I felt morally opposed to it, and I joined the radical slick magazine *Ramparts*, which became a magnet for disaffected intelligence types. There were explosive articles on the CIA's penetration of the National Students Association as well as foundations, the press and labor unions.

This effrontery did not go unanswered by the agencies. Recently released documents reveal that when I was doing the piece on FBI negligence in the JFK case, Hoover coiled and struck back with a full-scale investigation of me that drew off agents from the assassination inquiry (but then, that was a lower priority since the Director had made up his mind overnight that Oswald had acted alone). He redoubled his efforts after I authored an article detailing how a 1930s kidnapping case that sealed his reputation as a gangbuster, that of George "Machine Gun" Kelly, was tainted by the framing of his wife, Kathryn Kelly. After an attempt to criminally ensnare me failed, Hoover scribbled, "It's a shame we can't nail this jackal." The CIA was equally vindictive, creating Operation CHAOS to pull dirty tricks on *Ramparts*. Briefed by an operative on what had been accomplished, a high CIA official quipped, "Eddie, you have a spot of blood on your pinafore." But it didn't stop there: *Ramparts* was burglarized by a private intelligence network acting as an Agency proxy, a cutout stratagem that is used to this day.

Hoover was so rattled that a former minion would blow the whistle on him in print that he thereafter ordered all agents to sign a secrecy agreement permitting the Bureau to censor any articles or books they might write after leaving. The CIA was a step ahead of the FBI in this regard, having long required that its operatives submit to scissoring if they ever wrote on the subject of their CIA activities. This of course restricted the flow of information to those in authority charged with watching over the agencies vested with police powers. But in the Hoover days no public official dared to exercise that authority. It was well known that the FBI chief was bulletproof because he possessed a huge repository of files on everyone who was anybody, revealing where the bodies were buried. Not so well known was the extent to which the Bureau riddled the publishing industry with informants who were in a position to kill or discredit offending articles and books. When *Playboy* magazine was set to run my piece on Hoover's obliviousness toward the national crime syndicates, for example, an FBI mole sabotaged it. When I submitted a book manuscript to G. P. Putnam's Sons on the FBI's hegemony over local police, a Hearst press mole close to the publisher dismissed it on the grounds that I was engaged in "rotten activities."

When I became a critic of the Warren Report, which adopted Hoover's precipitant judgment that Oswald was a lone assassin, he whined that I had acted solely to find fault with him. In truth, I was not making a career out of being contumacious but had carefully thought it out. I had vetted the report and its twenty-six volumes through the eyes of a homicide detective and found too many anomalies in the forensic evidence, too many credible witnesses who reported shots from a frontal zone—the now-famous grassy knoll—to ignore. This didn't diminish my admiration for Earl Warren, since he had been boxed in by having to rely on the FBI as his investigative staff. Recently the chief justice's grandson, Jeff Warren, disclosed that "Earl never closed the door on the possibility of a conspiracy."

As it turned out, the assassination inquest was revisited in 1967 by New Orleans District Attorney Jim Garrison, who deserves a fairer hearing than he got at the time. Demonized by a national media inspired in part by the FBI and the CIA, he forged ahead nevertheless with his conspiracy investigation. He asked me to help, and, as an insider in the DA's office, I knew he was on the right track. This conclusion was shared in 1977 by the House Select Committee on Assassinations. As committee investigator S. Jonathan Blackmer reported in a memo on Clay Shaw, the international trade executive who had been indicted but acquitted, "We have every reason to believe Shaw was heavily involved in the anti-Castro efforts in New Orleans in the 1960's and possibly was one of the high-level planners or 'cut out' to the planners of the assassination."

The ornate Elysée Palace in Paris is a long way from the marble-halled DA's office in New Orleans, but French President Charles de Gaulle spanned the distance when he endorsed a literary project aimed at promoting Robert F. Kennedy's 1968 campaign for the White House. De Gaulle, himself the target of a 1962 assassination attempt by dissident military officers, never believed the Warren Report (*Vous me blaguez!* ["You're kidding me!"] he exclaimed when told of its conclusion). The project, called *Farewell America*, was carried out by French intelligence with the imputed cooperation of the Kennedy inner circle. Since *Farewell* portrayed the conspiratorial forces it saw behind John Kennedy's murder, it was not surprising that a draft manuscript mysteriously landed on Jim Garrison's desk. But just as *Farewell* was on the verge of publication in America, RFK was fatally shot in Los Angeles. The project vanished as swiftly as it had appeared. But not before a French spook delivered into my hands the storied Zapruder film, taken by a spectator at Dealey Plaza in Dallas, graphically showing JFK being rocked backwards by a shot from the front, indubitable evidence of at least two shooters. How the French—or was it the Kennedy circle?—liberated the film from its vault at *Life* magazine, where it reposed without ever having been publicly screened, was not altogether clear. But *Farewell* had proclaimed, "The Zapruder movie belongs to history and to men everywhere." I tried to make that a reality by showing it on college campuses across the nation.

The shooting of RFK was a shock. I had run for U.S. Congress in San Francisco advocating reopening the JFK case with the slogan "Not to do so is not only indecent but might well cost us the life of a future president of John Kennedy's instincts." But I hadn't expected it to happen so soon, in the same 1968 California primary. Despite the exquisite timing—RFK was slain the moment he won in California and was poised to go all the way to the White House—I didn't reflexively judge that there had been a conspiracy. After all, the suspect, Sirhan Sirhan, was captured in the Ambassador Hotel's pantry with a smoking gun in hand. But then the LAPD's no-conspiracy wrapping began to come loose. It developed that the pair of heavies controlling the cops' investigation had been on detached duty with the CIA. More bullets were recovered than Sirhan could possibly have fired. The lethal shot to the head had been fired point-blank, which ruled out Sirhan by simple geometry. As Vincent Bugliosi, the famed Manson Family prosecutor who teamed up against the LAPD's version, hyperbolized to the press, "The time has come for us to start looking for the members of the firing squad that night." William Sullivan, whose FBI played second fiddle to the LAPD in the investigation, unintentionally punned, "The case had too many holes."

Shortly after the shooting, I interviewed an enigmatic figure who might have been an accessory before the fact. Jerry Owen was a fundamentalist preacher who billed himself as "The Walking Bible" because of his phenomenal memory and ability to quote scripture. I felt that his story of picking up Sirhan hitchhiking the day before the assassination was a fiction hiding a deeper relationship. Sirhan's notebook scribblings suggested that he had been under hypnotic influence—the Manchurian Candidate theory. I discussed this theory with Dr. Herbert Spiegel, arguably the preeminent American authority on hypnosis at the time. Spiegel diagnosed Sirhan, on the matrix of personality traits he had

displayed during a prior psychiatric examination, as so highly susceptible to hypnotic suggestion that he well might have been programmed
to shoot.

One of the institutions *Ramparts* uncovered in 1967 as a CIA money
pipeline was the Kaplan Fund. The IRS and a congressional committee suspected that sugar baron J. M. Kaplan was a major tax cheat, but
the CIA slammed the door shut in their faces on grounds of national
security. There was, however, a sidebar that was surpassingly intriguing: Kaplan's nephew, Joel Kaplan, was in prison in Mexico City, convicted of killing a business partner whose corpse was someone else's
and had set up Joel's framing by Mexican authorities. Posing as a relative, I visited Joel in the prison. This led to a liaison I set up to attempt
his escape. A number of schemes failed, but finally, on August 18, 1971,
one succeeded: a helicopter swooped into the prison yard and plucked
Joel free. With *Ramparts* editor Warren Hinckle, I rushed to Joel's Los
Angeles hideout and got the story. It seemed that his real crime, in the
eyes of the CIA, had been to use the Kaplan family's sugar and molasses mills in the Caribbean to benefit Fidel Castro, with whose cause
he sympathized. We wrote a book that fully described the entire political tale, which became the motion picture *Breakout*, starring Charles
Bronson as the smuggler who engineered the escape and John Huston
as J. M. Kaplan. But there was an endgame. J. M.'s attorney, the formidable Louis Nizer, intimidated Columbia Pictures by threatening legal action. By the time *Breakout* was released, all scenes implicating
the CIA had wound up on the cutting room floor. What audiences saw
was an entertaining potboiler.

Joel Kaplan's breakout was followed in June 1972 by the Watergate
break-in by a Miami CIA team moonlighting for the White House.
The involvement of the CIA team in the event put Hinckle and me on
the trail of by far the largest and longest Agency covert action ever
mounted from American soil. It was a difficult story for us to wrap our
minds around because of its sweep, but in the end we had a high-
definition picture of a secret war against Cuba mounted in defiance of
the Neutrality Act.

The secret war began in 1961, after the Bay of Pigs fiasco, with Bobby Kennedy, then attorney general and a "piano wire hawk," as its driving force. The Miami CIA station became the largest in the world. Functioning under the commercial cover of Zenith Technical Enterprises, it possessed its own camouflaged navy, which regularly landed infiltrators and sabotage squads on Cuba. But John Kennedy was playing a dangerous game, and the blowback may have cost him his life. By late 1963 he was on climactic parallel tracks. On track one, exile forces were poised in the Dominican Republic and Nicaragua for a second invasion of Cuba. On track two, the president was carrying on secret negotiations with Castro aimed at rapprochement, which was to be finalized "after a short trip to Dallas."

The secret war had its own blowback in the Watergate break-in of Democratic National Committee headquarters, which cost Richard Nixon his presidency. Under fire for continuing the Vietnam War, Nixon wanted to demonstrate that it was the dead Kennedys, not him, who bore the moral guilt. He set out to prove that JFK ordered the 1963 "murder" of Ngo Dinh Diem, the South Vietnamese leader who was the victim of a military coup, which led to the massive involvement of ground troops under Lyndon Johnson. But no such proof existed, so E. Howard Hunt, one of the White House "plumbers," forged an incriminating cable. And it was Hunt, the CIA handler of Cuban exiles in the secret war, who recruited the Miami burglary team. One team member, Frank Sturgis, told me that Hunt contended that the purpose of the break-in was to find evidence that Fidel Castro contributed to Democratic campaigns, which would motivate these veterans of the secret war. But that was patently absurd. It was my conviction that the primary intent was to find "evidence" of Kennedy chicanery. If anything went wrong, the CIA would appear culpable since the team was composed of its former hirelings, and one of them, Eugenio Martinez, who had carried out more than three hundred missions into Cuba, was still on its payroll. Nixon had no compunctions about compromising the Agency, which he distrusted all along because it had failed to launch the Bay of Pigs invasion while he was still vice president. On the

Watergate tapes he can be heard muttering, "The problem is it tracks back to the Bay of Pigs."

Nixon's downfall was triggered by the reportage of Bob Woodward and Carl Bernstein of the *Washington Post*, whose informant, "Deep Throat," spilled the innermost details of White House scheming. The pair has steadfastly refused to identify "Deep Throat" while he remains alive, but a lively guessing game ensued. A number of names emerged, most prominently Nixon's ambitious White House Chief of Staff Alexander M. Haig, and most recently Leonard Garment, Nixon's White House counsel, guessed that presidential aide John Sears was the informant. But from the clues dropped by Woodward and Bernstein, I am convinced "Deep Throat" was W. Mark Felt, whom I had known in the Seattle office in the 1950s when he was an FBI supervisor. After Hoover died, a month before the Watergate break-in, Felt, by that time deputy associate director, was for all practical purposes running the Bureau. He was in close contact with White House counsel John Dean and other Nixon insiders. The politically flexible Felt fancied himself heir apparent to Hoover, and subtly lobbied for the post. But in 1973 Nixon's caretaker director, William Ruckelshaus, caught him leaking stories to the press, including the *Washington Post*, and pushed him into retirement. For Felt, already in place as a *Post* informant, it could have been a matter of getting even. As *San Francisco Chronicle* columnist Herb Caen reported on February 13, 1978, "Ex-FBIer Bill Turner is certain that Watergate's 'Deep Throat' was former Asst. FBI Dir. W. Mark Felt, who wanted Hoover's job." Confirmation of sorts came much later when, as recounted in *Time* magazine on August 9, 1999, a young man who had gone to camp with Carl Bernstein's son, Jacob, was told "Felt's the one." If Felt was indeed Nixon's Judas, there is an ironic footnote. In 1980 Felt was convicted of conspiracy to violate civil rights by authorizing break-ins of the homes of leftist activists in Hoover's last years. He was given a full pardon by President Ronald Reagan, which prompted Nixon to send him champagne.

The stories and the stories behind them in this memoir are, I believe, absorbing and informative in their own right, and some seem stranger than fiction. But they have a common denominator: They are episodes in a chapter-by-chapter exposition of an intelligence mafia that flourished in the past, and not much has changed. So the significance lies in the axiom "The past is prologue." Hopefully, *Rearview Mirror* will serve as a template to measure what intelligence abuses are afoot today.

> *In a government of laws, the existence of the government will be imperiled if it fails to observe the law scrupulously. Our government is the potent, the omnipotent, teacher. For good or ill, it teaches the whole people by its example. If government becomes a lawbreaker it breeds contempt for law; it invites every man to become a law unto himself. It invites anarchy.*

> JUSTICE LOUIS D. BRANDEIS

1

ONE OF THE
BOURBON-AND-BRANCH BOYS

During his posting to Washington in the 1950s, British diplomat Kim
Philby dealt with FBI and CIA agents in the course of his duties. After
fleeing to Moscow—it turned out he was a Soviet spy—he quite nicely
expressed the difference in the type of men recruited by the two agencies: "FBI agents were whiskey-drinkers, with beer for light refresh-
ment. By contrast, CIA men flaunted cosmopolitan postures. They
would discuss absinthe, and serve Burgundy above room temperature."
The CIA ranks were populated with Ivy League types, tweedy pipe
smokers from the eastern establishment. On the other hand, the FBI
drew from more populist backgrounds. As often as not, its recruits had
gone to Catholic colleges, southern universities or Mormon institutions, all deemed safe from communist influence. Bureau officials dis-
dainfully alluded to the CIA director as "Princeton Ought-Ought" and
his brain trust as "high-domed theoreticians," while the CIA hierarchy
looked down its nose at Hoover as "that cop."

My background predestined me to become a bourbon-and-branch
boy. I was born and raised in Buffalo, New York, where my father
was the proprietor of a family printing business. I went to Canisius

College, a Jesuit school. At age seventeen, with World War II raging, I enlisted in the navy, who consigned me to the fleet marines for the invasion of Japan just before President Harry Truman ordered the atomic bombs dropped. Mustered out after turning down an appointment out of the fleet to the Naval Academy, I played semi-pro hockey as goalie for the Buffalo Frontiers. In 1950, after I graduated from Canisius, my hockey coach advised me that the New York Rangers had placed my name on their reserve list, which in those days was tantamount to being drafted. Playing in the National Hockey League had always been a Walter Mitty dream for me, so I was excited when sent to camp that fall with the Ranger's Kansas City farm club. But I wasn't signed, and it was clear that my pro prospects were dim. At twenty-three, with two years lost to the war, I was becoming senescent by hockey standards.

I applied for the FBI. Hoover's pay scale seemed lucrative: $5,000 a year as opposed to the $3,500 or so an NHL rookie made. As a kid growing up I had been fascinated by tales of the G-men pitted against the desperados who held up banks and pulled off kidnappings in the Midwest. I nearly didn't make the cut because I was two years underage, but that requirement was waived when a personal interview determined that I "exhibited poise" and was "quite cosmopolitan in manner," which by Philby's distinction should have put me in the CIA.

On February 5, 1951, I reported to Bureau headquarters in the Department of Justice building, joining forty-three others to form New Agents Class Number 9 for eight weeks of boot camp. We were brimming with anticipation over our reception, but as it turned out, we were treated like striplings entering reform school. After a brittle greeting, Assistant Director Hugh Clegg darkly declared that violations of Bureau rules, which he reeled off as if he had memorized a manual, would bring instant and severe penalties. He cited the case of an agent whose handbook had been stolen in a car burglary. "That agent is no longer with us," Clegg intoned. "Besides"—he was fairly spitting out the words— "he didn't even look like an agent." Heads spun, eyes in quest of what an agent didn't look like, and an air of uneasiness filled the room.

Later, new agents who had been Bureau clerks while finishing college counseled the rest of us on the subculture we were entering. Clegg, known as "Trout Mouth" behind his back, was intensely disliked by the rank and file, as were the many officials slavish to Hoover's distorted sense of discipline. It was explained that the hapless agent who was fired had broken no rule and the theft was beyond his control, but he was scapegoated because the Washington police had recovered the handbook and returned it to the Bureau, which, in view of their strained relations, was a capital humiliation. Anything that fell into the category of "embarrassment to the Bureau," the shibboleth used in disciplinary letters, was a cardinal sin, no matter what the excuse, because Hoover projected an image of perfection. In fact, an agent doxology had sprung up about the Director wearing a halo. An example of this is the story about the New York agents who cornered a fugitive at a subway entrance. A shootout ensued, and one agent was taken to the hospital with a leg wound. The next morning Hoover appeared before a civic group as scheduled. "Gentlemen," he began, "I am with you this morning even though my heart is heavy, for last night in New York one of my agents was killed in a gun battle." When the Director's words reached New York, agents drew straws to see who would go to the hospital and finish off the wounded agent. But stick it out, our informants told us, things would be better in the field. Just look out for periscopes because the submarines were out there.

It was customary for a graduating class to meet the Director, which turned out to be a ceremony equivalent to an audience with the Pope. Our counselors from the training section primped us like anxious mothers at First Communion. We were cautioned that Hoover considered red ties a mark of insincerity, so we wore other colors. They also said that he distrusted those with moist palms, so we were instructed to carry a handkerchief to wipe the right hand at the last moment. We were arranged in order of ascending height for the procession through his office, under orders not to initiate a conversation. Although sturdily built, Hoover was not as stubby as generally thought. But the bulldog mien—pursed lips, crooked smile, spatulate nose and fixed brown eyes—was unmistakable. When it was all over, the counselors were visibly relieved. No one had tripped on the deep pile carpet or been singled out as unfit. The carpet, I noted, was red.

Following a one-year stint in St. Louis, where rookie mistakes could be left behind, I was off to San Francisco and assignment to the "Clubs," the FBI locations used for monitoring wiretaps and bugs. One was in the downtown produce district fronting as a marine architect's office with blueprints visible in the window to passersby. In the basement, leased lines fed in from installations on local Communist Party functionaries, the party organ *Daily People's World* and other "security subjects."

In fact, there were so many lines feeding in that the San Francisco police thought it was a bookie joint. One night they burst in, withdrawing only after I flashed my credentials and explained that it was an FBI operation. The other "club" was across the bay in Oakland, high in a downtown office building. One of its taps was on Jessica Mitford, an English aristocrat turned Communist Party member (she later resigned). I overheard no party talk, but before long I was privy to all her habits, including a preference for Ipana toothpaste. But I had no idea what she looked like. A dozen years later, after leaving the FBI, I was mingling at a San Francisco cocktail party when I heard a mellifluous British-accented voice that I recognized from the past. But I couldn't place the face. When the owner of the voice identified herself as Jessica Mitford, by then a well-known author, I explained how I was familiar with the voice. Mitford laughed uproariously; it was a story she became fond of telling.

But indefinite duty in the "clubs" was not exactly what I had bargained for in the way of action, so I routinely requested to be rotated off. This earned me a disciplinary transfer to Seattle for "putting personal preferences above the needs of the service," but the real offense was that I had gone over the head of the San Francisco special agent in charge (SAC). This was not out of character, since in the navy I had famously disregarded the pecking order. Action was not long in coming: On March 12, 1954, I was involved in a shootout when three robbers wearing false noses and spectacles held up the Greenwood branch of the Seattle First National Bank, leaving one police officer dead and two wounded. But the Dillinger days were over, and bank stickups were by and large the metier of rank amateurs. So agents created the illusion of big-time crime.

I recall in particular the matter of Leroy Jefferson, who had been declared delinquent by his draft board for failure to furnish a forwarding address. The FBI's role was to find him and connect him with the draft board. Jefferson was easily traced, but when an agent knocked on the door of his apartment he slipped out a back window. Affronted, the FBI obtained a rare Selective Service arrest warrant and mounted a full-scale raid on the apartment, drawing a large crowd. When Assistant Special Agent in Charge (ASAC) Clarence Kelley, a square-jawed Dick Tracy type, boomed out for Jefferson to surrender, he meekly complied, incredulous that all the fuss was over his failure to keep in touch with the nice folks at the draft board. Once Jefferson had been cuffed and driven away, we all hurriedly drove off. So hurriedly, in fact, that Kelley was left stranded at the scene. He had to find a pay phone to call me to pick him up. He later went on to bigger things, becoming an FBI director in the post-Hoover era.

As for Jefferson, his future was a long stretch in prison, but not for the Selective Service infraction. The Federal Bureau of Narcotics had had him under surveillance as a major figure in the largest drug ring in the West. A few months after he was released on the FBI charge, he was quietly arrested in Los Angeles by FBN agents and the LAPD on felony narcotics-trafficking warrants, convicted, and sentenced to twenty years.

But the juxtaposition of the FBI's petty case with the FBN's major one jolted me into recognizing that Hoover was ignoring organized crime. In those days the FBI had no jurisdiction over illegal drugs, although Hoover only had to ask and Congress would have obliged. Instead, it was the FBN director, Dr. Harry Anslinger, who earned the sobriquet "that bastard" from the mob. Hoover camouflaged his negligence by launching with much fanfare a Top-Ten Fugitive program, but the criminal elite weren't targeted. As I recalled in a piece I wrote for the *Washington Post Magazine* of January 28, 1979, the FBI "kept its sights on the human tumbleweeds of crime: bank robbers, car thieves, freight car burglars, the whey-faced little men who passed bad checks in bunches, the hulking waterfront pilferers, . . . cheap thugs, barroom knifers, wife-beaters and alcoholic stick-up men."

When informants reported mob activity, I was instructed, "Put it in the GIIF (General Investigative Intelligence File)," a catchall for information on which no action was to be taken. I asked my supervisor, Julius Matson, why we were squandering resources on criminal tadpoles when the Mafia big fish went unnetted. "Don't mention the Mafia," he retorted. "Hoover doesn't acknowledge that it exists." At first I thought that it was because he had established his gangbusting reputation in the 1930s and didn't want to risk taking on the mob, which was a formidable and dangerous foe. That might have been part of it, but there was talk around the water cooler about the boss meeting with New York Mafia don Frank Costello, after an introduction by columnist Walter Winchell, on benches in Central Park and suites in the Waldorf-Astoria Hotel, where both were comped; the FBI chief was a heavy better on horse races, and Costello tipped him off on which races were fixed. So I wasn't surprised years later to learn how mobbed up the director's pals were. One was Lewis Rosenstiel, the head of Schenley Industries, who had donated the liquor company's stock to fund the J. Edgar Hoover Foundation, the stated purpose of which was "to fight Communism" (the foundation bought and distributed Hoover's two books on the communist menace). From their early bootlegging days together, Rosenstiel had been close to Meyer Lansky, the so-called chairman of the board of organized crime. As Lansky biographer Hank Messick put it in *The Nation*, April 5, 1971, "The overriding puzzle to the Hughes Committee [a 1957 New York investigative body created by the legislature] was Rosenstiel. How, they asked themselves, can a man be a friend of J. Edgar Hoover on the one hand and a chum of Meyer Lansky on the other?" Lobbyist I. Irving Davidson, who had ready access to Hoover's office because he represented the Director's crony, Dallas oil Croesus Clint Murchison, also had Mafia clients such as Carlos Marcello of New Orleans, who had ties to Frank Costello, and Pete Licavoli of Ohio, who contributed $5,000 to the J. Edgar Hoover Foundation. On annual "working vacations" to Murchison's resort, the Del Charro Hotel in La Jolla, California, with his significant other, Associate Director Clyde Tolson, Hoover played the horses at the Del Mar race track, also owned by Murchison. The Director got a free ride, Alan Witwer, the Del Charro manager at the time, told me. His tabs (one was for $1,900.00) were picked up by Murchison's Delhi-Taylor Oil Company and his Atlantic Insurance Company. Whether Hoover knew it or not, 20 percent of the Murchison Oil Lease Company was owned by Gerardo Catena, chief lieutenant of the Genovese Mafia family. Another Murchison buddy with whom Hoover fraternized was Dub McClanahan, a Texas oilman and gambler who was a business partner of Carlos Marcello. Also in Hoover's social set was Alfred L. Hart, a former executive of Gold Seal Liquors, a Chicago distributor owned by the crime syndicate's Charles "Cherry Nose" Gioe and Joey Fusco. Hart had moved to California and bought his own liquor distributorship and the Del Mar track, which he then sold to Murchison. In 1968, Robert Goe, a newspaperman serving as Los Angeles Mayor Sam Yorty's flack, told me how Cartha "Deke" DeLoach, his FBI counterpart, once dropped by his office and raved about his boss's wonderful friend, Al Hart. "My God, Deke, don't you check your own files?" Goe interrupted.

There was also a theory that Hoover was neutralized by organized crime because it had evidence that he was gay. Certainly the fact that Hoover was constantly seen with Clyde Tolson, who had risen mercurially through the ranks to become associate director, invited rumors of a gay relationship. At social functions agents were frequently braced with "The Question," the standard answer to which was a coy admission that it was an "unwholesome" bonding. In 1968, Chandler Broussard, a *Look* journalist, gave some context to the relationship. Broussard was briefly related through marriage to a dashing ladies' man named Guy

Hottel, whom Tolson had brought into the Bureau to act as a buffer between himself and Hoover on their recreational excursions. One winter the threesome checked into the Gulfstream Hotel in Miami, Broussard told me, to partake of the Christmas horse-racing season. After settling in, Tolson and Hottel announced to Hoover that they had female dates that evening. With that, Hoover flew into a tantrum, locking himself in the bathroom and banging on the walls. The burly Hottel had to break down the door and slap the Director several times to bring him to his senses. My impression is that Hoover was a misanthrope devoid of erotic impulses, that he was frigid, and that he felt no passion either way.

The only information that he was actively gay was anecdotal, from questionable sources. Author Anthony Summers was told by Susan Rosenstiel, who went through a bitter divorce with Lewis, that in 1958 she attended a private party in a Plaza Hotel suite in New York hosted by Roy Cohn, the Red-hunting attorney who was a closet gay, and that Hoover was there dressed as a woman. Although fairly certain that it was the FBI chief, Susan reported no Clyde Tolson, no anal sex. A transvestite is not necessarily gay, and it is quite possible that Hoover, if Susan Rosenstiel's account was accurate, dressed in drag at Cohn's behest. He habitually was subservient to his rich friends. Alan Witwer recalled that at a chili feed at the Del Charro Hotel, the uncouth Texas oil magnate Sid Richardson greedily finished off a bowl and turned to Hoover. "Edgar," he commanded, "get off your fat ass and get me another bowl of chili."

On a larger scale, in 1969 Hoover ordered three New York agents who had cooperated in the prosecution of Roy Cohn on conspiracy, mail fraud, extortion, bribery and blackmail charges summarily transferred out of town on Cohn's demand. Summers also wrote that mob courier Irving Resnick divulged that Meyer Lansky had "pictures of Hoover in some kind of gay situation with Clyde Tolson." But Resnick never saw the pictures, and their existence was never verified, which is not to say that Lansky didn't have Hoover compromised through his covert associations with crime syndicate bigwigs. As Summers also disclosed, in the 1960s the Royal Canadian Mounted Police, taping a conversation between a mobster in Canada and Lansky in the United States, were astounded to hear Lansky read from an FBI report that had been written the previous day.

I remain an agnostic on the subject of Hoover's gayness.

On November 14, 1957, there was an event so resounding that I thought Hoover could no longer duck the organized crime issue. Seventy-five Mafia capos and their lieutenants from cities across the country converged on the small town of Apalachin, New York, for a summit council to resolve a territorial dispute. The conclave was held on the estate of Joseph Barbara, on whom State Trooper Edgar Crosswell had been keeping a watchful eye. When Crosswell observed the assemblage, he called for reinforcements and closed in, bagging, among other capos, Santos Trafficante of Florida, Joseph "Joe Bananas" Bonanno, the Midwest rackets coordinator, and Simon Scozzari of Los Angeles. Some fled through the woods and escaped.

Although continuing to deny that there was a Mafia, Hoover reacted to the embarrassing headlines by creating what was called the Top Hoodlum Program, which turned out to be an artful dodge. Each field office was instructed to compile a list of the ten top hoodlums in its territory and actively acquire intelligence on them. But hoodlums weren't necessarily members of organized crime. The program was so arbitrary that in New York, Chicago and Los Angeles ten would be a short list, while in outposts such as Butte and Anchorage there would be not one of any stature. Tellingly, there was no provision for the field offices to exchange intelligence on a national scale.

Two years after Apalachin, in October 1959, I was on an inspection team that descended on the Los Angeles office. My particular assignment was to review the major crimes files and conduct a survey of the Top Hoodlum Program. There were multivolume files on those the agents considered the ten most devilish hoods in the City of Angels. Some of the intelligence had been accumulated through surveillance, records checks, plain old footwork and wiretaps, most notably on the Runyanesque Mickey Cohen.

But the most useful evidence had been lifted wholesale out of LAPD files. This was not surprising since Captain James E. Hamilton, citing the FBI's default, had established the Law Enforcement Intelligence Union, composed of metropolitan police departments across the country, whose mob specialists exchanged information on a timely basis. Once, for instance, Tony Arcado and Sam Giancana, then numbers one and two in the Chicago hierarchy, deplaned in Los Angeles after traveling under fictitious names, only to be trailed and questioned by the LAPD intelligence division. "Now everyone will know I'm here," groused Giancana. "I can't do any business, so I might as well go home."

One of the LAPD cases was, I thought, ready for a federal courtroom. Miami Mafia capo Frankie Carbo had tried to grab a "piece" of welterweight boxing champion Don Jordan by threats of violence against the promoter and his manager. "And when I mean hurt, I mean dead," Carbo said, spelling it out. There followed a series of meetings in Los Angeles in which Philadelphia Mafia figure Blinky Palermo and Los Angeles enforcer Joe Sica continued the threats, but the LAPD had wired the manager, Jackie Leonard, for sound. The case had federal scope and seemed like a slam dunk, so I recommended that the Los Angeles FBI office give it top priority. Two years later Carbo, Palermo and Sica were convicted of extortion and conspiracy in a federal court, and the sentences were stiff.

In 1997 the current FBI director, Louis Freeh, whose trophies as a New York agent included top Mafioso John Gotti, disclosed to Congress the cost of Hoover's negligence. "We cannot allow the same kind of mistakes to be made today," he testified. "The failure of American law enforcement, including the FBI, . . . permitted the development of a powerful, well-entrenched, organized crime syndicate [that required] thirty-five years of concerted law enforcement effort and the expenditure of incredible resources to address."

Hoover substituted quantity for quality. He would make an annual trek to Capitol Hill to razzle-dazzle the appropriations subcommittee, each year boasting that the FBI had reached a "new peak of achievement" in "statistical accomplishments," meaning convictions, fugitive apprehensions, fines, savings and recoveries. But the means by which the new statistical heights were achieved often twisted justice. In one case that was particularly egregious, a police officer in a small town reported that a man known as a fence was selling hand tools, screwdrivers, wrenches and the like, stolen from McChord Air Force Base, which constituted theft of government property. The fence assured the seven purchasers, who were mechanics, gas station owners and attendants, and ordinary citizens, that the tools were government surplus. We took written witness statements from them to be used as evidence against the fence, and they were uniformly anxious to help the FBI. But it was near the end of the fiscal year, and the pressure was on to arm Hoover with his statistics. Our supervisor took the statements to the federal prosecutor, declaring, "Here are seven more." The prosecutor assumed the group was implicated with the fence, who was already in custody, and authorized charges of receiving stolen property. The supervisor didn't stop there, however, ordering me to round up an arrest team but wait two days so that Fugitive Form Letters could be sent to Washington designating the seven to be, in Hoover's words, "fleeing felons." After two days we arrested them in their homes, but not before one of my impromptu team members tried to quit in disgust.

There was one comparatively minor case, however, of which I was extraordinarily proud. A Jewish survivor of the Holocaust had scraped together enough money to buy $3,500 worth of surveying equipment to start his own business. The equipment was stolen from a federal site, and unless it could be found, he was out of business. I canvassed all of my criminal informants, and one just happened to know who did it and where the equipment was cached. So I "stole" the equipment back and, without introducing it as evidence at the trial for fear of blowing the informant, obtained a conviction on a preponderance of circumstantial evidence. The perpetrator, a repeat offender, went to prison, and the victim got his equipment back. He was near tears as I unloaded it from the Bureau car.

But I didn't feel warm and fuzzy about apprehending a young Indian man who had been drafted into the army and deserted, which set the FBI to the hunt. I had played hockey and socialized with several Indians from western New York tribes and was the second white man invited to play in the Seven Nations lacrosse league, so I thought I knew a tad about the reservation way of thinking. I suspected my fugitive had become homesick and returned to his native reservation on the Olympic Peninsula. But no one there professed to know his whereabouts, which I understood, because many Indians viewed law enforcement as the strong arm of a subjugating authority. At the break of dawn the following morning, as I reconnoitered the area I noticed that the door of an abandoned shack, which had been open the previous day, was closed. Leaving my gun in the car, I approached the shack and peered in a window. At this moment the sleeping figure on the floor awoke and bolted out the door. I tackled him and drove him to the nearest jail, notifying the military police. It was another "fleeing felon" statistic for Hoover, but a dehumanizing experience for me. Years later, after the 1973 Oglala Sioux uprising at Wounded Knee on the Pine Ridge Indian reservation in South Dakota, I was able to make amends of a sort by training a "college corps" of investigators helping the legal defense team against the FBI. Tension hung heavy over the reservation, and on my first night, patrol cars drove back and forth all night in front of the small Indian home in which I was staying. My hosts identified them as Bureau of Indian Affairs "goons" trying to intimidate me.

I wanted out of the statistical nightmare, but I didn't want to be reassigned to the security squad, whose legal jurisdiction was limited to conspiracies to overthrow the government by force and violence. The squad's only target of consequence was the Communist Party USA, which was not a tiger but a pussycat. When monitoring wiretaps on CP members in San Francisco and Oakland, the only "overthrow" I heard was when they were talking about softball games at family picnics. Notes I took during in-service training in Washington in 1953 show that nationally CP membership had skidded from half a million before World War II to a measly 24,000, many of whom were inactive. The CP was so impoverished that the bulk of its income came from dues paid by Bureau informants. Yet some thirty agents comprising the security squad shadowed the local members, ordered taps on their phones, wrote pro-lix reports, and surreptitiously entered the homes of functionaries to photograph documents. In those early days of COINTELPRO (Coun-terintelligence Program) dirty tricks, which were intended as harass-ment, the squad bombarded their subjects with nuisance calls and anonymously phoned employers to reveal that they had a commie on the payroll. Some agents possessed a near-pathological hatred of their subjects. One, an ex–Oregon State basketball player, decked a CP member who objected to being followed too closely. The climate in which this thrived was created by Hoover, who was virtually paranoid when it came to "Commonism," as he pronounced it. In a 1958 book, *Masters of Deceit*, ghostwritten by his public relations department, Hoover contended that the Communist Party "is bolshevizing its mem-bership and creating communist puppets throughout the country." It was this kind of turgid nonsense that prompted poet Kenneth Rexroth to brand the volume "a work of literary flatulence." But when Hoover spoke, most people listened, and his redundant rhetoric on the Red Menace provided Senator Joseph McCarthy of Wisconsin the plat-form from which to launch his reckless attacks on individuals and in-stitutions. In my opinion, McCarthy would not have gotten as far as he did without a steady diet of FBI abstracts based on innuendo, gossip and unsubstantiated allegations fed to him by Hoover (from his Senate bully pulpit McCarthy was not held to legal standards of proof). In fact, they were social pals, both free-loading guests of Clint Murchison, who contributed generously to McCarthy's campaigns, at the Del Charro. The senator loved to pose with his arm around the Director, truly an odd couple. While Hoover imposed on himself a two-martini limit—if not a $2 one at the betting window—McCarthy was a grace-less sot who peed outside his cabana and jumped in the pool naked.

On the other hand, I considered espionage by the Soviet Union and Eastern-bloc countries a live threat, and when a slot opened on the counterespionage squad I secured it. One phase was surveillance of "legals," who were legitimately attached to embassies and consulates but were suspected of spying. The other was trying to ferret out "illegals," trained agents who had slipped into the United States and were living seemingly normal lives under fictitious identities while carrying out assigned missions. This was on the order of solving Rubic's Cube, requiring patient digging. For example, I vetted Canadian Pacific ship passenger manifests from the 1930s, hoping to come up with the name of an agent "on ice." And I checked death certificates for infants, since agents sometimes appropriated their identities. The Los Angeles office identified an on-ice agent to us after discovering microfilm in a hollowed-out shaving brush the suspect had left behind in a hotel. How many were out there was anybody's guess. On November 19, 1993, I was a panelist at a national conference on the JFK assassination in Dallas, discussing the intelligence links of Lee Harvey Oswald. The panelist who took his place next to me was slight of build, with a goatee, horn-rim glasses, turtleneck sweater and safari jacket—in all, a professorial look. I had never seen him before, but his badge read "Oleg Nechiporenko." Of course, Colonel Oleg Maximovich Nechiporenko, late of the Soviet KGB. In the 1960s he had been posted to Mexico City, the nerve center of Soviet espionage in the hemisphere, under diplomatic cover. In September 1963 he interviewed Oswald when he applied at the Russian consulate there for an expedited visa.

"Thirty years ago who would have thought that I'd be sitting next to an ex-FBI officer in Dallas?" the KGB veteran asked.

"Around that time, Colonel, I worked counterespionage on the West Coast," I said. "Is it possible we didn't find all of the illegals you sent in?" A wisp of a smile crossed his face.

"That is correct," he replied.

But in 1960 I firmly resolved to leave the Bureau. Three years earlier, I had handed in a letter of resignation to accept a job in private industry, but the special agent in charge of the Seattle office, Richard Auerbach, tore it up, saying, "Things are going to change soon." Over the years agents had hung on, encouraged by the latest rumor that Hoover was going to retire (the most redundant one was that construction on his retirement home in La Jolla, near the Del Mar racetrack, was beginning). Auerbach, a political protege of Senator Styles Bridges of New Hampshire, a consumed anticommunist, was so wired into Washington that he was called the "Director of the West Coast." By 1960, however, it was clear that his inside information was just one more rumor, and I resolved to resign. But I couldn't bring myself to write the customary "hearts and flowers" letter telling Hoover how wonderful it had been. I had ten years invested in the FBI and decided to redeem them by pressing for reform. I had no illusion that when the first critical word was uttered I would become an "enemy of the Bureau" to be blackballed forever. I thought of General Billy Mitchell, who had been court-martialed for advocating air power and later vindicated by events.

Hoover couldn't erase my credentials. In the previous year I had received something quite rare: three personal letters of commendation—one in an espionage case, another for developing an informant who tipped off a bank robbery before it happened, and a third for performance on the Los Angeles inspection. My annual performance ratings were excellent, and I had been recommended for promotion to headquarters as a supervisor (which I didn't know about at the time). When I ultimately petitioned Congress (the high authority on how a public agency discharges its public trust), I could not be waved off as a "disgruntled employee," the label bureaucrats pin on those who dissent.

At this point a serendipitous thing happened: I was transferred to Oklahoma City to replace a sound man trained in wiretapping, bugging and burglary who had quit out of loathing for the special agent in charge. The SAC was Wesley G. Grapp, detested by the agent corps as Hoover's most ruthless enforcer. As Auerbach put it, "Grapp is the only SAC in the Bureau I can't say one nice thing about." Two years earlier he had been dispatched to Oklahoma City in the wake of a rash of "embarrassments to the Bureau," and he cut a wide swath of suspensions and disciplinary transfers known as the Oklahoma Massacre. Grapp embodied all that was wrong with Hoover's Dickensian personnel policies. My plan was to poke the tiger from inside the cage by reporting to Oklahoma City and then, after a decent interlude, requesting a transfer. Grapp's reaction was predictable.

Sponsored by archconservative Senator Karl E. Mundt of South Dakota, he was tall with dark hair in a pompadour, a glowering mien, and a pompous air. I was aware of how he had hounded a perfectly decent agent, James P. Kelley, out of the Bureau. Kelley's offense was that he was an officer in the U.S. Navy reserve and refused to resign his commission. There remains a question how Hoover, as a young Department of Justice clerk, avoided military service himself during World War I. He would later say that he was doing espionage work deporting German aliens, although there is no evidence he did anything more than push a pen. After the cessation of hostilities, he obtained a reserve officer's commission in the U.S. Army, which he resigned at the outbreak of World War II when he decided he could be of more value to the war effort with the FBI. And he wangled deferments for his agents on the same grounds, but he was embarrassed when hundreds of them judged it more patriotic to enlist in the armed forces. Hoover viewed the defections as personal acts of disloyalty, and thereafter pressured reserve officers to resign their commissions. When Grapp pushed the point by peppering him with petty accusations, Kelley resigned from the FBI. But not before securing another job, a strategy I planned to follow.

While I was waiting to brace Grapp with the transfer request, I put out employment feelers. A New York agent suggested the Internal Revenue Service, whose intelligence unit was expanding, but I was reluctant to go with a tax collection agency. An ex-agent in Chicago urged me to talk with the CIA, which dispatched a recruiter to Oklahoma City. He gave his name as Byron Crosman, and he looked like what I had pictured as the quintessential CIA operative: tall and slender with patrician features set off by steel-rim glasses and short, graying hair, wearing a black pinstrip suit with rep tie, and affecting a cane to aid a slight limp. Harry Lime personified.

I told Crosman up front that I was going to contest Hoover's policies and soon would be a bearskin on his wall, to which he replied, "You'll notice that I didn't blink in astonishment." He of course knew all about Bureau personnel practices because so many agents had jumped ship and gone over to the CIA that Hoover angrily accused his counterpart, Allen Dulles, of raiding, and the rupture between the two agencies was impeding the exchange of intelligence (we were instructed never to contact the CIA directly; if we had any information of potential value it had to be sent to Washington).

Crosman proposed a slot for me in the Office of Security as a roaming countersurveillance technician checking for taps and bugs on U.S. embassies around the globe. When he forwarded the recommendation to headquarters, an official asked, "Does he know that the FBI will fire him if they find out his interest in us?" But it was a moot question because I dropped the idea of living out of a suitcase as a career. Subsequently, the bungled Bay of Pigs invasion in April 1961 sealed my decision to forego the Agency entirely. It was difficult to understand why the CIA was trying to violently overthrow a government simply because it was socialistic.

Grapp reacted in character when I asked for the transfer. "Do you realize the consequences of this?" he angrily demanded, firing off a memo to Hoover recommending that I be put on probation simply because I had asked. Hoover complied, ignoring the rule in the manual that explicitly permitted transfer requests, and, in a prime example of Bureauthink, claimed I was placing personal preferences above the needs of the service. Theoretically, Hoover's door was open to any agent who wanted to see him, so I sent a letter seeking a meeting without mentioning that I intended to raise the subject of organized crime inertia in addition to personnel matters. Back came the reply: "Due to previous commitments it will not be possible for me to see you."

It would not be until ten years later that a sitting agent would tell Hoover face to face that his priorities were warped. The messenger was William C. Sullivan, a rumpled intellectual who was assistant director in charge of the Domestic Intelligence Division. On September 30, 1971, following a bitter exchange of letters in which Sullivan argued that the Ku Klux Klan was a more formidable menace that the Communist Party, the two locked eyes across the Director's mahogany desk.

"It's very clear you have no faith in my administration," Hoover is quoted by Sullivan in his memoirs.

"Right," Sullivan retorted. "I think you'd be doing the country a great service if you retired."

Hoover would have none of it, whining, "I never thought that you'd betray me—that you'd be a Judas too."

Sullivan calmly responded, "I'm not a Judas, Mr. Hoover, and you certainly aren't Jesus Christ."

Sullivan's allusion to the Ku Klux Klan reminded me of Hoover's own attitude toward integration. Until I went on the 1959 Los Angeles inspection, I had never seen a black or Asian face either in an agents' bullpen or a clerical pool. In reviewing the fugitive files—hunting fugitives was a comparatively simple assignment—I found that one agent, named Jesse Strider, had worked on the fugitive files but had repeatedly overlooked leads to their whereabouts. With no intention of writing up Strider, I asked his supervisor if there was some reason for the lax disregard. Pointing to the bullpen, the supervisor said, "See that Negro over there? That's Strider. He chauffeurs the Director when he comes to Southern California." I subsequently learned that Hoover had black "agents" in New York and Miami dedicated to driving the Director's limousines. In Washington, Sam Noisette was a kind of batman to Hoover, handing him a fresh towel after he had used his private toilet, wielding the flyswatter (the boss had a phobia about germs and flies), and helping him with his coat. But not one of them had attended the FBI training academy, and bestowing the title "special agent" was like calling an elevator operator a vertical systems engineer.

Hoover had a plantation mentality, but when RFK took office and pointedly asked how many black agents there were, he got the message. Seducing the black journal *Ebony* into running a piece called "The Negro in the FBI" in its September 1962 issue, Hoover recruited Aubrey C. Lewis, a black, Notre Dame, All-American football player, and showcased him as the "newest Negro fledgling, one of the most promising men recruited for action," implying that a long line of others had preceded him. When an *Ebony* reporter asked where the other black agents were assigned, Hoover replied vaguely, "On cases in every part of the country." Pressed as to their number, he hedged that he couldn't disclose "the tricks of the trade."

Sullivan's volte-face was complete, for he had been an architect of COINTELPRO and ghostwriter of the infamous letter to Dr. Martin Luther King, with a taped intercept of a sexual tryst enclosed, suggesting he commit suicide. According to a Freedom of Information Act (FOIA) document, Sullivan was angered in 1969 when he arrived for a lecture at Cornell University only to be greeted by a student chorus of "We want Bill Turner!" Years later, after he was forced into retirement by Hoover, Sullivan called me to reveal, "You've been a target all along," number three on Hoover's hit list behind Quinn Tamm, a former FBI assistant director who championed the independence of local police from Bureau domination, and Jack Anderson, whose expositive newspaper columns didn't spare Hoover. Sullivan promised that the next time I got to Boston he would, over lunch, detail Hoover's entire campaign to "screw" me. I regret not having made a special trip. On November 9, 1977, a few days before he was scheduled to testify before the House Select Committee on Assassinations—he had overseen the investigations of the JFK and King murders—he was shot and killed by a high-powered rifle bullet while walking in the fields near his New Hampshire home. The shooter, the son of a state police official, stated that he mistook Sullivan for a deer. I was skeptical, since I knew Bill Sullivan didn't have antlers and four legs, but the explanation was officially accepted.

No sooner had I locked horns with Grapp than through the office door walked an FBI legend, Nelson "Skip" Gibbons, whose exploit in single-handedly unmasking a Soviet spy was recounted to in-service training classes as an example an alert, resourceful agent: Assigned to rural Michigan, he became suspicious of a man who had come to town to obtain a copy of a baptismal certificate at a Catholic church. The suspect took a bus west and Gibbons tagged along, radioing the Detroit office that he had a possible spy in sight and asking for help. The Detroit supervisor scoffed, so Gibbons continued on his own.

Suddenly, the suspect doubled back and made a beeline for New York City. It turned out that he was Kaarlo Rudolph Tuomi, an illegal agent of Soviet military intelligence; he had gone to the Michigan town seeking a new identity. Tuomi turned double agent, exposing his entire network, and in June 1963 headlines proclaimed "FBI Smashes Soviet Spy Ring." It was the FBI's counterespionage tour de force. Hoover gave the inside story exclusively to the *Reader's Digest*, which was virtually a house organ for the Bureau, but Gibbons was not mentioned by name. By this time he was long gone, Hoover memorializing his departure with the notation, "Good riddance to bad rubbish."

Skip Gibbons had fallen from grace simply because he followed his doctor's advice. Hoover had decided to shed some poundage in the interest of good health, and, in his typical arbitrary fashion, ordered every agent to strictly conform to a weight chart. At an annual weigh-in, Skip, who had played football at St. Bonaventure University and kept himself in top shape, was a few pounds over the chart's desirable weight. He was instructed to lose five pounds, but his doctor judged his weight "medically proper." For failing to conform, he was charged with insubordination and put on the "Bureau bicycle," a series of rapid transfers designed to pedal him out of the service. Oklahoma City was Skip's second stop in a matter of months. Grapp greeted him, "I'm going to give you ulcers," to which Skip's Irish wit flashed, "I don't get ulcers, I give them."

Skip joined forces with me in contesting Grapp's abuse of power, which prompted Hoover to pull off the chief inspector, Roy Moore, from New York and dispatch him to Oklahoma City. Moore's first move was to ask us to resign, but we refused. So he conducted a sham of an investigation, never leaving the office to check out our allegations about Grapp's high-handed treatment of local officials and an Air Force colonel, and retreated to Washington. As documents obtained under FOIA reveal, Hoover wanted to fire us on the spot but was deterred by the fact that both of us were military veterans, which would give us the right to a hearing before the Civil Service Commission. The Bureau never wanted to send its dirty linen to a public laundry. So it suspended us without pay, transferring Skip to Butte and me to Knoxville, an isolation play.

The Department of Justice was the next avenue of appeal, and the word Skip received from agent informants inside headquarters was encouraging. The new attorney general, Robert F. Kennedy, was brashly asserting his hegemony, giving orders to Bureau officials without going through the Director and barging into the gym reserved for the exclusive use of FBI personnel. It was rumored that the Kennedys would put Hoover out to pasture and replace him with Byron "Whizzer" White (who later was appointed to the U.S. Supreme Court). Possibly a push from the inside would help squeeze Hoover out the door. I sent a telegram to RFK explaining the situation and asking to see him. As it turned out, however, the Kennedys considered it impolitic to dump the Director until after the 1964 election. The return telegram from RFK read, "Suggest you contact Director, Federal Bureau of Investigation on this matter." It was sent collect, and I had to pay $1.45 for its souvenir value. Bobby knew how to be a brat.

The next level was Congress. Using Skip's name (with his permission), as well as mine, I wrote various members seeking a congressional investigation of the FBI to separate the reality from the myth. One missive went to Senator Estes Kefauver of Tennessee, who had held hearings on organized crime in 1951, in which I stated that Hoover not only refused to do anything about the menace but was hostile to agencies that did. I contended that "morale in the Bureau is at an all-time low," driving out the best and the brightest. In sum, Hoover was running an "autocratic empire isolated by myth from outside inspection." Similar letters were addressed to Senators Jacob Javits of New York and Henry Jackson of Washington as well as others with oversight responsibilities. An informant in FBI headquarters called to advise me that the members of Congress were forwarding the letters to the Bureau for comment, which they received from no less a person than Deke DeLoach, the PR flack who doubled as lobbyist. A sandy-haired Georgian with a reputation for bullyragging, he showed up in their offices to declare the whole thing an administrative problem of no concern to Congress. Meanwhile, the informant said, Hoover's strategy was to keep Skip and me confined to Butte and Knoxville in the hope we would resign. So I stepped up the tempo and tone of the letters, determined to bring things to a climax. Just as I was about to file a federal lawsuit demanding that the Bureau show cause why I was under virtual house arrest—I had volunteered to go on a civil rights "special" to Mississippi but was turned down—the informant phoned again with glad tidings. A letter of dismissal was in the mail.

Clutching the letter, I flew off to Washington to shop for an attorney. Number one on the list was the fabled Edward Bennett Williams, who had defended Senator Joseph McCarthy and Teamsters boss Jimmy Hoffa, among other celebrity clients (Bobby Kennedy had vowed to jump off the Capitol dome if Hoffa was acquitted; after the verdict Williams sent him a parachute). From a pay phone in a hofbrau across Pennsylvania Avenue from FBI headquarters, I dialed Williams's number and was put through to Vincent J. Fuller, a rising young attorney in the firm. "Come right over," Fuller invited. When I finished telling the story and laying out the documentation, he snapped, "Sounds like a Gestapo." Williams took the case pro bono.

Williams warned me not to expect to win a Civil Service Commission hearing, to which I was entitled only because I was a World War II veteran (Hoover had long since convinced Congress that his own personnel system was superior to that of the Civil Service), because the CSC bureaucrats wouldn't dare rule against the FBI. This was confirmed by my inside informant, who divulged that the CSC had assured the Bureau before the dismissal letter was sent that its allegations against me would be upheld. But it was not until years later, when I secured files under FOIA, that it became apparent how flagrantly the deck was stacked. On June 7, 1961, which was eight days before I received the dismissal letter, Assistant to the Director John P. Mohr, Hoover's handsome number three man behind Tolson, reported that he personally met with Edward H. Bechtold, the CSC's Veterans' Service Staff Chief, who after "a detailed discussion . . . stated he felt the

CSC would sustain our discharging Turner." Bechtold went so far as to vet a draft copy of the letter "and felt they would be satisfactory with one or two changes." The ex parte connivance was brazenly improper, but it was repeated by the CSC field examiner who presided at the hearing, Michael E. Sedmak: He confidentially assured Bureau officials there was no way I would prevail.

The experience of Senator Javits typified the frustrations Congress faced in trying to deal with the FBI. His aide disclosed that he had been incensed that his inquiries of the Bureau had been used as a basis for firing me. When DeLoach dropped by to argue the need for tight discipline, Javits shot back that he had been in the armed forces and understood the need for discipline, but in my case any such need had been drastically exceeded. He called me over to the Senate reception room after his famous Berlin speech, and we went over the issues again. "Well," he said, turning to his aides, "let's take it up with Bobby or Jack." RFK temporized that he assigned his top troubleshooter, John Seigenthaler (later editor of the *Nashville Tennessean*), to look into it, but there was never an indication that Seigenthaler took more than a cursory peek. The Kennedys were stuck with Hoover, and they had to stick by him.

So with the fix on, the CSC hearing was anticlimactic. It took place in a stuffy room in the CSC's old granite pile of a building, with outsiders, including reporters, excluded. The FBI brought in a gaggle of officials to rebut my charges to Congress. One was DeLoach, who was designated to deny that the FBI was soft on organized crime. DeLoach boasted that the FBI had furnished 1,588 pages of reports to a special group prosecuting the Apalachin cases, but when cross-examined about how much of this volume was of any use, his only answer was to glare at me and launch into a philippic on Hoover's glowing reputation and the agency's high esteem to the point that Sedmak felt compelled to instruct him to limit himself to answering questions. When I put in the record that one of the Apalachin prosecutors, Richard Ogilvie (later governor of Illinois), had deemed the FBI uncooperative and "outmoded in its operations," John Mohr branded Ogilvie "an enemy of the Bureau." Such was the fate of all who contested Hoover's FBI.

The FBI also used retaliation as a weapon against those who didn't hew to the party line, as the hearing brought out. Grapp had accused me of being unable to get along with Oklahoma law enforcement; in particular, the Ada Police Department. So I wrote the chief, Homer Gosnell, who replied by return mail that "we of the Ada Police Department have a lot of respect for you and enjoyed working with you very much." Gosnell assured me a warm welcome any time I could manage a visit. And he called the agent who succeeded me in covering his department into his office, declared that he considered me "one of the best agents that had ever called on the department," and if the Bureau held otherwise, they were sadly mistaken. As FOIA documents show, Gosnell's honesty riled John Mohr, who ordered an end to training of the Ada Police Force by FBI instructors and asserted that "the Bureau will not favorably consider any applications for the [FBI] National Academy from the Ada Police Department." Mohr was equally vengeful toward the Oklahoma City FBI female clerical staff, which refused to furnish affidavits critical of me, freezing their pay.

In due time the CSC did rule in favor of the FBI, although it kicked out a majority of the charges. It agreed that I had "shown a poor attitude" toward the FBI and its Director by leveling the charges, which implied that any government employee who blew the whistle could expect to be hung out to dry. Obviously, it had struggled with my contention that personal letters to Congress, upon which the Bureau based its entire case, were "none of the Bureau's business," meaning they were constitutionally protected. The CSC skirted this issue with a "short answer" that tenure in the government is not a right, which was the mantra of the McCarthy era. To which it added, perhaps with a touch of guilt, that I should not be barred from other government employment just because the Bureau wasn't big enough for both Hoover and me.

Ed Williams filed an appeal in federal court on the First Amendment right "to petition the government for a redress of grievance," arguing that "the right of Congress to information without interference from the executive branch" had been breached. The bad luck of the draw got us an unreconstructed Mississippian as judge, Burnita Mathews, who decided for the FBI without comment. A similar misfortune befell us in the appellate court, a three-man panel dominated by two wizened conservatives, one of whom retired immediately thereafter. The pair outvoted Judge Charles Fahey, a solicitor general under Roosevelt, who in dissent concluded that I had been discharged in a manner "inconsistent with the protection accorded by Congress . . . and by the First Amendment." That left the Supreme Court, where Williams filed for a writ of certiorari to allow a full hearing. We fell one vote short of the necessary four (Earl Warren sided with us). But Williams had committed a bad error that might have cost us the game: he filed the petition a day late, and the court was a stickler for timeliness. As a FOIA document reveals, the FBI was aware of the tardy filing and believed that its victory came gift wrapped. In its May 1965 issue, the *Yale Law Journal* commented that the failure of the courts to spell out what restrictions they perforce attached to communicating with Congress left "uncharted waters" into which government employees could venture only at their peril.

After Hoover died suddenly on May 1, 1972, Congress found the will to impose major reforms. For the first time, the FBI had a charter specifying what it could and could not do. And in recognition of how dangerous Hoover's empire building had been, the term of future directors was limited to ten years.

But Hooverism was so imbedded in the insular culture of the Bureau that it lived on. In 1988, racist agents in the Chicago office forged the signature of black agent Donald Rochon on a death and dismemberment insurance policy, pasted a photo of an ape over his son in a family portrait, drowned a black doll in effigy, and ordered unwanted merchandise delivered to his home. When Rochon complained, he was censured. As Rochon's attorney, Patricia Motto, commented after repeatedly failing to get the FBI to seriously discipline the offending agents, "You start to feel like you're dancing with Hoover's ghost."

Later that same year, a female agent (the first one was admitted into the Bureau after Hoover's death), Suzane J. Doucette of the Arizona office, protested to headquarters that the SAC had placed a choke hold on her and touched her "in ways that are very sensitive." Instead of checking out her complaint, the Bureau retaliated against her, and she was subjected to on-the-job harassment. After testifying before a Senate subcommittee in May 1993, Doucette was suspended indefinitely without pay; it took a lawsuit to force the FBI to settle with her.

The macho mentality endures in operations. In 1993 the Bureau, in a fit of impatience, set off a conflagration of the Branch Davidian sect compound in Waco, Texas, which cost the lives of over fifty people, including eighteen children. The preceding year in Ruby Ridge, Idaho, an FBI sharpshooter gunning for a hunkered-down civilian militiaman killed his wife, with babe in arms, instead (the Bureau tried to cover up by altering its report; on October 19, 1995, Director Louis Freeh admitted to Congress that he had made a Hoover-like mistake in simultaneously promoting Larry Potts to assistant director and censuring him for Ruby Ridge. These twin actions enraged the paramilitary right and may have motivated the 1995 Oklahoma City federal building bombing. In 1997, FBI Laboratory scientist Frederic Whitehurst blew the whistle on shoddy practices and the slanting of evidence against defendants, which threatened to taint criminal prosecutions, among them the Oklahoma City bombing. The Bureau reacted in Hooverian fashion, but public hearings sustained Whitehurst's charges, and the FBI was forced to settle with him for $1 million.

But whistleblowing remains fraught with peril. From 1987 through 1998, agent Joseph G. Rogoskey worked undercover on a secret operation where he allegedly "witnessed acts of serious misconduct and violation of federal law by employees of the federal government during the course of their employment." When his Bureau superiors refused to act, Rogoskey sought to inform President Clinton, Secretary of State Madeleine Albright and the House and Senate committees charged with oversight of the FBI. But Bureau executives muzzled Rogoskey by invoking the mantra of national security, which frequently is no more than bureaucratic security. Then they tried to discredit him by giving him a suspension and calling for a fitness review. He was threatened with firing if he failed the review, which could make it appear that he was psychiatrically disabled, the old Soviet technique for dealing with dissenters.

In 1961, however, there was no whistleblower protection. Following the CSC hearing, in which he testified for me against Grapp, Skip Gibbons was handed yet another transfer, from Butte to Anchorage. For a year the Bureau harassed him, hoping he would resign. Instead, the onetime hero simply decamped from Alaska. Inspectors found him back in Michigan, where he had uncovered the Soviet spy, Kaarlo Tuomi.

"What are your intentions?" they asked.

"What are yours?" he shot back.

Reluctant to fire the ex-Marine and wind up with another CSC hearing, the FBI gave him a medical discharge for "nervousness" at a pension of $250 a month. He went off to Jackson Hole, Wyoming, and became a certified ski instructor. I was fond of calling him the only government-subsidized, officially nervous ski instructor in the world.

As for Wesley Grapp, as long as Hoover remained in power he was untouchable. But when Hoover died and L. Patrick Gray took over as director, agents bombarded him with protests against the most ruthless officials, and he acted. An inspection team determined that Grapp, then SAC in Los Angeles, had bugged his own personnel and defied Gray's grooming relaxations, dispatching an agent whose sideburns he deemed too long on a nonsurveillance into the molten summer heat of the Mojave Desert in a car without air conditioning. Grapp was busted and ordered to Minneapolis as an ordinary agent. Roger "Frenchy" LaJeunesse, a senior Los Angeles agent at the time, told me he called ahead to see what preparations were being made for Grapp's arrival. "Don't worry, Frenchy," a Minneapolis agent reassured him. "When Grapp gets here he's being sent on a long road trip to North Dakota. It's cold as hell out there now, and his car won't have a heater." Perhaps sensing the fate that awaited him, Grapp didn't show up; he had his attorney negotiate an early retirement. When he tried to join the Society of Former Special Agents of the FBI, he was blackballed.

Gray's in-basket was also full of agent complaints against John Mohr, and he was shown the door. The Department of Justice investigated Mohr for using FBI employees to wash, gas, repair and service his Cadillac, among other personal services, and about sums unaccounted for in the agents' FBI Recreational Association fund. But he was made of Teflon, and nothing stuck.

In October 1971, only months before Hoover died, an historic Conference on the FBI was held at Princeton University's Woodrow Wilson School of Public Affairs. It was the first time in memory that any independent body, including Congress, had ventured to stage a full-scale open inquiry into the agency's policies and practices. Scholars, lawyers, journalists, police commissioners and former Justice Department officials participated. Hoover was invited, but refused to send a representative. I presented two papers, "The Inside Story: An Agent's Dilemma" and "The FBI and Other Police Forces," and took part in panel discussions. The papers and discussions were published in a book entitled *Investigating the FBI: A Tough, Fair Look at the Powerful Bureau, Its Present and Its Future* (Doubleday, 1973). It was studied in manuscript form by Director Gray and undoubtedly influenced many of his corrective actions.

But there were few fundamental changes. As Louis Freeh recently put it, "We have a long and unfortunate history to overcome." He was speaking of the Bureau's ingrained racial and gender discrimination, but he might as well been referring to the FBI as a whole.

2

JFK: THE BIG STORY

Less than seventy-two hours after John F. Kennedy was slain in Dallas on November 22, 1963, the night scene in Dealey Plaza, the site of the shooting, was unforgettable. I had flown in that day from San Francisco as the president's funeral procession rolled slowly down Pennsylvania Avenue in Washington, on assignment from *Saga* magazine to look for a story on the security breakdown. At the mouth of the plaza, I memoed my editor in New York on my portable Remington typewriter, is

> the modern Dallas County Court Building, its upper windows latticed with the grillwork of the jail bars. It is dark, and there is an eerie scene, illuminated by the high-mounted street lights and by the portable floodlights of the television crews. [Jack] Ruby has been taken here, and photographers, reporters and onlookers are waiting for the next development. And here is the Texas School Book Depository, diagonally across from the Court building. Its facade is neatly compartmentalized into sets of windows. One the right side, as one faces it, in the sixth set of windows from street level, can be seen the outline of a large box. It is said that the assassin lurked behind it, biding his time. At the curb, by the spot where the bullets struck, the citizens of Dallas

have deposited floral bouquets and corsages. At the Court building an ambulance wails to a halt—the large doors are raised to admit it. There is a surge of the press and the curious—another killing. "Sorry boys," says a bulky plainclothesman, "It's the fourth floor." The fourth floor, I learn, is the women's floor.

Upon arriving in Dallas, I had gone straight to Dallas police headquarters. Reporters from all over the world were on a feeding frenzy, hell bent to come up with a new angle. Flashing my press credentials, I was able to get in a word with Captain Glen King, the top assistant to Chief Jesse Curry. He absolved the police of any blame in not knowing that the suspect, Lee Harvey Oswald, belonged to the pro-Castro Fair Play for Cuba Committee, as had been reported in a wire service story datelined New Orleans. "Up until this Ruby thing," he said, alluding to nightclub owner and police buff Jack Ruby's fatal shooting of Oswald, "we were in good shape." King turned me over to Inspector Sawyer of the Special Service Bureau (SSB), an intelligence squad that "keeps a finger on the pulse of the town." According to Sawyer, the SSB concentrated on heavy hoodlums and prostitutes, turning over anything having to do with subversive activity to the local FBI. "They work 365 days year on that type of thing," he noted. The SSB had nothing on Oswald.

It appeared that Oswald had not tested the vigilance of the Dallas police. From the fragments of information coming in, he had been an underground man living under the pseudonym O. H. Lee in a nondescript rooming house in the Oak Cliff section. I was absorbed with that mystery when I spotted, in the milling throng, a familiar face. It belonged to Jack Flanagan, a senior agent from Oklahoma City who, two years earlier, had caught me early one morning Thermofaxing a copy of my initial letter to Hoover. He knew what I was up to.

"Hoover will crucify you," he counseled. "Why don't you go after someone like John Mohr?"

"No, Hoover's the one," I replied. "There wouldn't be a Mohr without a Hoover."

Jack had looked at me as if I was taking off on a kamikaze mission.

Now, in Dallas, he explained that he had just flown in on a "special" and hadn't even checked in at the local FBI office. We exchanged pleasantries, but I kept it short. I knew I was on the Bureau's "no contact" list of "enemies" and didn't want to compromise Jack by being seen together.

Over drinks with reporters at the Press Club of Dallas, I picked up some leads on the security breakdown story. A local brought up the name of police officer Welcome Eugene Barnett, who was stationed in front of the Depository Building when the shots rang out. I found Barnett directing traffic near the Adolphus Hotel. "If the moon fell on Dallas," the sandy-haired young man said, "it would land at my feet." He had been instructed to watch for troublemakers. As the president's motorcade swung past him, he heard a sharp report, like a firecracker. After about three seconds there was another shot. Dealey Plaza reverberated with the sounds. He looked over his shoulder toward the roof of the depository but saw nothing. The Secret Service men in a car behind the president's limousine were looking around, unable to fix where the shots were coming from. In what seemed like another three seconds after the second shot, a third sounded. A woman ran up to Barnett and yelled, "Over there in the bushes!" pointing to the landscaped flank of the plaza now familiar as the grassy knoll. While several policemen scurried in that direction, Barnett ran to the rear of the building, convinced that the first two shots had come from the roof and that the perpetrator might try to escape out the back door. But no one came out.

Barnett's account was intriguing in that it indicated shots from two locations, which meant at least two shooters. This was reinforced by his tight spacing of the shots. It didn't seem that the suspect could have fired three rounds in roughly six seconds with a bolt-action rifle fitted with a telescopic sight, which would have caused parallax. But I was in Dallas on a two-day deadline on the security story. The FBI had a definite responsibility to alert the Secret Service, which was charged with presidential protection, to the presence in the area of anyone who could possibly pose a threat. I knew that the standard procedure was to instruct all agents to contact informants and other sources to identify any such risks. Oswald, known to be a defector to the Soviet Union and pro-Castro activist, was on the face of it a political extremist. But a Secret Service spokesman I contacted, Jack Warner, flatly denied that the FBI had sent over a skinny (a background file) on Oswald. It had sent over a "risk list," but Oswald's name was not on it.

If not, why not? From a neutral phone I began contacting sources close to the FBI. One, Elmer Jacobsen, an ex-agent in Minnesota, had a source in Bryan, Texas, connected to the Dallas office, who reported that after Oswald returned to Dallas in October 1963, two agents, W. Harlan Brown and James Hosty, approached his mother, Marguerite, to obtain his address. She gave it to them and they interviewed him. Then, ten days before the assassination, Hosty interviewed him again.

So there was a scoop on the crime of the century: The FBI was in contact with the suspect but didn't tell the Secret Service or local police about his background. I rushed back to San Francisco to bang out the copy for the March 1964 issue of *Saga* in time for a press run in late January. What couldn't be included, since I had no evidence at the time, was that Hosty was running Oswald as a confidential informant. Several months later Jacobsen rather offhandedly mentioned that the Bryan source also had tagged Oswald as an FBI security informant, which would have been reason enough to withhold his name from the Secret Service. Jacobsen added that after the assassination, Oswald's FBI status had been given to the Secret Service in Washington. But there is no evidence that the Secret Service, whose chief, James J. Rowley, was an ex-FBI agent close to Hoover, ever passed on this vital bit of information to the Warren Commission.

In the meantime, Bureau officials learned that I was writing the article and were sliding down the fire pole to respond. As FOIA releases reveal, they had known for several months that *Saga* was doing a profile of me as the first agent to blow the whistle on Hoover. What they didn't know was that it had been converted to an assassination assignment. As Supervisor William E. Clark, who rode the "Turner Desk" tracking my every move as if I were a menace to the republic, wrote to Deke DeLoach, "we have been trying to follow this discreetly, although *Saga* is staffed with very undesirable people." What caused DeLoach to sit up and take notice was Clark's news that the New York office discovered from a source in the publishing industry that the forth-coming issue of the magazine would run my security-breakdown ar-ticle. DeLoach picked up the phone and called "a good contact of ours" in Manhattan who corroborated the bad news. Later that day, an advance copy of *Saga* arrived from New York, prompting the head spinmeister to notify John Mohr, "The cover prominently displays the article by Turner and a quick review of it reveals it is a strong attack upon the FBI." By this time J. Edgar Hoover had been given a heads-up. "Where is the memo of review?" he impatiently demanded to know.

But it was too late to try to thwart publication, so the Bureau shifted into a damage-control mode. Mohr called the Dallas office to order a full-scale probe that rivaled the one it was conducting into JFK's mur-der. Airlines were canvassed to determine what flights I had taken. A check of major hotels determined that I was registered at the Sheraton-Dallas from November 25 to 27 in room 1205, and was alone. Toll records were requisitioned to see whom I had phoned from the room. The registration card with my signature was forwarded to the FBI labora-tory for handwriting comparison. Such were Hoover's priorities that manpower needed on the Turner case was diverted from the investiga-tion of the assassination of the president.

The Dallas agents were also detailed to interview the three police officers quoted in the article. One, Captain King, recognized my photo as a magazine writer to whom he had denied that the police had any record of Oswald. His memory was vivid, he said, because afterwards an FBI agent from outside Dallas told him he should know that "the individual who had just left his office was an ex-FBI agent who had left the Bureau under a cloud of some type and was understood to be in a controversy with the Bureau currently." The agent was, of course, Jack Flanagan. I had wondered whether he would cover his ass by tattling because he was under a cloud himself, having arrived in Oklahoma City on a disciplinary transfer after a female relative married a security

33

subject and he didn't report it. As it turned out, he had also tipped off the Dallas FBI office the same day that I encountered him. King's revelation prompted the Dallas SAC, G. Gordon Shanklin, to call Washington to say that he vaguely recalled Flanagan phoning him with news that I was in town representing McFadden Publications, the parent of *Saga*, but didn't realize the significance of it due to the hectic media crush. But, as came to light years later, Shanklin had more than the media on his mind. In 1975, before a congressional committee, agent Hosty testified that on December 7, some two weeks before the assassination, Oswald dropped off a note with the FBI receptionist telling Hosty to come to him directly rather than bothering his wife, Marina. The note reached Shanklin, who stuck it in his desk drawer. After Ruby shot Oswald, Hosty recounted, Shanklin summoned him to his office and agitatedly thrust the note at him, yelling, "Get it out of here. I don't even want it in this office. Get rid of it!" Shanklin was plainly upset that the note documented an FBI link to the accused assassin — in less than a week Hosty would, according to my informant, meet with Oswald. Hosty flushed it down a toilet.

For his part, Hoover was furious with Shanklin for attaching "so little attention" to my journalistic presence in Dallas that he did nothing. The lapse caused the Bureau a month's lag in finding out about the article, which left no hope of sabotaging it. The editors not so subtly titled it "The FBI Could Have Saved President Kennedy's Life," and when it hit the newsstands it promptly sold out, accompanied by widespread media press coverage. What undoubtedly stung Hoover badly was the national prominence the article gained in the widely syndicated column of Drew Pearson, regarded as the dean of the genre. Although Hoover had maintained a surface civility with him — even exchanging polite letters — he privately griped that Pearson was one of the pack of "journalistic prostitutes" who dared to write critically of the Bureau. In his column of January 29, 1964, Pearson scribed:

> This week, William Turner, for ten years a G-man, reports in *Saga* magazine: "Lee Oswald . . . was probably aided by jealousy and lack of

co-operation and communication between law enforcement agencies.
. . . I learned that a Dallas FBI agent had especially interviewed
Oswald only ten days before the assassination. . . . I also learned that
eventually the FBI did give the Secret Service a "risk list" of people
the Bureau feared might harm the President. But Oswald's name was
not on it.

It was left to Hoover to strike back through gossip column pals for
whom he had provided lively copy in the past. In his "Tower Ticker"
column in the *Chicago Tribune*, Herb Lyon reported, "G-Man Chief
J. Edgar Hoover is burned up at Ex-Agent William Turner's mag piece
that the FBI goofed in not rounding up Lee Harvey Oswald before The
Deed." And Ed Sullivan, who was best known for his TV variety show
but penned a "Little Old New York" strip, ran part of a "Dear Ed"
letter from the Director that read, "I've seen your column in the *New
York Daily News* in which you mention the current magazine story by
former Special Agent William Turner. . . . But the investigation of Lee
Harvey Oswald had given absolutely no clue indicating Oswald was a
potential assassin. Sincerely, Edgar."

As the Warren Commission went about its inquest, the wire services
reported bit by bit that it was headed in the direction of a no-conspiracy
verdict. On December 16, while the commission was still dealing with
housekeeping matters, Gerald Ford, then a congressman, piped up that
he had been called by a wire service chief he knew who said, "Jerry,
I'm surprised that we got, and the other wire services got, stories out
the very same day." The reference was to a confidential FBI report
Hoover had handed to President Lyndon Johnson a week earlier, which
concluded that Oswald and Ruby had each acted alone. "The minute
he said that," Ford declared, "it led me to the belief that there had
been a deliberate leak from some agency of the federal government,
and now they wanted to confirm by commission action what had been
leaked previously." In fact, it was Ford himself who was the FBI's spy
on the commission, leaking information to Deke DeLoach, who in
turn made sure it reached the wire services. Hoover had saddled the
commission with his own premature verdict.

So there were no surprises when the Warren Commission Report was rushed to publication before the November 1964 elections. It concluded that Oswald had acted alone, and that Ruby was a lone avenger. Indications to the contrary were laid to rest under the heading "Speculations and Rumors." As for my article's disclosure that the FBI had interviewed Oswald ten days before the assassination, the report contended:

> The last FBI interview with Oswald, before the assassination, took place in New Orleans in August 1963, when he asked to see an FBI agent after his arrest by police for disturbing the peace, the outcome of his distribution of Fair Play for Cuba handbills. Neither Special Agent Hosty nor any other FBI agent saw or talked with Oswald between his return to Dallas, on October 3, and November 22.

This denial was based solely on the word of Hoover, which bothered several of the commission members. One, former CIA Director Allen Dulles, remarked, between puffs on his pipe, that he himself would lie to protect an Agency informant.

But Hoover was not entirely off the hook. In a section on presidential protection, the Secret Service official in charge of physical security testified that he believed "the accumulation of facts known to the FBI should have constituted a sufficient basis to warn the Secret Service of the Oswald risk." This prompted the commission to censure the Bureau for taking "an unduly restrictive view of its role in preventative intelligence work prior to the assassination." It decided that "A more carefully coordinated treatment of the Oswald case by the FBI might have resulted in bringing Oswald's activities to the attention of the Secret Service."

Hoover went ballistic. He severed relations with Earl Warren, striking him from the Director's Special Correspondence list on which he had been placed for cooperating with the FBI as governor of California, and ordered agents to spy on him. Then, quietly, he scapegoated seventeen agents, including the hapless Hosty, with letters of censure, suspensions without pay and disciplinary transfers to Bureau gulags.

He deemed them guilty of not investigating Oswald thoroughly enough to forward his name to the Secret Service.

On November 18, 1964, Hoover, still seething over the Warren Commission's slap on the wrist, called a group of eighteen women reporters to his office and staged an impromptu press conference. It was an unprecedented scene, since the Bureau ordinarily got its message out through press handouts and planted stories. Hoover unloaded on the commission for unfair criticism of his agency, then launched into a tirade against Dr. Martin Luther King, labeling him "the most notorious liar in the country" for complaining of Bureau lassitude in civil rights probes in the South.

The nation's top cop had shot himself in the foot. Although LBJ feared to fire him ("I'd rather have him inside the tent pissing out than outside pissing in"), his performance was so outrageous, the malice so transparent, that it marked the beginning of a long and steady slide in prestige. Puff pieces in the media became fewer and fewer as open discussion took their place. On September 25, 1965, *The Saturday Evening Post*, which rarely took on controversy, ran an article by James Phelan proposing that Hoover might soon have to be replaced. And on April 9, 1971, *Life*, whose late publisher, Henry Luce, had been one of Hoover's most passionate supporters, came out with a cover story depicting the Director as a Roman emperor. "After Almost Half a Century in Total and Imperious Charge," the piece was captioned, "G-man Under Fire."

By this time Hoover had slipped into a bunker mentality that bordered on the paranoid. In 1966, on the third anniversary of Oswald's death at the hand of Ruby, a UPI dispatch datelined Dallas crossed his desk reporting that yellow chrysanthemums had been left at the grave with the message, "He has left all the world confused." The dispatch quoted Oswald's mother, Marguerite Oswald, as saying the flowers were left by "a former FBI agent." On it Hoover scrawled, "She's utterly irresponsible, although it could have been Turner."

On May 1, 1972, I completed a lecture tour on Hoover's FBI at the State University of New York at Cobleskill. When I went to bed that night at a local hotel, I tossed and turned. So I arose before dawn, drove to Albany, and caught the first plane headed west. When I got into my car at the San Francisco Airport, a radio news bulletin announced, "Flags are at half-staff for J. Edgar Hoover." He had died in his sleep, apparently of natural causes, in the early morning of the international communist holiday.

The man whom JFK didn't live to fire was gone.

3

BUGS AND BLACK BAGS

"Don't forget," quipped the FBI's master burglar, George Berley, a dapper, silver-haired graduate of Fordham University who had been my instructor in the fine art of break-and-enter, "possession of burglary tools in the state of Washington can get you up to ten years." It was October 1958, and I was about to return to the Seattle office outfitted with a set of noninventory lock-picking tools. Berley's class in surreptitious entry had been part of an intense three-week course in the theory and practice of wiretapping and bugging, euphemistically referred to as Sound School, for which I had been drafted because of a background in electrical engineering. Berley conducted his classes in the attic of the Department of Justice building, out of sight of curious tourists taking the FBI tour and several floors over the heads of successive attorneys general, who hadn't the slightest notion that the Bureau was committing illegal break-ins, termed *black bag jobs* after the satchels used to lug the tools. No one heard the grinding wheels in Berley's hideout as each student customized his own set.

The Sound School curriculum included practicing planting bugs—in Bureau parlance, "mikes"—in the walls of a jerry-built room, which required some skill in carpentry, plastering and matching paint. We learned all about the infrastructures of the telephone companies in order to install taps and how to cultivate telcom security agents in order to obtain the data about a subscriber's line necessary to install a tap. On Saturdays, when the Justice building was virtually deserted, we experimented in locating one wire out of the spaghetti-maze running through the conduits. Wiretapping was a criminal violation of the Communications Act of 1934, but the FBI rationalized that, although conversations were intercepted, they were not divulged—a key element in the law—outside the Justice Department. "The Act was directed against telephone company employees," a Sound School instructor explained to us in a tone suggesting that the law wasn't meant for the FBI. Nothing was said about the legality of bugs, which were far more insidious than wiretaps because they picked up everything that was said in a room, not just phone calls. With the rare exception, it was necessary to commit a burglary to install a bug, which made it not only a statutory crime but a constitutional infringement. And when the bug fed a wireless transmitter, the crime had to be repeated periodically to replace the batteries.

On his annual trek to Capitol Hill to regale the House Appropriations Subcommittee with the accomplishments of his agency, Hoover dutifully reported that at any given time there were approximately one hundred wiretaps in service nationwide, all installed with the permission of the attorney general to "thwart espionage, sabotage and grave risks to national security." This was not precisely the case. For instance, the Washington Field Office had one on the personal line of French Ambassador Herve Alphand, who, the agent listening in assured me, was "quite a ladies' man." How many more "love taps" there were, I am not sure. But those modest one hundred wiretaps that Hoover reported were the result of tinkering with the numbers. I recall a case in which an American citizen was recruited as a spy by Soviet agents operating out of Mexico City (which was Nechiporenko's base at the time). The man was "on ice," meaning he was instructed to lead a normal life until activated in the indefinite future by someone calling on the phone and giving a password. A tap had been in place on his home phone to intercept the call when it came. But as time dragged on and no call came, the FBI Laboratory, which was in charge of electronic surveillance, became impatient. The tap was not yielding continuous intelligence, and, as one of the Hoover Hundred, it needed to produce, if not here, then somewhere else. Disconnect the tap, the lab instructed me. At the same time, I was told to install a bug known as a MISUR (microphone surveillance) to supplant the tap. My Sound School notes reflect that while the attorney general had to approve each tap, the authority for planting mikes lay with the Bureau only. Since the Bureau free-lanced buggings, their number exceeded that of taps exponentially.

Installing a tap had simply required climbing a telephone pole and bridging the subscriber's lugs in the pole box. But putting in a bug, of course, required a trespass, which led to a Woody Allen comedy. The first step was to replace the "drop wire" running from the pole box to the house with one sent by the lab, which had an additional pair of fine wires imbedded in it. We borrowed a utility truck from the local power company. A senior agent assigned as driver sat with me on the crest of a hill awaiting the all-clear transmission from agents in radio cars, who had the man and his wife under surveillance at their places of employment. An agent monitored incoming calls at the police department to cut off any report of a burglary in progress in the neighborhood. Finally the radio crackled with the all-clear signal. My driver, sweating with nervousness, revved up the engine and let out the clutch. Too suddenly. When we lurched forward, there was a loud metallic noise followed by a thump. The transmission had fallen out.

But we came back another day. Wearing a hard hat, belt and climbing irons, I substituted the lab's special drop wire for the phone company's. Neighbors did not seem to notice that although I had a power company truck, I was working on the phone lines. A few days later, with no sign that we had been detected, I picked the lock of a side door and, accompanied by another agent, entered the home to hook up the bug. I immediately spotted a problem in the form of a parakeet in a cage right by the telephone, where the bug was to be planted. "Ed," I whispered to my accomplice, "don't say 'pass the pliers' or anything else that goddam parakeet can repeat later." When we were in the basement making the final connection, we heard the dread sound of a door opening upstairs and footfalls moving from room to room. Had we been discovered? In accordance with policy, we carried nothing that would link us to the FBI if captured—no credentials, no badge, no gun, no FBI Recreational Association card (FBIRA dues paid by agents were used as a slush fund by Hoover). We would be on our own. I decided I would act like a burglar by knocking out whoever it was and fleeing. The footfalls started and stopped, moving from room to room for what seemed like an eternity but was only a couple of minutes. We cringed in a corner as the footfalls arrived at the head of the basement stairs. Then they moved on, and a door opened and slammed shut. After a few minutes we strode purposefully out of the house and drove off, as if it all was in a lineman's day.

The bug was connected to the monitoring post in the FBI office by a line leased from the phone company under the thinly disguised name Federal Research Company. Back at the post, I turned on the amplifier and sat back to listen to the parakeet. To my surprise the overriding sound was music and ads—the drop wire acted as an aerial, picking up a nearby commercial radio station. So I designed a low-pass filter and made one last trip to the neighborhood to climb the pole and install it. After that, the parakeet came in fine, as did the rest of the family. The lab was notified that the bug was in place, and a memo prepared for the "Do Not File" file in which sensitive operations such as black bag jobs were kept in an unmarked safe and later destroyed. J. Edgar Hoover wrote me a personal letter of commendation, but I never did find out whether that one phone call ever came in.

Nor was I ever told the purpose of the black bag job we did on the Japanese consulate in Seattle in 1957. Barely a year before I became his student in Sound School, George Berley flew out to crack the safe in the consulate's office suite, which was on an upper floor of a downtown office building. We had gotten the door key from the building

superintendent, who had been led to believe he was performing a patriotic service. My role was to act as a lookout on the street with another agent while Berley was in the suite. He had brought with him
from Washington photographs of the consul and his staff, obtained
from the State Department, so we could warn him by radio should one
show up in the middle of the night. But Berley seemed to be taking a
long time, and after three hours I went up to see how he was doing. He
had taped a slug of radioactive cobalt to the rear of the safe, then positioned a piece of photographic film on the dial. It had taken a while,
but finally the film silhouetted the alignment of the tumblers. Berley
spun the dial back and forth and the door swung open. Whatever documents he was looking for were there. He carefully measured their position in the safe so that they could be put back precisely. Then he photographed them with a document camera, replaced them and shut the
door, and we were out of there. Berley took the first plane to Washington with the loot, which I guessed were Japanese codes. Why a Cold
War ally was targeted I never figured out, although it seemed logical
that the Seattle consulate was selected because security at the embassy
in Washington was far tighter.

Black bag jobs were fairly common across the country. Security squad
agents routinely invaded the offices of the Communist Party and other
radical political groups or the residences of functionaries to photograph
membership lists and other internal documents. And of course they
were an integral part of planting a bug. In metropolitan areas, such as
New York, some Bureau burglars were kept so busy they earned a substantial supplemental income in the form of cash awards. And, having
been trained and equipped for the shady business, Sound School alumni
in the field offices were repeatedly badgered by other agents to bootleg
a job on, say, a prostitution or theft case. These were called "suicide
taps" and "suicide bag jobs" because discovery would mean an instant
pink slip.

The fact that the Bureau sanctioned black bag jobs was a tightly
held secret even within the FBI, and no one on the outside was privy to
it. The operations were performed with such meticulous attention to

good housekeeping that the victims never knew they were. But the wraps began coming off in 1961 when Hoover, pressured by Robert Kennedy to do something about organized crime, overextended himself. He had seized on the name La Cosa Nostra (Our Thing), which a minor mobster had uttered, pretended it wasn't the Mafia, which he had earlier insisted didn't exist, and trumpeted, "The battle is joined. We have taken up the gauntlet flung down by organized crime." Because of protracted neglect, however, the FBI was faced with a dearth of intelligence on the national crime syndicate. It made up for lost time by creating a plague of bugs.

By this time I had made a U-turn on the question of listening-device illegality. Berley's cavalier remark after I had completed his break-and-enter course about the criminal penalties for burglary had set me to thinking. Hoover didn't know best, after all; there was no reason his Bureau should be above the law. Wiretaps were justifiable at times, since they didn't require break-ins. In the 1960 kidnap-murder of Colorado brewery scion Adolph Coors, Jr., for example, I installed a tap on the phone of the parents of the suspect, Joseph Corbett, Jr., who was a fugitive (he was eventually apprehended by the Royal Canadian Mounted Police in Canada). But surreptitious home and office invasions mocked the law and the Bill of Rights, and my Jesuitical training reminded me that the end didn't justify the means. And so, over lunch at Washington's tony Metropolitan Club, I discussed the conundrum with another Jesuit product, Ed Williams. According to Evan Thomas in his biography of the legendary attorney, *The Man to See*, I "told Williams about the director's vast secret—and illegal—electronic eavesdropping campaign against the Mafia in Chicago, New York, and Las Vegas." In Las Vegas, Hoover had ordered bugs to be placed not only in the executive offices of the Desert Inn and the Fremont Hotel, trying to detect skimming in the casinos, but in bedrooms of those two establishments as well as the Sands, Flamingo, Riviera, Dunes, Horseshoe and Stardust hotel-casinos. What did the pillow talk of guests have to do with skimming?

The FBI had originally developed the ability to listen in on hotel

44

rooms as part of its national security coverage. I recall an occasion in which three Russian military attaches visited the Seattle area, which they were allowed to do as long as they didn't venture into restricted zones. The trio made reservations at the Benjamin Franklin Hotel, which was serendipitous for us because it was one of three leading hotels in the city where, with the public-spirited cooperation of management, certain rooms were prebugged. When the Russians checked in, they were put in the special room, with the one next door reserved for us to listen in. We got an earful, since they did in fact plan to sneak a look at the off-limits Whidbey Island Naval Air Station. But with the capability in place, the Bureau didn't scruple to use it for more ignoble purposes. A prime example was the 1963 and 1964 bugging of Dr. Martin Luther King, Jr., in Washington's Willard Hotel and the Hyatt House in Los Angeles. Tapes and transcripts of the sexual disporting in the rooms were offered to select politicians and media in a brazen attempt to smear King, who was personally anathema to Hoover.

In February 1964, Ed Williams, retained by the hotel-casino proprietors, socked the FBI with a $4.5 million damage suit that probably contaminated gambling-connected prosecutions for some time to come. Collaterally damaged was the Central Telephone Company of Nevada, which was hit with a $6 million action. Phone company officials grudgingly admitted that, beginning in 1961, they had filled FBI orders under the thin cover of Henderson Novelty Company, "a musical rental service," for twenty-five leased lines connecting the bugs with a remote FBI monitoring post. Eventually the cases were settled tamely, with the casino proprietors forgoing monetary damages and the Bureau agreeing not to prosecute any crimes it might have overheard.

Although the casinos caper attracted wide press coverage, the point was not made that while the bugs were an invasion of privacy, planting them required criminal trespass. This was true whether the bugging was aimed at organized crime, political activists or figures like Dr. King. But a year later, in 1965, another threat of exposure of illicit eavesdropping loomed in the person of Senator Edward Long of Missouri. He scheduled hearings before his Subcommittee on Administrative

Practice and Procedure to explore the "armory of electronic snooping" possessed by federal agencies. Alarm bells sounded in Bureau head-quarters—the family jewels were in jeopardy again.

The FBI troubleshooter who materialized in Long's office was Deke DeLoach, whose most recent escapade had been playing the tapes of King's "love feast" to Bureau friends in Congress. DeLoach had a brassy proposal for Long: place in the record an FBI statement absolving it-self of illegal electronic snooping. But the subcommittee's waspish counsel, Bernard Fensterwald, Jr., rejected the gambit out of hand, suggesting instead that a Bureau official testify under oath. No, DeLoach countered, that "might open a Pandora's box insofar as our enemies of the press [are] concerned." Fensterwald, who had asked me to brief him on the subject, then recommended that I testify, based on my FBI training and experience, which would have indeed sprung the box. DeLoach went ballistic, denouncing me as "a first-class SOB, a liar, and a man who had volunteered as a witness only to get a public fo-rum." Fensterwald pushed for my testimony, but his boss had been compromised, in what must rank as the irony of ironies, by an FBI wiretap. Oh so discreetly, Hoover tipped Long that his voice had been captured in conversations with organized crime members. As a result, the FBI emerged unscathed by the hearings, while the Internal Rev-enue Service bore the brunt of Long's scrutiny. The only drama was famously provided by San Francisco private eye Harold Lipset, who demonstrated how a tiny bug could be hidden in a martini olive.

As the Long hearings droned on, Teamster boss Jimmy Hoffa asked me to come to Washington to assess what evidence against him might have been tainted by illegal electronic surveillance. He had been con-victed in Chattanooga a year earlier, in 1964, of jury tampering, and the matter was on appeal. I had ambivalent feelings about Hoffa. I had participated in the Seattle FBI investigation and prosecution of his predecessor, Dave Beck, on corruption charges. Beck had lived it up in a pretentious home on Lake Washington while sucking the union treasury dry. In contrast, Hoffa had lived modestly in Detroit and im-measurably improved the welfare of the rank and file. His fault—and it was a major one—is that he had deep mob ties. In my mind, however, the issue of FBI malfeasance was overarching. When I met Jimmy Hoffa in the marble-palace Teamsters national headquarters, he was a pale imitation of the cocky verbal gunslinger depicted in the media, the specter of prison clearly on his mind. After a discussion of the details of his case with his attorney, William Buffalino, and two Teamsters officials joining in, Hoffa set me loose in a cavernous conference room with stacks of files on the table. It didn't take much flipping through the files to figure out that the FBI had him under blanket electronic surveillance while he was in Chattanooga preparing for the trial and during it—I recognized the names of four Sound School graduates among the hundred or so agents brought in on a "special" from all over the country. Coupled with other clues, it was a cinch that when Hoffa went to the bathroom in his hotel suite, agents with headphones heard the flush. I briefed one of Hoffa's attorneys that there was ample suggestion that the Bureau had used TESURS (technical surveillance, meaning wiretaps) as well as MISURS, the proof of which would be found in a tightly held JUNE file. (The JUNE files were the depository for the most highly sensitive information.)

What I didn't know at the time was that Hoover had reportedly made an abortive attempt to sabotage the Hoffa conviction out of hatred for Bobby Kennedy, who in November 1964 had been elected U.S. senator from New York, concomitantly currying favor with Lyndon Johnson, who considered RFK a future rival for the presidency. This startling bit of intelligence was contained in an October 1967 letter written on FBI stationery, composed by Los Angeles agents, and addressed to Attorney General Ramsey Clark. They sent me a copy of the letter, followed by a discreet phone call in which they explained that they sought to oust Hoover and his high command and block the ambitious DeLoach from succeeding Hoover. They asked me to contact Clark and vouch for the letter's authenticity, which I did despite a feeling that the agents were naive in thinking that anyone who served at the pleasure of Lyndon Johnson would do anything. Sure enough, as my FOIA file reveals, the only action Clark took was to send my letter along with that of the agents to the Bureau. Had the Department of Justice delved into the accusations, the FBI would have been turned upside down. In the eight-page broadside, John Mohr was accused of documentable fraud and Wesley Grapp of being so invulnerable that he "openly stated that Hoover and Tolson, whom he knows intimately, and some of their friends are homosexuals." With regard to Hoffa, whose conviction was the crowning achievement of RFK's tour as attorney general, the letter alleged that in December 1966 Deke DeLoach, at Hoover's instance, told William Loeb, the ultraconservative publisher of the Manchester, New Hampshire, *Union Leader*, who was openly sympathetic to the Teamsters' boss, that Kennedy "had a special wiretapping team which operated against Hoffa during his trials. DeLoach suggested to Loeb that if Hoffa were to press the Justice Department to investigate what had been done by Kennedy during the Hoffa trials, they would un-cover wiretapping." The Los Angeles agents, obviously on Kennedy's side, wrote Clark that this "traitorous act" by DeLoach was done "at the great risk of losing this most important case."

No evidence ever surfaced that Kennedy ran a rump wiretapping operation folded into his "Get Hoffa" squad, although he occasionally used International Investigators, Inc., an Indianapolis-based team of former FBI agents known as the Three Eyes, for off-channel assign-ments (that is, assignments not in the usual course of business). In 1966, the Supreme Court rejected Hoffa's appeal and he went to prison. Ironically, in the same year a gutsy solicitor general, Thurgood Marshall, informed the Supreme Court that as a result of the FBI's promiscuous bugging without the attorney general's authorization, as had been un-covered in Nevada, scores of important prosecutions would have to be dropped (one beneficiary was Bobby Baker, LBJ's political crony, who had been found guilty of influence peddling). Yet in 1969, during the course of a renewed appeal hearing for Hoffa, a Justice Department attorney insisted he "had never heard" of a special file on FBI wiretaps and bugs, contending that the Hoffa people just wanted to "rummage in government records." But Hoffa's attorneys subpoenaed the right man to the stand, Charles Dolz, the Bureau's head of records, who admitted under oath that there was such a file—the JUNE file. In 1971, Richard Nixon commuted Hoffa's sentence and he was freed. In 1975, he disappeared, presumably kidnapped. The FBI suspected that a New Jersey Mafia faction that had thrown in with his successor, Frank Fitzsimmons, put out a contract on his life because he was making moves to regain power. The case remains unsolved.

A year after the Hoffa consultation, I finally found the forum that DeLoach had feared Senator Long's hearings would give me. It came in the form of an upstart national magazine named *Ramparts*, which styled itself the Catholic Laymen's Journal but was widely regarded as radical slick. The editors loved to expose government chicanery, so my piece, which they pejoratively titled "I was a Burglar, Wiretapper, Bugger, and Spy for the F.B.I.," was a natural fit. It ran in the November 1966 issue, which hit the stands only weeks before the general election. Drew Pearson picked up on it, noting that the hotel-casino bugging was the marquee issue in the Nevada governor's race, where incumbent Grant Sawyer, a Democrat, was pitted against Republican Paul Laxalt. Sawyer challenged Hoover to furnish proof that the FBI had caught any members of the underworld skimming and deplored the bugging as a "police-state tactic." Pearson wrote that "both Gov. Sawyer and his opponent, Lt. Gov. Laxalt, might well read this month's issue of *Ramparts* magazine and its article on wiretapping by William W. Turner, a former FBI man. It's an amazing revelation. Turner tells how Hoover operates a 'sound school' to teach agents how to place bugs, also to pick locks and make illegal entry for the purpose of placing bugs."

At least Sawyer read the article, for he asked me to come to Las Vegas and do a series of television ads describing Hoover's use of tapping, bugging and burglaries. Holed up in the Sands Hotel, I composed my own copy, then delivered it before the camera. The film was flown to Carson City, screened for Sawyer, and put on the air that night. When the series was finished, the Sawyer campaign arranged a press conference at which I drove home the point that bugs, unlike wiretaps, "can seldom be installed without the surreptitious invasion of a person's office or home." The story received prominent play in newspapers throughout the state, among them the *Las Vegas Review-Journal*, whose front-page coverage prompted Hoover to scrawl on the clip that crossed his desk that I might be a "former" agent, but "infamous would be more accurate." What might have sharpened his pique was that at the same press session I ventured that despite President Johnson's bugging ban in the wake of the Las Vegas lawsuits, the Bureau was still up to its old tricks, quoting Senator Estes Kefauver that "Hoover is more powerful than the president." As then–Attorney General Nicholas Katzenbach belatedly found out, the FBI had stopped the bugging—but only in Nevada.

Sawyer lost his bid for a third term when a Republican tsunami swept over elections in the West. But Hoover wasn't finished with me, seeing an opportunity to throw me behind bars in a drawing that had illustrated the *Ramparts* article. It had been reproduced from a Bureau technical handbook and depicted a "Microphone Installation Employing Acoustical Impedance Matching," which, despite the arcane jargon, was as elemental to bugging as the slingshot was to weaponry. According to a FOIA release, a Hoover deputy found an obscure subsection of the espionage statute that prohibited anyone with lawful possession of a document relating to the national defense from failing to deliver it on demand by a U.S. officer entitled to receive it. The FBI's legal counsel told the deputy that there might be a technical violation but that there was also a practical problem. "We felt that Turner would deny having anything," the deputy memoed, "move it to some other location than his home before we could search it under warrant, and then proceed to write another article about the whole affair." The deputy ruefully concluded that "it does not appear there is any legal action we could take against Turner without risking greater embarrassment by far than we have thus far sustained from his writings."

Embarrassment was what Hoover, now in an image-protection mode, dreaded the most. Perhaps realizing that he had narrowly escaped a national fuss, he called a halt to all black bag jobs, whether to plant bugs or to filch intelligence. It was not until August 1973, more than a year after his death, that the story broke loose on a national scale. It began when a beleaguered President Nixon tried to make the Watergate break-in seem like business as usual by contending that FBI burglaries had been widely authorized by the Democratic administrations of John Kennedy and Lyndon Johnson (which was not the case). An Associated Press reporter in Washington called to ask what I knew about burglaries during my career, which spanned the Eisenhower years. I repeated what had appeared in *Ramparts* seven years earlier, only this time, with Nixon's allegations the lever, it was big news. As soon as the story went out over the AP's national wire on August 24, headed "Ex-Agent Bares Break-Ins Under Ike," media vehicles pulled up at my home as if a Mafia wake were being held. The reporters left with a news land mine that hadn't appeared in *Ramparts*: the safe job on the Japanese consulate in Seattle. As the *San Francisco Examiner* framed it:

> Turner's revelation of the burglary of the Japanese consul was already causing foreign policy ripples today. The Japanese Foreign Ministry expressed shock and puzzlement at the report. The Tokyo newspaper *Yomiuri Shimbun* quoted foreign ministry sources as saying, "This is news to us. If it is true, it is regrettable." For its part the FBI was silent.

It turned out that the Bureau had a compelling reason to remain silent: even before Hoover's death, Deputy Associate Director W. Mark Felt and intelligence division chief Edward S. Miller had gone behind his back and ordered resumption of black bag jobs. A particular target was the elusive Weather Underground, a small radical band violently opposed to the Vietnam War. The Bureau was frustrated because it couldn't locate Weather members, so it burglarized the homes of relatives and friends in the hope of picking up clues. Felt and Miller's bootleg operation came to light in 1975 when Senator Frank Church's committee probed the "rogue elephant" tendencies of the intelligence agencies. FBI Director Clarence Kelley, who had steadfastly insisted the burglaries had ceased in 1966, when Hoover ordered a halt, fumed "I was lied to" and conceded he couldn't guarantee that burglaries weren't still going on. In 1978, President Jimmy Carter's Justice Department obtained indictments against Felt and Miller for conspiring to violate the civil rights of the victims, and two years later they were convicted but spared jail sentences. In one of his first acts as president, Ronald Reagan pardoned the unrepentant pair. As I put it in an essay in the *Los Angeles Times*, the pardons

> might well be the raising of the flag signaling an all-out assault on the intelligence-gathering restrictions that lately have been imposed on the FBI and CIA in an effort to strike a balance between national security and civil freedom. The president apparently marches to the same ideological drummer as Felt and Miller, and, in tune with his belief that Vietnam was a "noble" venture and the Russians are still out to conquer the world, unleashing the intelligence agencies appears to be a consuming goal.

Recently FBI Director Louis Freeh, citing a terrorism menace, lobbied to remove the restriction imposed under the 1970s reforms that wiretaps be approved by a judge. Freeh undoubtedly saw the expediency in removing judicial oversight but was advocating one more step back toward lawless law enforcement. If the past is prologue, black bag jobs won't be far behind. And with them scary new technology. A laser beam "bug" aimed from a distance at a windowpane can "hear" the room conversation. "Smart dust," originally developed for weather research, consists of packed sensors, tiny computers and wireless communicators that can float in the air for hours and monitor for light and sound. The FBI's Internet surveillance tool, called Carnivore, is subject to abuse. Carnivore could, in the words of an FBI lab report, "reliably capture and archive all unfiltered traffic to the internal hard drive," not just e-mail to or from a criminal or security suspect in accordance with a court order. Although the FBI promised not to capture wide swaths of Internet communications, there is no provision for independent supervision. As the "suicide taps" and unauthorized break-ins of my era attest, the Bureau has a history of believing rules were made to be broken.

4

RAMPARTS REDUX: BLOWING THE CIA'S COVER

Plain-spoken Harry S. Truman, reflecting on his presidency, observed that he never had any idea "when I set up the CIA, that it would be injected into peacetime cloak-and-dagger operations." Nor did I have any idea, in submitting a manuscript on J. Edgar Hoover to a small California magazine, that I would be drawn into a journalistic tour de force stripping the cover from far-flung CIA operations. Old Harry, in retirement in Independence, Missouri, might well have silently applauded.

It began in November 1964 when Hoover, in an unprecedented outburst, branded Dr. Martin Luther King "the most notorious liar in the country" because he had criticized FBI foot-dragging on civil rights investigations. The thought of the top cop slurring a widely respected civil rights leader who was about to be awarded the Nobel Peace Prize enraged me. I sat down at my Underwood upright typewriter and banged out an article on why the FBI chief had to go and who might qualify to succeed him. "One of the paradoxes of the latter-day Bureau," I wrote, "is that its impressive conviction rate has not extended to civil rights violations in the South. . . . The Bureau has not made impressive headway in solving the wave of home bombings, church burnings and other acts of terror visited on Negroes. Indeed, until the firm hand of Bobby Kennedy was laid on the FBI's shoulder, the sight of an agent delving into civil rights matters was a curiosity."

I was pondering where to send the article, called "After J. Edgar, Who?," when I spotted on a friend's coffee table a copy of *Ramparts*, billed as the Catholic Laymen's Journal. The magazine was based in Menlo Park, a short trek down the San Francisco peninsula. I called the publisher, Edward Keating. "Send it right down," he said. He ran it in the March 1965 issue. According to a FOIA document, Hoover scribbled "What a rat!" when he found out.

Hoover's trepidation that I might find a continuing home for my writings was realized when the *Ramparts* editor, Warren Hinckle, assigned me to do a cover article on the farm labor situation in California. The root of the problem was the bracero program, authorized by Congress during the labor shortage of World War II, which permitted agribusiness to bring in field workers from Mexico for the harvest seasons. They were paid miserable wages, with the fringe benefit of rat-trap housing, which was justified by the myth that the home-grown labor force was nomadic and unreliable. Cesar Chavez and his fledgling United Farm Workers union (UFW) were trying to organize, insisting that they could provide a stable work force if paid decent wages. The piece, which appeared in the August 1965 issue, was titled "No Dice for Braceros." Its thrust was that there existed a domestic labor pool that could—properly organized—be even more reliable than the bracero program, which simply imported Mexican poverty. The cover depicted California Governor Edmund "Pat" Brown wearing a sombrero with a Mexican blanket slung over a shoulder, strumming a guitar. Brown was noted for playing vacillating tunes, and he had caved in to the agribusiness lobby on the bracero issue.

Within days of publication I was approached by three Protestant clergymen asking what action they might take. Off the top of my head I suggested that they picket cruise ships in port in San Francisco to block the loading of grapes. The longshoremen, I was certain, would not cross the picket line. The clergymen picketed, the longshoremen didn't cross, and the ships went grapeless. A few weeks later at a cocktail party, Harry Bridges, the head of the International Longshoremen's & Warehousemen's Union (ILWU), buttonholed me to say that the shipowners had filed a million-dollar lawsuit charging an illegal secondary boycott.

"I'm sorry, Harry," I apologized. "I didn't know about secondary boycotts."

Bridges wasn't angry. "Don't worry. I'll handle the suit," he said. "You handle the writing."

Which is what I did. Comedian Steve Allen asked Ed Keating if he could "borrow" me to ghost a book on the farm labor situation under contract from Doubleday, with all proceeds to go to Chavez's UFW. He hadn't found any humor in the bracero program and had done considerable research on the subject. But his television show had food processors for sponsors, and I called him to make sure he knew they wouldn't be happy with the book the way I intended to treat it. "Don't pull any punches," he assured me. The result was *The Ground Is Our Table*, which the *San Francisco Chronicle* lauded as "a well-documented, compassionate study of the plight of the American farm workers."

At this point *Ramparts* was undergoing a transmogrification. It had been started as a quarterly in 1962 by Keating, whose wife held a large stake in U.S. Gypsum. The early issues carried such highbrow reading as an essay by the Trappist monk Thomas Merton on Ghandi-type pacifism and a critique of James Cardinal McIntyre of Los Angeles for fostering racism in his sprawling diocese. One literary critic commented that *Ramparts* could "take its place on the shelf with the *Hudson Review*," a lofty literary quarterly. But then the magazine shed its Catholic identity and expanded into secular muckraking in the style of H. L. Mencken's *American Mercury*, the "Huntley-Brinkley Report" on NBC News noted with some wonder. This was largely the doing of Warren Hinckle, who took over publication after rounding up financing from limousine liberals when Keating went broke. Spurred by a series of news-making articles, the circulation jumped from 2,500 copies initially to 250,000 at its pinnacle. The cover price: 75 cents.

A San Franciscan who lived in a Victorian house and was unhappy in the suburbs, Hinckle promptly moved the editorial offices some thirty miles up the freeway to 301 Broadway in San Francisco, eliminating the quotidian trudge to Menlo Park. The site was an industrial-looking one-story structure two blocks from the glitz of North Beach and across from a freeway on-ramp with a "Begin Freeway" sign (columnist Herb Caen quipped it was the only American freeway named after an Israeli prime minister). Then in his twenties, Hinckle was a graduate of the University of San Francisco, where he edited the student newspaper, *Foghorn*, turning a weekly into a daily to the dismay of his budget-conscious Jesuit proctors. He was a beat reporter on the *San Francisco Chronicle* when Keating offered him a riskier paycheck but more freedom of style.

In style, Hinckle was in fact a throwback to Mencken. He wore an eye patch, the consequence of a boyhood auto accident. His attire was a brown velvet suit and buckled patent-leather pumps. In his office he kept a parrot mockingly dubbed Henry Luce after the troglodytic *Time-Life* publisher. But he spent as little time as possible at his desk, preferring instead the funky bar at Cookie Picetti's on Kearny Street, where he bought rounds for the cops and politicians who hung out there (many a manuscript arrived at the typesetter's marked with wet circles). In his memoirs, *If You Have a Lemon, Make Lemonade*, Hinckle recalled that Eldridge Cleaver, the Black Panther luminary, loved drinking in a place loaded with cops, but "said that people at *Ramparts* wondered why I drank only in right-wing bars but were afraid to ask. I asked Cleaver if he had ever heard of a good left-wing bar, and, that issue settled, we had another drink."

Despite his reputation as an enfant terrible, Hinckle had few rivals as a writer and editor. He knew a story when he saw one, and how to go for it. At heart he was the quintessential ink-stained wretch. But he was a stickler for fact checking, to the point of annoying writers whose manuscripts came back riddled with question marks. He was the Jimmy Breslin of San Francisco, only more so. His pungent, catchy style was unsurpassed, as when he lampooned Cardinal McIntyre: "A former

Wall Street stockbroker, who later took a strong position in commodity futures of Heaven, McIntyre ran his corner of the Catholic Church like the giant money-making machine that it was. Questioning his methods was as fruitful as arguing with success, and twice as unappreciated, as the Cardinal, nearing 80, took the act of kissing his ring as a metaphor for kissing his ass, and would countenance no behavior to the contrary." But to catalogue Hinckle—and *Ramparts* for that matter—as ideologically partisan was to miss the mark entirely. When a *New York Times* profiler suggested the magazine was New Left, Hinckle huffed that the term "referred to an amorphous collection of people with no agreement on anything." Nor would he settle for liberal. After *Ramparts* achieved recognition as a stinging critic of the Vietnam War, Hinckle met with Vice President Hubert H. Humphrey, a putative liberal, in Air Force Two as it sat on the tarmac at San Francisco Airport. He returned to the office in a snit—Humphrey had not budged an inch.

"Don't ever call me a liberal," he fumed. "It's the goddam liberals who brought us the war."

Ramparts scored its first big scoop when managing editor Robert Scheer had the presence of mind to recognize a true-blue defector from the war when he saw one. Scheer, who as a Berkeley graduate student was closer to the New Left than anyone, had caught Hinckle's eye for his ability to pry money loose from the local Daddy Peacebucks types. One day an ex–Special Forces master sergeant named Donald Duncan crossed his field of vision. Wearing a yellow golf cardigan, and ruggedly handsome with glacial blue eyes, Duncan had been knocking on the doors of Berkeley peace groups trying to drop a bomb on the war but was, quite understandably, dismissed as an infiltrator. But Scheer stopped, looked and listened, and the result was a smashing story of how Duncan had briefed Secretary of Defense Robert McNamara on why the massive bombing was a dud and how Americans engaged in the torture, killing and maiming of civilians, wiping out entire villages, faking body counts, and in doing so creating more Viet Cong than they eliminated. There was Duncan on the cover of the February 1966 issue, resplendent in full Green Beret regalia, combat medals hanging from his chest, being quoted as saying, "The whole thing was a lie. I quit."

The Duncan article made *Ramparts* a magnet for the disaffected, and Hinckle realized that the oddly assorted crew of former soldiers, intellectually compromised professors, FBI agents and CIA contract operatives beating a path to his door could recount personal stories that would put *True Confessions* to shame. As he observed in his memoirs, "It was characteristic of these renascent individualists that—although their entire world view had shifted—their psyches remained unchanged. Suddenly on the left side of the fence, they were as constant to their training and lifestyles as they had been on the right. They remained straight arrows, although flying in the opposite direction."

After Duncan's shrift ran, Hinckle challenged me, "It's your turn. See if you can top the Green Beret." He was referring to my checkered career as an FBI burglar, bugger and wiretapper, and I duly churned out the story (as reported in the previous chapter). At this juncture the 1966 political season loomed. In California Pat Brown was running for a third term, opposed by Republican Ronald Reagan, in his first race. The match-up was a natural for *Ramparts*, since the superannuated actor had gone off the political deep end, although he was toning it down for the campaign. Personally, I had no respect for Reagan. Originally a New Deal Democrat and president of the Screen Actors Guild, he turned on his leftist colleagues, becoming an FBI snitch and in 1947 a friendly witness before the House Un-American Activities Committee in its witch hunt against the film industry, which blacklisted some of the most talented actors and writers. In 1954 he began an eight-year stint as host of the television series "General Electric Theater," touting the virtues of unfettered free   enterprise so convincingly that he became the poster boy of monied conservatives. A gaggle of them formed a Kitchen Cabinet, brought him in as chef, and handed him the menu. They sagely knew that California was star-struck and would have no compunctions about voting for a fading screen idol. After all, hadn't actor George Murphy, a hidebound Republican, tap-danced his way into the U.S. Senate only two years before?

Hinckle deployed a *Ramparts* task force to interview key players in both camps. I interviewed Reagan's rotund press secretary, Lyn Nofziger, at the campaign headquarters on Wilshire Boulevard in Los Angeles. A hardnosed newsman, Nofziger gleefully wanted to know why I didn't have a beard like the rest of the *Ramparts* hippies, when in truth Scheer was the only one I knew with facial hair (later, when he joined the Reagan White House, Nofziger sported a beard himself). I left the session with Nofziger not only with a handful of campaign literature but the distinct impression that oilman Henry Salvatori, a member of the Kitchen Cabinet and moneybags to Fred Schwartz of the Christian Anti-Communist Crusade and other Jerry Falwells of the day, fancied himself the next shadow governor of California. I also interviewed Jerry Brown, Pat's son and future governor, who was then marking time in law practice, and Willie Brown, a rising young assemblyman who went on to become its powerful speaker and the fashion-plate mayor of San Francisco, among other Democratic pols.

The article, which ran in the October 1966 edition, was titled "Golly gee, California is a strange state!"—after Brown's habit of exclaiming "Golly gee" when informed of practically anything, and featured Mickey Mouse in Disneyland on the cover. There was a glimpse of Reagan:

> It was a scene right out of . . . well, it was right out of an old Ronald Reagan movie. The handsome, good-guy candidate, dressed proletarian-style in a black sports jacket, baggy gray slacks and beat-up shoes, was walking ramrod-proud down the dusty main street of a rural town. He had just delivered a speech on the "good things" about America. On the podium with Reagan was a young man, his face scarred by a shrapnel wound: an eager-eyed tight-lipped veteran of Vietnam, proudly wearing his G.I. uniform. A carefully placed California flag was cradled tenderly in his arms. The handsome candidate put his arm around the young G.I., who shoved the flag into the candidate's well-manicured hands and said, "You go get yourself some of those Berkeley Cong, Mr. Reagan."

But a snapshot of Pat Brown was not so upbeat:

Brown would have worked perfectly as the anguished father in one of those serious movies about juvenile delinquents. He is a well-meaning guy who is perpetually befuddled by the gap between the intentions of his actions and the results. His style is best defined by his favorite saying, "Golly gee," a phrase well known to those who for the past eight years have attempted to cajole, coerce and seduce good Pat into becoming something that he never could be. Having first come into office on an impressive wave of progressivism, charged by the voters to remake the political life of California, he is now an almost pathetic figure, muttering helplessly as chaos mounts around him, and he is increasingly threatened by a rival who seems to have a monopoly on fresh ideas and political vitality.

The article made little attempt to depict Reagan as a dangerous right-wing ideologue with extremists running his camp, but pounded away at Brown as a hopeless vacillator whose mind was ultimately made up by external forces, as witness his capitulation on the Vietnam War issue to the will of Lyndon Johnson.

When I read the article, which was written anonymously by Hinckle and Scheer, in galleys, I was baffled. I asked what they thought they were doing putting a pro-Reagan spin on the information the task force had brought in.

"Brown's so wishy-washy he has to go," Hinckle explained. "Reagan will make a fool of himself, and in four years we'll be able to elect a real Democrat."

"You won't be electing anyone from a concentration camp," I shot back. "Reagan's the front man for a scary mob, and he's a master of pretend."

Amiable and bumbling, Brown was a decent man with decent instincts, and I regretted that the magazine was out to torpedo him. It so happened that in the fading days of the campaign, as I was researching an article on the paramilitary right, precursor to today's militias, I stumbled upon a link between the Minutemen, perhaps the most potentially violent group, and the Reagan campaign. I called Bill Bennett, a former San Francisco cop and Democratic activist who was close to

Brown. He agreed the link was a bombshell and called Brown at his Beverly Hills home.

"The governor was grateful for the information," Bennett reported back. "But he says it's too late, and he's too tired to do anything."

A week later Brown was trounced by Reagan, who went on to decimate the state's mental health system, to bring the Vietnam War home by using military helicopters to tear gas demonstrators, and, as president, to preside over the illegal Iran-Contra diversion. But by this time *Ramparts* had taken aim at a new target, the CIA, in what would prove to be a long-running and fateful engagement. The opening volley was fired in the April 1966 issue with an article quirkily titled "What the hell is a university doing buying guns, anyway?" It was based on the revelations of a Michigan State University professor, Stanley Sheinbaum, who was privy to a CIA-sponsored program using MSU as cover and logistical support in the late 1950s and early 1960s. This was a period in which the Agency, having created a puppet ruler in South Vietnam in the person of Ngo Dinh Diem, kept his corrupt regime in business. Some $26 million a year was pumped through the MSU pipeline to arm and train a large state police apparatus, including the dreaded Vietnam Bureau of Investigation, which would ruthlessly ensure Diem's grip on power.

According to a partial document release in a 1982 lawsuit under FOIA, then-CIA Director William F. Raborn, Jr., reacted to the expose by ordering his director of security, Howard J. Osborn, to get a "run down" on *Ramparts* personnel on a "high priority basis." Raborn gave Osborn only two days for his staff to research a brief on *Ramparts*. With this command the Agency breached its restriction under the National Security Act of 1947 to refrain from domestic operations, and it never turned back. Dossiers were assembled on the editors and reporters, myself included. Osborn's deputies spent a good part of that spring digging into the magazine's finances with an eye to shutting it down. As Angus McKenzie disclosed in *Secrets: The CIA's War at Home*, another purpose of the probe "was to place *Ramparts* reporters under such close surveillance that any CIA officials involved in domestic operations would have time to rehearse cover stories before the reporters arrived to question them." Raborn was obsessed with the idea that we were in the process of uncovering more Agency covers.

He was right—we were peeking under the covers. One suspect was the Asia Foundation, a few blocks away in San Francisco. In January 1967 I showed up at the foundation's reception desk asking to speak with someone concerning its activities, as I was researching foundations. As CIA documents released under FOIA show, the man who handed me a calling card reading John Bannigan and invited me into his office was a staff officer. When I left, he checked with CIA headquarters at Langley, Virginia, and, to his surprise, learned that I was with *Ramparts*. As he reported to Langley, "Turner was pleasant, deferent and otherwise a picture in studied innocence throughout the conversation. At the same time, he asked exactly the 'right' questions."

But if the right questions didn't elicit the right answers, it didn't matter. A showstopper of a story came in over the transom about the venerable National Student Association, run by a congress of mostly left-leaning longhairs in vests, the last milieu on earth one would expect an intelligence agency to receive a warm welcome. But the CIA was there, Michael Wood insisted, and he was in a position to know since he was an NSA fund-raiser. While I was setting off bells at the Asia Foundation, a skeptical Warren Hinckle was meeting with Wood at the Algonquin Hotel in New York, the bar of which served as the magazine's meeting room. Wood had agonized for months about spilling the beans, finally deciding to do so while in the throes of an overwhelming guilt trip. Unbeknownst to the membership, Wood said, the NSA leadership had over the years jet-setted around the world to student conferences, feeding back to the CIA the results of confidential contacts with trusting foreign counterparts. The subsidies, which ran into tens of million dollars a year, were funneled to the students through a maze of Agency fronts and foundations. Until Wood came forth, no one suspected the CIA would turn students into spies.

Hinckle dispatched another task force to the field, which developed sufficient verification of what Wood had to say to prepare a story. The conundrum was: why had the CIA coopted the left, and why was the left playing along? The picture that emerged was that the career Ivy Leaguers in the Agency, themselves a bit liberal, at least on domestic issues, had in the 1950s crafted a plan of imperialistic scale to gain covert control over American professional organizations of journalists, educators, jurists and businessmen. These sectors were populated with staunch anticommunists of the so-called democratic left who could be inserted in positions here and abroad to undercut communist influence by selling the liberal alternative. A prime target was the Third World, where a little money fed through a front went a long way toward pocketing trade unions and other components of the political landscape. In scope and intent it was the kind of Pax Americana foisted on the world against which John Kennedy would warn. To set the tone for this Kulturkampf, the Agency set up the Congress for Cultural Freedom in Paris and encouraged new writings by such literary lights as Mary McCarthy, Robert Penn Warren, Robert Lowell, Hannah Arendt and Lionel Trilling, acknowledged liberals all. It may have been that they were extremely credulous, but in any case, the CIA manual deemed it a sign of successful propaganda when the "subject moved in a direction you desire for reasons he believes to be his own." The seductive effect of the Agency's plan on witting progressives was articulated by one NSA leader who argued against our going to press with the story on grounds that the CIA funds were used for valuable liberal projects, even anti–Vietnam War teach-ins (besides, he said, he might lose his draft deferment). Another NSA honcho rationalized in a similar vein: disclosure would be damaging to the "liberal" internationalist wing of the CIA, which was willing to dole out money to domestic progressive causes. It was like saying that dope dealers who tithed Mother Teresa were in reality good guys.

The article was scheduled to run in the March 1967 issue, but as it was being written, in what theoretically was great secrecy, word filtered back that the CIA antenna was picking up our signals. A *Ramparts* double agent inside the NSA revealed that at that very moment the

Agency was assembling the key NSA hierarchy in an Arlington, Virginia, motel and was briefing them on a plan to neutralize the story, which was several weeks away from publication due to the fixed production schedules of monthlies. The strategy was for the NSA to hold a press conference disclosing, in a limited hang-out, that in the past the CIA had laid some money on the NSA but that its current leadership had terminated that inappropriate arrangement. By trivializing the situation, the Agency hoped to contain the secret of how extensively its networks had penetrated American institutions. By the time *Ramparts* came out with the full account, it would be seen as a rehash of old news, preserving the family jewels.

When Hinckle heard of the CIA scheme, he pulled off a preemptive strike that was at once brilliant and simple: he bought full-page advertisements in *The New York Times* and *The Washington Post* to run on Valentine's Day that began, "In its March issue, *Ramparts* magazine will document how the CIA has infiltrated and subverted the world of American student leaders over the past fifteen years." The ad was so crammed with details that the CIA would be unable to diminish its impact. When a *Times* reporter phoned the NSA leaders, who were gathered with their CIA handlers preparing for a press conference the following morning, to ask a few questions, panic set in. They ditched their handlers and caucused, deciding to call in the media and tell all. They even alleged that the CIA had "pressured" them to deny the truth of *Ramparts'* charges.

Like hounds to the spoor, the media took up the hunt for CIA cover institutions and dummy fronts. Reporters were queued up two-score deep outside Internal Revenue Service headquarters waiting to scour tax records for yet another collaborating conduit; they were trading foundation tax reports as if they were bubblegum baseball cards. After a few weeks of this frenzy the covers were denuded, baring the participation of such enterprises as the National Council of Churches, the International Commission of Jurists, the American Friends of the Middle East, the Ford and Rockefeller Foundations, Harper & Row, the United Auto Workers, the Metropolitan Opera and Time, Inc. An amazed Hinckle remarked, "It is a rare thing in this business when you say bang and somebody says I'm dead."

Reaction elsewhere was hardly muted. President Lyndon Johnson ordered an immediate end to CIA covert subsidies to student groups and appointed a committee to look into allegations that the Agency was operating domestically against its charter. Vice President Humphrey lamented, "This is one of the saddest times our government has had." *Newsweek* viewed the affair as the CIA's "most damaging scandal since the Bay of Pigs," and observed that to high CIA officials "almost as galling as the story was the vehicle of its disclosure — *Ramparts.*" For its part, the magazine won the George Polk Memorial Award for excellence in journalism, an honor, Hinckle wryly noted, "shared this year with the essay department of *Time* magazine. Any remarks about strange bedfellows would be fatuous, idle and undignified."

The CIA's old boys at Langley were once again in high dudgeon. As Evan Thomas recently revealed in *The Very Best Men,* his book on the CIA mullahs, James Angleton, the orchid-growing, martini-sipping chief of counterintelligence who wracked the CIA for years with his paranoia about a mole, believed that the article was a "Soviet plot" and vowed to figure out a way to shutter *Ramparts.* Desmond FitzGerald, chief of clandestine services, was already in action. Des Fitz, as his colleagues called him, was the Agency's Great Gatsby, just as Richard Helms was its Lone Ranger. A veteran of the Office of Strategic Services, the World War II forerunner of the CIA, he went to Harvard law school and married the socially prominent Marietta Tree (who later divorced him). Recruited by the CIA, FitzGerald became an imaginative hatcher of lethal dirty tricks that can politely be called harebrained. It was he who proposed in April 1963 that on a trip to Cuba attorney James Donovan, who had negotiated the release of the Bay of Pigs prisoners, plant a bomb concealed in a seashell, to be fabricated by the CIA laboratory, which could be detonated when Fidel Castro swam by while skin diving. When the lab vetoed this idea as impractical, he came up with an alternative: have Donovan present as a gift to Castro a skin diving suit that the lab had impregnated on the inside with deadly

65

tubercle bacilli. Again, no go. In Paris, on the night of the JFK assassination, FitzGerald operative Nestor Sanchez met with Rolando Cubela, a Cuban double agent who had expressed a willingness to kill Castro, and gave him a ballpoint pen fitted with a hypodermic needle from which the poison Blackleaf-40 could be injected (Cubela never used the pen, and later asked for a scoped rifle). According to Evan Thomas, when FitzGerald got wind of what *Ramparts* was up to, he assigned case officer Edgar Applewhite to try to discredit the editors any way he could.

"I had all sorts of dirty tricks to hurt their circulation and financing," Applewhite told Thomas twenty-five years later. "The people running *Ramparts* were vulnerable to blackmail. We had awful things in mind, some of which we carried off, though *Ramparts* (eventually) fell of its own accord. We were not the least inhibited by the fact that the CIA had no internal security role in the United States."

When Applewhite returned from his mission to brief FitzGerald on his dirty tricks (he would not reveal to Thomas what they were), the CIA chief was amused. "Eddie," he said, "you have a spot of blood on your pinafore."

What stained the pinafore remains pretty much a mystery. As far as I know, there were no serious casualties among the editors and staff during that period, nor do I recall any suspicious-looking seashells lying about the office. There had been a burglary of the editorial offices, about which more later. Personally, I was audited by the IRS over a $35 dispute (I told the auditor, one Mrs. Black, that I was sure another government agency had put her up to it, which she didn't deny), and there was an attempted break-in of my Mill Valley home that had none of the earmarks of a commercial job. But the only potential for blackmail among the personnel was some legendary drinking and pot smoking. As for the financial part, the CIA's in-house history of the NSA affair reveals that "possible examination by the Agency of *Ramparts* income tax returns was discussed by IRS but was not accomplished." Probably because there was nothing there: Hinckle recognized well the proclivity of government agencies to use the IRS as a weapon, and the returns were as clean as a whistle. But that same history divulged that after the news of the impending article hit Langley, two hundred of FitzGerald's finest worked for two weeks around the clock on damage control. Their efforts went for naught, and in the end, as Thomas put it, the Agency's "whole system of anticommunist fronts in Europe, Asia, and South America was essentially blown."

It was a measure of the panic gripping Langley that Richard Helms, who had succeeded Raborn as director, now formed a Special Operations Group (SOG) focused on *Ramparts* and designed Operation MHCHAOS to run parallel with FitzGerald's off-channels campaign. Heading the SOG was Richard Ober, another buttoned-down Ivy Leaguer with reddish hair and complexion, who was designated by Helms to succeed the director of security, Howard Osborn, as chief of the Ramparts Task Force. The move was made to prevent any leaks to the media: Ober was a veteran counterintelligence officer—the elitist of the elite, and he functioned in the tightest security (so secret that even his closest associates were supposed to deny knowing him) with a select staff of twelve. Ober had tried in vain to imagine a way to stop *Ramparts* from publishing the NSA piece, and it was he who conceived the idea of staging the preemptive press conference by the student leaders that Hinckle finessed with the full-page newspaper ads. It was almost the stuff of fiction to pit the shadowy Ober in a war of wits against the conspicuous Hinckle with his eye patch.

Ober wasn't outed until 1975 when he was summoned to testify before the Rockefeller Commission investigating intelligence agency abuses. He admitted to parts of MHCHAOS but kept silent on its most sensitive secrets. The "MH" signified that the operation was worldwide, zeroing in on not only *Ramparts* but, eventually, the entire antiwar press, while "CHAOS" stood for what it spelled. Ober persuaded the IRS to send over tax data on the magazine and its personnel, and one of his analysts thought he had found a discrepancy (although there is no record of what was done about it). He pulled out all the stops to try to find foreign funding and influence, which might have justified a domestic spying operation, but struck out. Undeterred by legal niceties, Ober wrote a memo proposing "certain operational recommendations." While the text of this document remains classified, some idea of its sweep can be gained from other sources. CIA officer Louis Dube, deposed in the course of a Freedom of Information Act lawsuit, disclosed that all *Ramparts* staff writers and researchers, as well as other persons somehow linked to the magazine, were thoroughly investigated. On March 4, 1967, Dube said, a report was received at Langley from a person who had attended a *Ramparts* staff meeting at which interviews with high-ranking executive branch officials were discussed, which suggested that infiltration was one of Ober's methods. Twelve days later Ober's men picked up a CIA agent in Washington who was a good friend of a *Ramparts* reporter, took him to a hotel, debriefed him, gave him a cover story, and sent him back to get more information from the reporter. At the same time, Ober was trying to recruit five former *Ramparts* employees as informants. My own CIA file, which is noteworthy for what is redacted, shows that under CHAOS there was a continuing interest "in any information on members of the staff; their travel, contacts and activities."

Ober also mounted a propaganda campaign against *Ramparts* using CIA assets in the media. As an example, nationally syndicated columnist Carl Rowan, an erstwhile director of the CIA-affiliated United States Information Agency, wrote shortly after the NSA exposé broke, "A few days ago a brief, cryptic report out of Prague, Czechoslovakia, was passed among a handful of top officials in Washington. It said that an editor of *Ramparts* magazine had come to Prague and held a long, secret session with officers of the Communist-controlled International Union of Students." The intent obviously was to imply that the magazine was communist-influenced, which was comic to anyone who knew the editors. But the content was necessarily skimpy on details because it was fictitious (Rowan refused to discuss the subject).

Ober was also absorbed with cutting off *Ramparts'* advertising revenues, thinking that would cause a financial coronary. On April 28, 1967, Dube recalled, the spymaster tried to find out if the Agency had any contacts in a position to persuade advertisers to drop their accounts. Ober apparently was abiding by the Madison Avenue convention that magazines survived through advertising. But he should have realized that *Ramparts* wasn't conventional. Those glossy full-page ads were mostly knockoffs from conventional magazines that *Ramparts* ran gratis and without permission to give a look of prestige and prosperity (upon learning that one of their ads had graced a page of the magazine, Pan American World Airways executives were incensed). In reality, advertising revenue was a trickle; the magazine was sustained by subscription and newsstand receipts.

Richard Ober had other designs up his sleeve—what Dube tagged "heady shit." But Dube refused to expand, and to this day the Agency clings to the excuse that disclosure would expose their "methods." One can only assume that these methods were so down and dirty, perhaps even criminal, that they would be hugely embarrassing.

Hinckle sensed that floating in the stream of unsolicited manuscripts coming in as a result of the exposés were a few whose authors were plants, and that infiltration of the staff was a likelihood. To forestall publication of an article that would blow up in our faces and to screen out infiltrators, he charged me with manning a "spook desk" on the theory that it took an old intelligence agent to recognize one. Hinckle called it the Ramparts Bureau of Investigation, but if the truth be known, I relied more on intuition and the articles' content than shoe leather to judge their authenticity. The RBI was put to the test almost immediately when an approach was made by a young man who claimed to be a kind of Don Duncan of the CIA, a junior officer who quit in disgust over its tactics. Some of his bona fides were checkable, such as graduating from Berkeley in anthropology, a discipline that was catnip to the CIA, but the main test was talking for hours on a park bench in Richmond, near Berkeley, to avoid prying ears. He did not come across as evasive or deceptive, and there were no discrepancies in his account, based on what I already knew about the Agency. His story ran in the April 1967 issue as "How I Got In, and Why I Came Out of the Cold," although he understandably did not want his name used. I knew him as Caldbeck. He fancied himself politically liberal but fully approved the CIA's intelligence-gathering responsibilities. He described how he had graduated from the tradecraft school at Camp Peary near Williamsburg, Virginia, that taught clandestine skills, including burglary. He had gone on to demolition training at Isolation Tropic, a hidden base near Elizabeth City, North Carolina, where he learned such things as how to make a granary explode and how to incinerate a bus. If Caldbeck had been awarded a CIA medal for applying these black arts in the field—agents can look at but not touch the medals—he modestly refrained from mentioning it.

Then Caldbeck's conscience hit the wall over a recruiting practice that targeted foreign students attending U.S. universities, some on Fulbright exchange scholarships, who would return to their native lands as CIA agents-in-place. Caldbeck was assigned to the San Francisco station, probably because of his fluency in Asian languages. His territory was the West Coast, which included schools from UCLA to Washington. He was "sheepdipped," that is, he was a CIA agent operating as a military officer with the cooperation of the Department of Defense. He recounted how he had been instructed to recruit the students, many of whom were from Third World countries and could be expected to rise rapidly to influential positions after their return. Caldbeck selected his prospects from lists sent out from Langley, presumably obtained from the State Department.

"I wasn't too interested in the Taiwan Chinese," he said, "although I did recruit one guy whose mother was high in the legislative councils on Taiwan."

He focused on students from mainland China and other nominally hostile countries. He went on: "From various sources I obtained reports, descriptions and evaluations of them, so that by the time I received permission from headquarters to attempt to recruit them, I knew them like a book. In the face of this interpersonal relationship, I often had to use the Agency's bag of dirty tricks to nail down a person's compliance. As an example, I might give him $10 'expenses' for his help in performing some innocuous task and get him to sign a U.S. government receipt. Then I would kite the amount to $1,000 by adding zeros and threaten to expose his 'valuable assistance' to us if he didn't cooperate. In time I began to despise this kind of deceit, especially when used against the young and the naive idealists. Their faces began to haunt me. The attrition among agents on both sides was high, and they probably sensed it. Some, obviously terrified at the thought, simply failed to meet me as arranged and dropped from sight. Others were arrested, and they disappeared. The ones that remained had been transformed into cynical, hardened spies." The CIA would neither confirm nor deny the article.

When the Oxford-educated Senator J. William Fulbright, who sponsored the exchange program bearing his name, read the article, he asked me to visit his office. "I knew the CIA was recruiting the U.S. scholars going abroad to study," he said. "But I never once dreamed they were going after foreign scholars studying here." Other than protest to the Agency, the senator didn't have a clue as to what to do about it. "I'm just a country boy," he cracked. "Guess I'll go back to Arkansas."

But Jacob M. "Jack" Kaplan was no country boy in the way he used the CIA to stalemate the IRS. The Manhattan-based Kaplan was the proprietor of Southwestern Sugar & Molasses, whose operations stretched throughout the Caribbean. He was a political benefactor of such fashionable liberals as Hubert Humphrey and Chester Bowles. At the same time, he ran the $20 million J. M. Kaplan Fund, which showered money on such do-good causes as the New School for Social Research, Henry Street Settlement and free Shakespeare in Central Park. But other beneficiaries were not so deserving: the Kaplan Fund was secretly being used as a CIA conduit for subsidies to "safe" social democratic alternatives to communist and hard-line socialist regimes in the Caribbean region. Kaplan funded the Institute of International

Labor Research, a creature of the CIA, through which hundreds of agents fanned out across the Caribbean posing as sociologists, students and consultants. Their mission: solidify the opposition.

But there was a quid pro quo, albeit illegal. On August 31, 1964, a feisty Texas congressmen, Wright Patman, was holding hearings on the lax policing of tax-exempt foundations by the IRS. He caused a one-day sensation when he charged that the Agency was interfering to keep the IRS from pursuing possible multimillion-dollar tax violations by the Kaplan Fund because it was being utilized as a conduit for "foreign operations of the CIA." He reeled off the names of several phony foundations reportedly set up by the Agency to run money through the Kaplan Fund and other foundations. Declared Patman, "[Our] study of the J. M. Kaplan Fund's operations indicates a large possible tax liability as well as violations of Treasury regulations and abuse of its public trust, including self-dealing to the detriment of the Fund's stated charitable purposes." If the specter of prison flickered in Jack Kaplan's mind when he heard those words, his apprehension was short-lived. After the hearing ended that day, Patman huddled with representatives of the CIA and IRS, emerging to announce he would "delve no further" because "no matter of interest . . . relating to the CIA existed." The national security curtain had been dropped on a major tax-cheat investigation.

The curtain stayed down for the next three years. Then, as the CIA exposés rolled off the pages of *Ramparts*, Hinckle and I were confidentially contacted by a man who claimed he was an accountant and fiscal advisor for the Kaplan Fund. He had documentary evidence, he said, of the financial skullduggery that went on behind the Agency's shield. It had been going on for a decade, and he was appalled at what Jack Kaplan was getting away with. At the same time, he was afraid. I told him I was an ex-FBI agent and would use appropriate security measures. Where did he want to meet? In true espionage fashion, he chose Grand Central Station.

After the agreed-upon signals and password, I shook hands with a well-tailored gray-haired man, briefcase in hand, who looked every inch the senior professional. Albert Arbor delivered what he had promised: reams of internal records that detailed Kaplan's extensive tax-avoidance manipulations. Stock losses suffered by Kaplan or corporations he controlled were frequently transferred to the Kaplan Fund retroactively so that it would take the loss. For instance, on June 8, 1959, Community Newspapers, Inc., which was owned by Kaplan, bought 1,000 shares of Minute Maid at $24.20 a share. When the stock closed down $1.08 that day, Kaplan had the brokerage house change the ownership to the Kaplan Fund. By December 31, 1959, the price of Minute Maid had plunged to $18.34 a share, and the Fund had sustained a considerable loss. On the other hand, if Minute Maid had gone up, Kaplan would have put it in his own account and pocketed the profit.

Kaplan also used the New School to control stock in companies he was trying to take over. As an example, on May 11, 1955, he lent the school $150,000 interest free for the express purpose of buying 2,500 shares of Minnesota and Ontario Paper Company. Since he was the principal contributor to and trustee of the New School, he could direct how the shares were voted. But the lending of money at no interest by a foundation was an egregious violation of the tax code.

Armed with the Arbor windfall as evidence, Hinckle and I trooped into the Washington office of Edward Bennett Williams, who was serving as *Ramparts'* unpaid libel lawyer, to show him the galley proofs of the Kaplan Fund article we were about to publish. We repaired to the conference room, where Williams thoroughly vetted the text while I stared at a protracted map of the world on the wall. Finally, he pronounced the documentation so tight that we would ultimately prevail in any lawsuit.

"But how much do you rely on newsstand sales?" he asked.

"We couldn't survive a month without them," Hinckle replied.

In that case, Williams said, Jack Kaplan had the power to close us down. He would have his attorney, the famed Louis Nizer, seek an injunction that would freeze the receipts from newsstand sales (the law has since been changed).

Warren flew off to Denver, where the magazine was printed, and, in the interest of living to fight another day, substituted a different article in the issue going to press. The story of the "CIA exemption" was filed away.*

But the galleys didn't stay filed away for long—they were embezzled and handed over to the CIA. According to a recently released Agency memo dated December 11, 1967, the miscreant was former *Ramparts* staff writer John Raymond, whom Scheer had charitably hired months earlier because he needed the money. But finances at the magazine were getting tight, and a few marginal staffers, Raymond among them, were let go. Apparently bent on retaliation, Raymond invited a CIA "reliable source" to his apartment and handed him the Kaplan galleys as well as the notes of our Vietnam correspondent, David Welsh, an ex–*Detroit News* reporter, on how Lyndon Johnson made sure his old Texas buddies, George and Herman Brown of Brown & Root, got the lion's share of construction contracts for a huge American military base in the country. Raymond told the CIA source that he wanted to "expose" *Ramparts* so that its "financial support will dry up and the magazine will fold."

This was exactly the aim of the CIA, and presumably Raymond's materials were avidly read at Langley. But the *Ramparts* economic downdraft had nothing to do with newsstand sales. Although Hinckle's spendthrift ways didn't help, investor booster shots of money, for which there was a continuing need, were not coming in as they had. The reasons were perverse. Martin Peretz, who years later bought the *New Republic*, had plunked down close to $1 million in support of the CIA articles but objected to a *Ramparts* editorial on the 1967 Israeli-Egyptian Six-Day War that he didn't consider sufficiently pro–Tel Aviv.

---

*In 1975 Kaplan's plan to tie up newsstand sales and put *Ramparts* out of business was confirmed. In New York City a writer friend, Betsy Langman, whose family owned Gimbel's department store and was prominent in philanthropic circles, insisted that I join a group for lunch in the restaurant at the top of the Pan Am Building. In the group were the president and business manager of the New School for Social Research. When Betsy introduced me they were cordial as could be. But when she added, "This is the *Ramparts* Bill Turner," their smiles froze. But they were good sports, recounting that when Jack Kaplan somehow got wind of the impending story, he summoned them to his office to brainstorm what to do about it. And the decision was indeed made to have Louis Nizer put a legal clamp on newsstand revenues.

Other monied liberals were scared off by the magazine's backing of the Black Panthers, as personified by Eldridge Cleaver, a staff writer. To be sure, the Panthers' rhetoric was fiery (H. Rap Brown declaimed that "violence is as American as apple pie"), their outfits of black jackets and berets menacing. But they claimed they were simply protecting the black population of Oakland from a predatory police force; their good works included organizing day care centers and free breakfast programs. Cleaver himself was the best-selling author of *Soul on Ice*, a searing cry against racism.*

It is interesting to note that during this period J. Edgar Hoover had replaced a moribund Communist Party with the Black Panthers as the number one international menace. Failing to recognize that the Panthers were an indigenous movement, he pulled out all the stops in seeking evidence that they were being secretly funded by the People's Republic of China (he never found a shred). The FBI had a wiretap on Panther leader Huey Newton's phone (duly intercepting Newton calls to me) and deployed COINTELPRO against the group. Perhaps the most despicable tactic was the destruction of Jean Seberg, the movie actress celebrated for her role as Joan of Arc, because she was one of the Panthers' prominent white supporters. In 1969 a wiretap revealed that Seberg was pregnant. The FBI anonymously leaked the gossipy news, falsely identifying the father as a Black Panthers member. Following a publicity cloudburst, Seberg, who was emotionally fragile, took an overdose of sleeping pills, and the baby survived only two days after being born. She became obsessed over the baby's death, the more so when, several years later, she learned of the FBI's dirty trick. In 1979 she committed suicide. Her husband, French novelist Romain Gary, gave the epitaph, "Jean Seberg was destroyed by the FBI."

---

*In April 1968, Cleaver was involved in a shootout with Oakland police in which party member Bobby Hutton was killed. Charged with attempted murder, he was released on $50,000 bail pending trial. He maintained that the "shootout" actually was a trap set by the police. In December, as the trial loomed, Cleaver guided me into a *Ramparts* stock room for a private talk. He asked questions suggesting he was going to flee to Cuba via Canada, which, a few days later, he did. In 1975 he returned voluntarily from exile. The criminal case against him was weak, and he struck a deal with the prosecution in which he was placed on probation.

Like a space capsule making a water landing, *Ramparts* went out with a majestic splash. In October 1967, Che Guevara, a hero of the Cuban revolution who was leading a band of insurgents through the hinterlands of South America, trying to persuade peasants to rise up, was cornered and killed by a Bolivian army elite unit tutored by the CIA. The tinhorn Bolivian generals who had ordered his murder were putting his artifacts up for auction, chief among them his diary, with the CIA acting as a Sotheby's. Since Che was an icon to the world's oppressed—even American teenagers hung posters of his handsome beret-topped face on their bedroom walls—the diary would be a publishing coup. Hordes of publisher gunslingers descended on La Paz, the Bolivian capital, to put in their bid. A Magnum consortium played the high hand at $200,000, a moonshot price for that era.

Then a peculiar thing happened. The Bolivian interior minister, Antonio Arguedas Mendieta, dispatched a copy of the diary on the sly to Fidel Castro. He did it, he said, to spite the CIA, which toyed with his country as if it were a Lionel train. He charged that the Agency planned to doctor the text to make it seem a chronicle of revolutionary failure rather than an epic struggle. Bob Scheer happened to be in Havana to interview Castro when the diary arrived, and, to his utter astonishment, the Cuban president offered it gratis to *Ramparts* because he liked the magazine. As Hinckle would explain in his memoirs, "He found it amusing that we shocked so many people on the American left. He understood fighting slick with slick. He knew about guerrilla journalism. And he was betting *Ramparts* would slam Che's diary into the United States in a way that would pull the rug out from under the CIA's own publishing plans." Hinckle and Scheer rushed to New York and wangled a $40,000 deal with Bantam Books to publish an instant paperback simultaneously with a special edition of the magazine, which was printed in high secrecy over a weekend. The generals' junta was scooped, the diary's virginity remained inviolate, and *Ramparts* was $40,000 richer.

But $40,000 couldn't save the magazine. In December 1969, six months after the Che masterstroke, *Ramparts* filed for bankruptcy. The

CIA of course never had a credit problem: its current budget, despite the end of the Cold War, is estimated at some $27 billion. It justifies this staggering expenditure by conjuring up new menaces, but it probably hasn't forgotten one called *Ramparts*. The magazine was uniquely a product of its contentious times, and it is not probable that there will ever be another quite like it.

5

OPERATION CHAOS, INC.

In April 1967, the morning after Easter, barely two months after *Ramparts* broke the CIA–National Students Association story, I was the first to arrive at the editorial offices, which wasn't unusual since the editors were largely night people. I was greeted by a scene of feral vandalism. A serpentine trail of white goo from the fire extinguishers led from the receptionist's desk to practically every piece of furniture in the place. Chairs had been tossed through the plate glass front windows. An IBM Selectric typewriter lay askew in the toilet bowl, as if in scatological commentary on the magazine's articles. Documents yanked out of file cabinets were scattered on the floor.

A San Francisco police sergeant who responded to my call dutifully asked questions and took notes. No, there was no sign of forced entry. Any suspects? "All I can think of is a right-wing nut," I said, observing that nothing appeared to have been taken. When Warren Hinckle arrived a couple of hours later, he capriciously told a UPI reporter, "It must have been the CIA."

As it turned out, the CIA *was* involved. But not in the trashing episode—there had been a burglary two nights earlier that went undetected. It was committed by an ideologue in the employ of a right-wing network hitting an array of left-of-center targets, including people's advocate Saul Alinsky in Chicago and the United Farm Workers' Cesar Chavez in California. The stolen documents were distributed among agribusiness giants, corporate executives, conservative data banks, the FBI and the CIA. In truth, the private network was running a kind of CHAOS, Inc., since the *Ramparts* heist was a special order from the CIA. It is a classic illustration of how intelligence agencies use proxies in their operations.

None of this came to light until early 1975, when Hinckle called me from Cookie Picetti's bar. He had been approached by a man who claimed to have burglarized *Ramparts* back in April 1967, which was the month the offices were trashed.

"But he couldn't have done it," Hinckle flatly declared.

"Why not?" I asked.

"Because Gene Marine [a *Ramparts* editor] and I did it," he confessed. He explained that they had imbibed too many coffee royals at the Tosca Cafe on Columbus that night and made a besotted decision to ransack the offices for some perverse fun. Hinckle wanted me to rush down to Picetti's and talk to the burbling burglar as one former second-story man to another.

Jerry Ducote was impeccably groomed, with silvery hair and soft brown eyes, the manner of a con man, and a frame so huge I wondered how he could have wriggled through windows. He was, I thought, an improbable burglar. Although he contended he pulled off on average one burglary a month during the two years he was active, he obviously hadn't learned the trade at the FBI Sound School. Simple, he said. For ten years he had been a burglary and vice squad detective for the Santa Clara County Sheriff's Office. It was his habit upon collaring a burglar to make him demonstrate how he gained entry and how he opened safes and file cabinets. Ducote recalled that when he broke into the San Jose law office of John E. Thorne, who represented Black Panther leader George Jackson, he found the safe combination pasted under a secretary's desk drawer. In other capers he found that the office phone number backwards or the serial number of a file cabinet was the secret. He was careful to leave no trace of his presence. When he broke into the house of a woman aiding the farm workers, for example, he crawled in an open window, then blew some dust from the top of the refrigerator onto the windowsill so it would continue to look dirty. "Those lefties don't clean house well," Ducote remarked. "There's always a lot of dust around."

What dispelled all doubt that Ducote had victimized *Ramparts* was the handful of papers he pulled out of a brown attache case. Just a sample, he said. There were publisher's canceled checks, investigative memos on the CIA, and Hinckle's bar bills. "Son of a bitch," Hinckle bellowed, "you broke into *Ramparts* too!" Ducote fixed the date as April 6, 1967, two days before the Hinckle-and-Marine infamy on Easter eve. They had unwittingly covered up for Ducote, since *Ramparts* staffers with missing files assumed they had been stolen in the unsolved trashing.

Ducote named his handler in the political network as Stephen D'Arrigo, Jr., widely known as the "lettuce king of California," whose firm, D'Arrigo Brothers, was the largest grower in the Salinas Valley, called "the salad bowl of the nation." The ruggedly handsome D'Arrigo, a brawny man with a background in military intelligence, was a generous contributor to conservative Republican causes, including the 1966 gubernatorial campaign of Ronald Reagan. As a grower, D'Arrigo sought continuance of the bracero program and had frowned on my *Ramparts* article a year earlier, pushing for its termination. He instructed Ducote to bring out with him not only my files on the bracero article but documents on CIA covert programs, financial records, and editorial files, as well as the materials I had gathered on the John Kennedy assassination, about which I had begun to write. And, oh yes, Ducote said, the FBI wanted anything personally damaging to me.

A week after the black-bag job, Ducote said, he flew first class on TWA to Washington, D.C., at his feet twenty-five pounds of *Ramparts* papers crammed into a black leather map-carrying case borrowed from a pilot friend. He rendezvoused with D'Arrigo, who had taken an earlier flight as a security precaution, and the wealthy grower took him directly to the Capitol Hill office of Charles Gubser, a crusty congressman from D'Arrigo's district who was the ranking Republican on the House Armed Services Committee. Waiting until his secretaries went home, Gubser pulled the office blinds and mixed drinks. Ducote extracted the *Ramparts* swag from the map case. Thumbing through it, Gubser stopped short when he came to a memo describing a CIA covert program in western Europe that used military dependents as spies. "I'm on the military affairs subcommittee," the lawmaker cried, waving the memo. "How come the CIA never told me about this?" He picked up the phone and called Agency headquarters.

Gubser arranged for Ducote and D'Arrigo to meet a CIA agent at the Georgetown Inn. The agent turned out to be urbane and sophisticated. He studied the documents for two hours and was relieved to find that *Ramparts* didn't appear to know anything more about his compartmentalized organization than he did. The agent paid for dinner, thanking his California visitors for the "fruit basket." When he left, he cautioned that it might be better if they all remained on a first-name basis. It wasn't until he was on the plane going home that Ducote realized the agent hadn't even given his first name.

Two days after their return, D'Arrigo phoned Ducote. "The people in Washington have requested that we have another meeting," he said. "I've rented a room for tomorrow at the Hyatt House in San Jose." The CIA agent who showed up the following morning was a study in contrasts with his East Coast counterpart. He had short blond hair combed Prince Valiant–style over his forehead. He seemed edgy. He flashed his CIA credentials but kept his thumb over his name. He sat in silence on the side of the bed, poring over the *Ramparts* documents, flipping each page with a pencil eraser to avoid leaving fingerprints. He asked Ducote to open each file folder, refusing to touch them himself, and took copious notes. At one point Ducote, seeking to break the chill, asked if these were the usual Agency procedures. The agent glared at the burglar. "Don't you know that these documents are stolen?" he asked.

A month after his *Ramparts* caper, in May 1967, Ducote pulled off another burglary set up by Steve D'Arrigo. The victim was Cesar Chavez, whose incipient United Farm Workers union was viewed by the big growers as a clear and present danger to the bracero system. This time Ducote was assigned a partner in crime, allegedly Henry Sterling, a spindly, nervous man with a bobbing Adam's apple, who, like Ducote, had been active in the John Birch Society. On the appointed night, Ducote, garbed in a safari outfit, and Sterling pulled into the parking lot of the Carousel Restaurant on the outskirts of Delano, the Central Valley town where Chavez was based. They were driving a white Chrysler rented by Sterling. Soon a tan Chevy Impala with a citizen's band antenna sprouting from its roof and the logo of the Three Brothers Ranch on the doors stopped alongside. At the wheel, wearing a tailored cowboy jacket, was allegedly Jack Pandol, one of the state's largest grape growers and supporter of a variety of right-wing causes. Governor Reagan had appointed him to the State Board of Agriculture.

Wordlessly, Pandol handed Ducote an envelope stuffed with $1,400 in used $100 bills, the pay for the night's work, and a key. "I had no idea how he got the key," Ducote told us. But he did know that it fit the rear door of the Philippine Social Hall in Delano, a faded clapboard structure that Chavez was using as a hiring hall and command post for the national grape boycott he was trying to mount. Entering at 2:00 A.M., Ducote and Sterling took fifteen minutes to lug off four boxes filled with records covering several years: the names and addresses of dues-paying UFW members, the mailing list of financial contributors across the country, and strategy files containing the plans and national contacts for the grape boycott. As a result, the boycott schedule was severely set back. And the names on the lists were entered in CIA and FBI data banks, enabling COINTELPRO-type operations against the UFW's backers.

But, like the Watergate burglary to come, the UFW job didn't go off without a hitch. On the way out the door with the last box of loot, Sterling tripped over two farm workers sleeping on the floor. Panicked, he pulled out a .32-caliber pistol and pointed it at the terrified pair, then ran to the white Chrysler. As the car sped away, one of the workers peered through a window and observed the license number, then called police. Incredibly, Sterling had rented the Chrysler in his own name, and in a matter of hours a statewide APB was out for him. By brandishing the pistol, he had increased the crime from burglary to armed robbery.

Ducote remembered that when he found out about the APB he called Steve D'Arrigo in a sweat. Sterling was shaky, and if he talked under police questioning it might lead to the entire ring. Within an hour, Ducote and a local attorney named Robert Baker took off from San Jose Airport in the D'Arrigo company plane. The grower had already made calls to the FBI and arranged for them to meet with the Delano police chief in the anonymity of Bakersfield. When they landed, a Delano police car was waiting alongside the runway; the chief, James Ailes, was in it. The trio drove to a bar where, while Ailes sipped a tomato beer, ex-cop Ducote spoke his language. He argued that Sterling was no common thief but a good thief—he had taken only materials that would prove the communist taint of the farm workers' movement. "I had trouble keeping a straight face," Ducote grinned. "The chief had no idea I was the other burglar." Ailes was impressed. He mentioned that he had already received a call from the FBI expressing an interest in Sterling's welfare. He canceled the APB and didn't pursue charges. Cesar Chavez protested that there was a "massive coverup" to protect the big names behind the plot, but this was before Watergate, before the term *break-in* became a part of the political lexicon. In fact, Reagan's lieutenant governor, John Harmer, became so emboldened by the laissez-faire climate that he printed letters stolen in the UFW burglary in a pamphlet attacking Cesar Chavez (Harmer later denied knowing that the letters were stolen).

Ducote had first gained political notoriety several years earlier when he sued the city of San Jose for flying the United Nations flag, which made him an instant idol of the local Birchers. He became county chairman of the Birch Society, then clambered up the political ladder to become a member of the California Republican Central Committee and star of the California Young Republicans. Columnist Joseph Alsop described him as an extremist who helped shove the California Republican Party away from the moderation of Earl Warren and into Goldwater-Reagan radicalism.

Assured of his political reliability, several wealthy growers saw in Ducote's law enforcement background an opportunity to exploit him as a private spy. The approach was made in 1965 by a brilliant self-styled "communist hurter" named R. Ken Wilhelm, secretary of the Santa Clara County Farm Bureau, who became his case officer. The 300-pound Wilhelm had, according to Ducote, a conspiratorial turn of mind. He boasted of his contacts in the FBI and CIA and kept a red telephone on his desk that was reserved for "national security purposes." He periodically took it apart to check for bugs. The target assigned for Ducote's debut was the *People's World* newspaper, the West Coast Communist Party organ, in San Francisco. The growers wanted to cop its mailing list to see if any farm workers were on it. It was known that *People's World* annually updated the list, throwing the old one away. For days Ducote staked out the paper's trash bin at a rear door. Late one night, he recounted, a man came out the door with a thick mailing list in his hands and dumped it in the bin. No sooner had he gone back inside than Ducote was at the bin clawing for the prize, but so were four other men in topcoats. Each flashed identification, thinking the others were without authority. They turned out to be from the FBI, Army intelligence, the House Un-American Activities Committee, and the police intelligence squad. The cop solved the dilemma by offering to make copies of the mailing list for everyone. At that the five marched to a nearby bar to have a comradely drink.

There was nothing illegal about retrieving something that had been thrown away. But when Wilhelm took Ducote to an outfit called Western Research, located in an office building on San Francisco's Market Street, things took a darker twist. I was familiar with Western Research, having used its services more than once when I was an FBI agent. In essence it was a repository of information on political progressives, who were blacklisted by such paying clientele as blue-chip corporations Southern Pacific Railroad, Pacific Gas & Electric, Standard Oil of California, and the Hearst press. But agents from the FBI and the CIA, the police and military intelligence had only to display their credentials for free access. Wilhelm introduced Ducote to a Western Research official, Lawrence Cott, who later would go to work for conservative maven William F. Buckley, Jr. As they sat amidst the green file cabinets, Cott leaned forward and whispered to Ducote, "A lot of people would appreciate it if you could get the mailing list of the San Jose Peace Center."

"There is only one way to get it," Ducote said.

"That's up to you," Cott replied. "Every security agency in the Bay Area would cooperate if we could get that list." Apparently Cott wanted to swap data with the security agencies.

A few days later Ducote received an envelope in the mail from Western Research with nothing inside but a torn half of a dollar bill. That was followed by a phone call instructing him to meet a man at the Little Bit, a hole-in-the-wall tavern in San Francisco's financial district. The bar was empty except for one man; a torn dollar bill was conspicuous among his change. Ducote proffered his half and it matched. "I understand you want to pick up something down in San Jose," the man said. "This may be of some help." He took a folded piece of paper from the inside coat pocket of his brown gabardine suit. As he did, Ducote spotted a .38-caliber revolver with a six-inch barrel—standard FBI issue. On the paper was a diagram of the San Jose Peace Center office drawn to scale, with the types of locks on the doors and windows identified. "It made breaking into the place a piece of cake," Ducote enthused.

Ducote said he received this type of detailed briefing before sixteen of the seventeen break-ins he would pull off. Through the agents with the torn dollar bills, he knew the precise dimensions of windows and doors, the model of burglar alarm, if any, and the exact filing-cabinet drawer he should open to find the desired documents. "I could have walked through those places blindfolded," Ducote said. "It was like landing a plane on radar." The question I had was why, if it was so easy, the FBI just didn't do it itself. A possible answer lay in the timing of Ducote's first surreptitious entry at the peace center. It came only a few months after I let the cat out of the black bag in *Ramparts* and Hoover called a halt to Bureau burglaries because there would be blowback if one went wrong. But if Ducote were caught, he alone would take the tumble.

After all of the break-ins, Ducote said, the booty was taken to Wilhelm's luxurious ranch-style home, from which it was delivered to Western Research for microfilming and distribution to the intelligence agencies. In fact, most of the groups Ducote hit—among them the ACLU, Student Nonviolent Coordinating Committee, American-Russian Institute, Catholic Social Justice and George Jackson's attorney, John Thorne—were of primary interest to the FBI. But the stolen data was disseminated not only to the Bureau and the CIA but to the House Un-American Activities Committee, which catalogued it; the ultraright paramilitary Minutemen, who mailed death threats marked with rifle cross hairs to every person on the mailing list of a Palo Alto peace group; and the American Security Council (ASC), based in Chicago.

When Ducote told me he had been steered to the ASC by his California handlers, I realized how nationwide this network had become. In a 1972 book, *Power on the Right*, I devoted an entire chapter, "Free Enterprise Wages the Cold War," to the ASC because it was loaded with buttoned-down superhawks lobbying for a bigger and better anti-ballistic missile system on the grounds that there was a large missile gap with the Soviet Union (the gap turned out to be mythical). The ASC also kept dossiers on liberal activists, leftists and antiwar protesters on a scale rivaling that of its model, the FBI. The ASC stored some six million names on index cards to supply what it called a "subversive information service" for its 3,200 member companies. The fruits of Ducote's nocturnal labors helped fill those files, and firms ranging from Sears, Roebuck and Quaker Oats to General Electric and Motorola used them.

While in Chicago, Ducote met with ASC board member Robert W.

Galvin, the chief executive of defense contractor Motorola. The odd couple was closeted in Galvin's office for three hours. According to Ducote, Galvin was vitally interested in Saul Alinsky, the Chicago-based social activist. At the time, Alinsky was pioneering the tactic of soliciting proxy votes from company stockholders against corporate involvement in war technology, and Motorola was a prime contractor for the anti–ballistic missile system. Alinsky was already a Ducote victim—the burglar had broken into his Carmel, California, residence and snatched his briefcase, which contained his false teeth and keys to his Chicago office. Ducote mailed back the false teeth but used the keys to enter the office and haul away Alinsky's files. Finding the boxes too heavy to lift by himself, Ducote enlisted the aid of a building security guard to carry them to a waiting cab. "And why not? After all, I had the keys." Ducote didn't doubt that Galvin was aware of the method by which he obtained the files. But Galvin tensed when he began outlining future Alinsky operations. "Because of the nature of this material, I would rather have you deal with one of my aides," Galvin said, ushering the burglar out the door.

Having the gift of gab, Ducote doubled as an itinerant fund-raiser for his California sponsors in the budding espionage apparatus. In Philadelphia he wangled a $1,000 donation from J. Howard Pew, the board chairman of Sun Oil, who opened his deep pockets for rightist causes. In Southern California retired LAPD sergeant Norman Moore, whose unofficial Fire & Police Research Association peddled dossiers on local leftists, referred Ducote to a client, George Hearst, Jr., publisher of the *Los Angeles Herald-Examiner*. Hearst, who was involved in a protracted labor strike, was impressed with Ducote's anti-UFW exploits. He wrote out checks for $2,000 and $1,500 to Moore's Fi-Po, as it was known, but the money came back to Ducote in cash, minus a $500 Fi-Po "handling charge." Moore also arranged an appointment with a Los Angeles emissary of Lamont Copeland, Jr., the DuPont heir who was on the sucker list of just about every archconservative group. Copeland approved a $2,000 cash donation over the phone. Ducote delivered the money at the bar of the swank Beverly Rodeo Hotel to two burglars whose services he had retained for a second entry into Saul Alinsky's Chicago office. Ducote also worked closely in political espionage matters with Patrick J. Frawley, Jr., the head of Schick-Eversharp and Technicolor, a member of Ronald Reagan's "kitchen cabinet," and an inveterate backer of ultraconservative crusades.*

Another contact was Henry Salvatori, the oilman who was Reagan's chief financier. On a transcontinental jet, over a game of gin rummy, Ducote titillated Salvatori with the latest personal dirt his burglaries had yielded.

But a damper was put on the private spy network by the ill-fated Watergate break-in of April 1972, and it wound down its operations. The game became too dangerous: Senator Howard Baker of Tennessee was trying to persuade his colleagues, albeit unavailingly, to investigate the interlock between government intelligence agencies and their private counterparts—what he called "the animal crashing about in the forest."

By April 1974 Ducote was unemployed but had no compunctions about working the other side of the street. Using the alias Fred Schwartz, an act of considerable chutzpah, since the real Fred Schwartz ran the Christian Anti-Communist Crusade, Ducote called the UFW and offered to sell back the documents he had stolen two years earlier. But the UFW called the FBI, unaware of its role in covering up the burglary. Two agents shadowed Ducote as he met with UFW attorney Jerry Cohen to display samples of his wares. Instead of buying, Cohen lodged a civil rights complaint with the U.S. Department of Justice, which ordered the Bureau to investigate and turn over the results to local law

---

*Frawley was a generous supporter of the American Security Council and the Christian Anti-Communism Crusade, to name two beneficiaries, as well as right-wing politicians like Reagan and George Murphy, who was dubbed "the Senator from Technicolor." After I did a profile of him in *The Progressive* for September 1970, depicting him as perhaps the most influential of the right-wing moneybags, he told the *Santa Monica Evening Outlook*, with a touch of paranoia, that the profile "was just setting me up to be assassinated—that's all." He was in fact deadly serious. When the profile was reprinted in the *Philadelphia Inquirer*, I received a letter from the colonel in charge of the Pennsylvania Military College asking me to use my influence with Frawley to secure a donation to the college. I forwarded the letter to Frawley with the notation, "The good colonel does not merit an 'A' in reading comprehension." No response.

enforcement officials for prosecution. Agents knew, of course, that Ducote was one of the perpetrators. A few weeks later they interviewed Ducote in a Bakersfield motel, and he confessed. The Bureau's report was complete, down to such details as Ducote's cigarette habit—Camels, chain-smoked—and beverage preference—sherry.

But the Bureau stonewalled, refusing to turn the report over to local authorities, undoubtedly fearful that its own role in the affair would be exposed. It wasn't until November 1975, when the Santa Clara County district attorney, who had gotten wind of the burglary conspiracy, threatened to prosecute FBI agents for obstruction of justice, that the report was surrendered. The agents (Charles Bates, the San Francisco SAC who led the hunt for Patty Hearst, and Buck Sample of the San Jose suboffice) were read their Miranda rights by investigators from the DA's office. It was Bates's second entanglement with political burglaries—he had been demoted from assistant director for moving too slowly in probing the Watergate break-in three years before.

A few days before Christmas 1975 the DA charged Ducote with twenty-two counts of fraud and concealing stolen property, stemming from his burglary career. The DA's men had found a stash of photocopies of Ducote's purloined loot next to his high school yearbooks in the basement of his home. "INCREDIBLE PILE OF STOLEN DOCUMENTS," headlined the *San Francisco Chronicle*. The question was posed how one man could have stolen so much from so many and gotten away with it for so long. The answer, at least in part, was FBI concealment. In court, miffed Santa Clara County officials testified that the Bureau deliberately misled them about the burglaries; that FBI officers baldly lied to local investigators; that when the Bureau finally was forced to turn over the Ducote report, it was doctored to sanitize prior knowledge; and that FBI agents admitted to local police they had "orders from above" not to cooperate in any investigation of Ducote.

But no criminal charges were ever brought against the FBI, and the men who directed and financed Ducote escaped scot-free. The attorney for Stephen D'Arrigo told the investigators that it "was hard to believe educated men could fall into this web, but at the time they thought they were doing their country a service." Kenneth Wilhelm denied everything, refusing to take a lie detector test because the mere mention of Ducote's name caused his blood pressure to soar. Jack Pandol, the grower who allegedly had handed Ducote $1,400 and the key to the UFW building, took the Fifth Amendment when questioned.

So Ducote took the fall alone. He wound up pleading guilty to reduced charges and served a year in the California correctional facility in Chino. From there he wrote me tongue in cheek, as one rehabilitated burglar to another, that he was suffering cruel and unusual punishment because "the swimming pool is too cold and the basketballs are lopsided." Upon release, he started a speakers bureau, signing up Warren Hinckle, myself, and Lenny Bruce's widow as lecturers. He truly was reformed. But then he lapsed and recruited Egil Krogh, a Nixon White House official who served jail time in the Watergate burglary.

After the case was over, the DA released to me the *Ramparts* files Ducote had stolen. Among them was my research on farm labor and the JFK assassination. I still have them sitting on my shelves, mute reminders that even today there may be more CHAOS, Inc. operations crashing about in the forest.

6

THE FBI PROPAGANDA MACHINE

On the muggy Los Angeles night of July 1, 1968, I arrived at the studio of "The Joe Pyne Show," a nationally syndicated television program, to be interviewed about my first book, *The Police Establishment*. Pyne was a contentious conservative, a Rush Limbaugh prototype, who was notorious for verbally mugging guests with whom he disagreed. It was obvious he thought he had me up a dark alley when he shunned even a perfunctory handshake. Certainly the theme of the book was enough to get his testosterone flowing: urban police forces across the country were bonded by a powerful lobbying and public relations network presided over by J. Edgar Hoover, then in his forty-fifth year as FBI director. Hoover gave every indication that he intended to go on and on; there was an aura of immortality about him.

Before the program began, Pyne huddled in the wings with his producer, giving me a chance to steal a peek at his cue cards. Sure enough, he was loaded for a personal attack on me rather than a discussion of the issues, and the ammunition could have come only from the FBI. When the cameras rolled, I answered questions before Pyne could ask them. He became more and more exasperated, finally snapping, "A hundred years from now, who are people going to remember, Bill Turner or J. Edgar Hoover?"

"Why, Hoover, of course," I retorted. "He'll still be director." Pyne became speechless, and cut for a commercial.

Several days before the program, documents released under the Freedom of Information Act (FOIA) disclose, the producer had called the local Bureau office soliciting "any information on Turner" because there were "some derogatory comments on the FBI" in the book. The Los Angeles Special Agent in Charge (SAC), Wesley Grapp, immediately sent an "Urgent" teletype to Deke DeLoach's publicity department recommending that an abstract of my dossier be furnished to Pyne. A supervisor had his staff prepare an anonymous letter for transmittal to Pyne with the understanding "that it is not to be attributed to the FBI." The supervisor felt confident that the television host would keep the secret because "we have cooperated on a confidential basis previously with Pyne." The letter was bumped all the way up to Hoover, who scrawled his distinctive "OK H" on it.

The Pyne episode illustrated how Hoover's FBI assiduously safeguarded its image by fair means or foul. It coiled and struck back personally at its critics instead of dealing with the issues raised. It planted puff pieces with favored journalists, "cooperating" with them in return. It waged a relentless campaign to paper over its blunders and idealize its accomplishments. (There was a Washington saying: "When other agencies blunder, they make excuses. When the FBI blunders, it just makes another movie.") If the legendary Edward Bernays had tricks up his sleeve in pioneering Madison Avenue advertising, Hoover had more in running his Pennsylvania Avenue propaganda machine. As John Kennedy once quipped, the "three most overrated things in the world are the state of Texas, the FBI, and mounted deer heads."

Such was the obsession with image that Hoover did not scruple to ignore justice or twist the facts if his reputation was at stake. Virtually every case that the Bureau cracked in the 1930s had to be rewritten to omit certain details that would detract from the legend being shaped. The "Lady in Red" who betrayed John Dillinger, the reckless bank robber elevated to Public Enemy Number One by the FBI chief, was an informant for a private detective agency, not the Bureau. The gunning down of Dillinger as he exited the Biograph Theater in Chicago had been preceded by a horrific blunder when Hoover's men, acting on a tip, cornered Dillinger at the Little Bohemia Lodge in Wisconsin but killed three guests while the fugitive slipped out the rear.

Alvin "Kreepy" Karpis, labeled "Public Rat Number One," was another archcriminal whose saga needed revision by the Bureau rewrite desk. The office-bound Hoover, baited by a U.S. senator that he had never personally made an arrest, ordered his agents when they were on the verge of arresting Karpis in New Orleans, to wait until he could fly down and do the honors. The official fiction was that Hoover ran up to Karpis's car as he got in it, grabbed him before he could reach a rifle on the back seat, and pronounced him under arrest. Bureau oldtimers gave me a different version: Karpis was collared by a young agent named Norman H. McCabe while Hoover lurked at a safe distance. In his memoirs, Karpis recalled seeing Hoover peek around the corner of a building and move in when one of his agents shouted, "Come on, Chief! We got him! You can come out now!" But the chief had no handcuffs and Karpis's wrists had to be bound with an agent's necktie. In addition, as with Dillinger, Karpis had previously escaped an elaborate FBI trap: he scurried down the rear fire escape of an Atlantic City hotel in his underwear while agents were storming the front.

The Bureau rendering of the demise of Charles "Pretty Boy" Floyd had him going down in a hail of FBI bullets in a shootout in an Ohio cornfield after robbing a bank. In 1974, however, an Ohio policeman, feeling free to speak after Hoover died, gave a conflicting version. There was no shootout. The policeman had downed Floyd with a shot to the shoulder. Melvin Purvis, who had led the pursuit of Dillinger, arrived as Floyd, disarmed, was sitting on the ground. Believing Floyd guilty of participating in a gun duel in which an FBI man was killed, he cold-bloodedly commanded agent Herman Hawless to shoot him to death. But when the FBI gave its official accounts of these exploits, the gaffes had been airbrushed out and the stories were picture perfect. Caught up with the hoopla of J. Edgar Hoover as a pop icon, the public didn't sense that what seemed too good to be true, was.

What happened to Kathryn Kelly, the wife of George "Machine Gun" Kelly, demonstrated the utter ruthlessness with which Hoover created and preserved the myth of FBI invincibility. On the night of July 23, 1933, one year before Dillinger met his fate, wealthy oilman Charles F. Urschel was kidnapped at gunpoint from his colonial mansion in Oklahoma City. The police advised his wife to call the FBI in Washington on a special "hot line" that had been installed as the result of the recent enactment of the Lindbergh Kidnap Law, which gave the Bureau primary jurisdiction in kidnapping cases. The call was patched through to Hoover's modest home in the Rock Creek district of Washington, awakening him. He picked up the phone and scratched notes. Then he called the small Oklahoma City office with orders for the agents to take over at once rather than wait for evidence that the perpetrator had taken the victim across a state line, as the law required. The abduction-murder of Charles Lindbergh's infant the year before had gone unsolved by local police, and Hoover was determined to crack the Urschel case to show what the FBI could do.

The Special Agent in Charge in Oklahoma City was the ubiquitous Melvin Purvis, the nemesis of Dillinger in Chicago the following year (Purvis became such a celebrity in his own right that a jealous Hoover drummed him out of the service). Purvis assigned the case to Gus Jones, a bovine man culled from the ranks of the Texas Rangers. How Jones's team solved the case after Urschel was released upon the payment of $200,000 ransom became the stuff of FBI lore. Urschel told how he had been held blindfolded on a ranch. Each morning at 9:45 A.M.—he tricked his captors into giving him the time—he heard an airplane fly overhead, except for a Sunday when there was a hard rain. Agents pored over flight schedules and found that an American Airways flight normally overflew Paradise, Texas, at that hour, but on the Sunday in question it had detoured around a menacing thunderhead. Suspicion fell on a ranch near Paradise owned by relatives of Kathryn Kelly, married to bootlegger George "Machine Gun" Kelly.

The son of a Memphis insurance executive, George Kelly earned his nickname from a habit of stitching his initials on a barn with a Thompson submachine gun. Brawny, blue-eyed and good-looking, with a dimpled chin, he wore well-tailored suits, Palm Beach hats and two-tone shoes in the manner of the dandies of the day. He had gone to college before becoming a Prohibition-era bootlegger, when he catered to Memphis society, delivering his product in an elegant pigskin briefcase. Kathryn Kelly was a sleek spitfire who, with her high cheekbones, auburn hair, flop hat and pearl necklace, bore a startling resemblance to actress Marlene Dietrich. But she was hardly a role model for young ladies. Her mother was a bootlegger, her aunt a prostitute, a cousin a moonshiner and an uncle a car thief. Two previous marriages had ended in divorce and suicide. Kate once confided to a friend that she flushed $10,000 worth of stolen jewelry down the toilet rather than let police catch her with it. To satisfy her expensive tastes she persuaded George to get into the lucrative business of selling gin on Indian reservations.

What may have convinced George to make the leap into kidnapping was that the Lindbergh abductor had realized $50,000 in ransom and so far had gotten away with it. When agents arrived at the Paradise ranch they found Harvey Bailey, a small-time crook who had accompanied George on the snatch, and some of the marked ransom money. But George and Kate were gone. They raced, hid and backtracked some 20,000 miles across the midlands. By the time the couple arrived in Memphis, they had buried all the loot and were broke. When George wired a contact to send money, the message was intercepted. Agents and Memphis police surrounded the cottage to which the money was destined. In his 1938 book *Persons in Hiding,* Hoover depicted Kate as the more threatening of the pair: "There was an early morning raid, by Special Agents and police, and the officers knew . . . the most dangerous by far was the woman. Surprise aided them. The pair was captured without resistance." According to Hoover, a cowering George cried, "Don't shoot, G-men!" The sobriquet stuck. But the Memphis police considered George the more dangerous. Their version, as told in "Shoot to Kill" in the January 1946 *Harper's*, revealed: "On a dining room table at which Kelly sat was an automatic pistol; on the floor were several sawed-off machine guns, his favorite weapon. At six in the morning, [police] detective Sergeant W. J. Raney slipped into the house. The bedroom door opened and there stood Kelly, gun in hand, ready. The detective, who had been trained to look at a quarry's hands and not his face, made one move. He shoved his shotgun barrel into Kelly's stomach and said, 'Drop that gun.' And Kelly dropped it." Nothing about "Don't shoot, G-men!"

In addition to arresting George, the FBI also charged Kate with kidnapping and conspiracy despite a paucity of evidence that she had willfully participated. The ransom letters were unsigned, they bore no latent fingerprints, and the typewriter used to write them was never found, so there was no scientific way to identify their author. But Hoover had no doubt that it was Kate. In *Persons in Hiding* he wrote that "when the ransom letters began to arrive, they carried an atmosphere of imagination and a casual use of hyphenated words entirely foreign to the average gangster," ignoring the fact that George had attended college. The letters reflected, Hoover said, "feminine thought and psychology," and it was manifest that "the words, the construction, the imagery, the supersentimentality mixed with utter cold-heartedness, could only have come from Kathryn Kelly."

Such misogynistic voodoo psychology was of course inadmissible in court, but there was other documentary evidence: cajoling and coercive letters postmarked Chicago that had been written to the *Daily Oklahoman* newspaper and the Urschel family while the Kellys were on the run. Without being able to prove that Kate had written these missives, the prosecution had insufficient evidence to convict her. Kate denied that she had written any letters or notes and insisted that she had accompanied her terrible-tempered husband only because she feared for her life and that of her child. She testified that she had begged George to release Urschel when she found out about the kidnapping, but he threatened her that it was "none of [her] business" and that the victim would be killed if the ransom was not paid. On the face of it, the letters supported Kate's denial: although typewritten, George's fingerprints were on them, and they were signed "George R. Kelly." Hoover disposed of this dilemma by contending that Kate, "by her dominance, caused Kelly to affix his fingerprints." The quandary of the signature was taken care of by a local certified public accountant, D. C. Patterson, who styled himself a handwriting expert and testified that he had compared the signatures on the letters with known specimens of Kate's handwriting. He concluded that she had forged her husband's name.

On cross-examination, the defense tried to impeach Patterson's competency. Kate's attorney asked Kate and George, who was being tried at the same time, to write their names and a few words on slips of paper. He challenged Patterson to identify the handwritings, but the "expert" begged off on the grounds that it would take too much time. The suggestion that Patterson was a quack prompted the attorney to ask the judge for a delay in order to have the handwriting independently analyzed. He refused, and after a mercurial two-day trial, Kate and George were found guilty. Both received life sentences.

From prison, Kate, resolutely affirming her innocence, solicited attorneys around the country to help reopen the case. It was not until she had spent twenty-five years behind bars that she succeeded. On March 19, 1958, James J. Laughlin of Washington filed a motion for a new trial based on the judge's failure to permit an independent handwriting examination. After a hearing, Judge W. R. Wallace ordered the FBI to produce its file so that he could evaluate the merit of Laughlin's argument. He freed Kate Kelly on bond pending the outcome.

I had always considered it odd that the FBI had used a local handwriting analyst of marginal skill in the prosecution of one of its most famous cases. It was a hard-and-fast rule that the FBI Laboratory be used. In fact, there were occasions when the Bureau refused to take over a case from local authorities because police laboratories had already processed the evidence. Why was the Urschel kidnapping an exception? After I arrived in the Oklahoma City office in the fall of 1960, I learned that the Kelly file was kept segregated in the SAC's safe. Shortly after I locked horns with Wesley Grapp, a senior agent named

Frank Alden slipped me a manila envelope to be opened at home. In it was the answer to the enigma of why the FBI had not used its own handwriting expert to testify.

The smoking gun was a copy of an FBI Laboratory report dated September 23, 1933, prepared by the lab's founder, Charles A. Appel, who a year later concluded that Lindbergh kidnapping suspect Bruno Richard Hauptman had written the ransom note in that case, and so testified. Appel's testimony helped convict Hauptman. But the reason he wasn't allowed to testify at the Kelly trial is that he disagreed with Patterson's conclusion. After comparing the letters to the *Daily Oklahoman* and Urschel with a known specimen of Kate Kelly's handwriting, Appel flatly declared, "The handwriting on the letters to the *Oklahomian* [sic] and to Urschel is not identical with that of Mrs. Kelly." He went on to say, "There are a great many similarities which on casual examination would lead one to think that these handwritings are the same. However, detailed analysis indicates that Mrs. Kelly did not write these letters." Appel added that none of the specimens submitted was "to any great extent disguised or changed from normal." It was George Kelly, Appel wrote, who may "have written these letters."

How Frank Alden accessed the locked Kelly file I never found out. But that manila envelope also contained documents confirming that the Appel report was never forwarded to the U.S. attorney in Oklahoma City prosecuting the case. It also held Wesley Grapp's recommendation, after Judge Wallace ordered the file produced, that it remain suppressed. In a communication to Bureau headquarters September 4, 1959, Grapp cynically reasoned that if the court ordered a new trial or hearing, the U.S. attorney might well commission a fresh examination of the handwriting, which would reveal Patterson's error and render the deceased Oklahoman the scapegoat. There would be no need to divulge the existence of the Appel report, which, Grapp stressed in a follow-up letter on October 15, 1959, posed great "potential as a source of embarrassment to the Bureau."

After I left the FBI in 1961, I received an unmarked envelope, presumably from Alden, which disclosed the recommendation of the new

SAC, Lee O. Teague, who had swapped places with Grapp, who went to Miami. An Oklahoma native who was highly respected by the field agents, Teague readily grasped the moral implications of the dirty little secret. Of Grapp's push for continued suppression, he wrote, "I recommend exactly to the contrary. . . . I recommend this office be authorized to bring to the attention of the U.S. Attorney the facts concerning the Bureau's laboratory findings." But the Bureau ignored Teague's entreaty.

It also ignored the court order to produce the Kelly file, so the case went into legal limbo. I gave the Appel report to Edward Bennett Williams, who planned to try to locate James Laughlin, Kate's attorney, and to do whatever else might reopen the case. In the end, however, he was reduced to publishing a brief account of the cover-up in his 1962 book, *One Man's Freedom*. Kate herself had retreated into silence. In 1959, shortly after being freed on bond, she was placed on the payroll of the Oklahoma County Home and Hospital outside Oklahoma City with the promise of a pension in fifteen years. It didn't take much imagination to surmise who was responsible for that sinecure, since the promised pension was in effect hush money. In 1962, after Ed Williams's book came out and an Oklahoma City reporter tried to interview her, the once swinging femme fatale, who had scribed witty items for the Terminal Island Penitentiary inmate journal, pleaded, "I'll lose this job if this constant barrage of publicity keeps up."

Eight years later I wrote an updated story in *Scanlan's Monthly*, Warren Hinckle's replacement for *Ramparts* (the magazine's brief life ended shortly thereafter when the Royal Canadian Mounted Police (RCMP) impounded an entire press run at the request of the Nixon White House, which was incensed at a cover photo showing the president in conference with supportive labor leaders whose criminal records were appended). Hinckle slyly titled the piece, which ran in the May 1970 issue, "J. Edgar Hoover Gets His First Woman." Since *Scanlan's* was short of travel funds, I called a private detective agency in Oklahoma City that had an ad in the Yellow Pages. Sure, they'd send an investigator out to the Oklahoma County Home and Hospital to show Kate a copy of the Appel report and try to get her to talk. The investigator reported that when he sought to see Kate he was intercepted by a shrewish woman named Beulah Pless, who said she was Kate's supervisor and praised her bookkeeping proficiency. But when the investigator asked to see Kate in person, a wall of hostility went up.

"She's paid her debt to society," Pless retorted. "She wants to be left alone."

The investigator persisted, citing the new evidence of her innocence.

"We don't care about any new evidence," Pless asserted, shooing the investigator off the premises.

FOIA-released documents reveal that as soon as the investigator drove off, Pless phoned the local FBI office to report the interview attempt. How he had introduced himself I don't know, but Pless claimed it was as "Bill Turner of the FBI." The office fired off a teletype to headquarters stating that a probe was underway to determine if it was really I. If it was, I could be prosecuted for impersonating a federal officer. Hoover was delighted with the prospect. "Press vigorously!" he scribbled on the teletype. Once again, as after the JFK assassination, I was the subject of a full field investigation. Agents displayed my photo to Pless, but she didn't recognize it. They canvassed hotels, motels, auto rental agencies and airlines, but my name didn't crop up. It was a dry well. On the teletype breaking the bad tidings, Hoover groused, "It is a shame we can't nail this jackal."

As for Kate Kelly, she never did get the hearing. Her court file, number 10478-CR, with its yellowed pages, continues to gather dust in the archives of the Oklahoma City federal court, devoid of the Appel report, mutely subservient to the legend of J. Edgar Hoover and his G-men.

Once the legend was manufactured, it fell to Louis B. Nichols, a glib, swarthy man who entered the Bureau in 1935, to perpetuate and burnish it. Nichols organized an entire division, euphemistically called Crime Records, as an image factory. Nichols was a Hoover sycophant, showering Hoover with gifts and naming his son J. Edgar. In 1950, when former Harry Truman advisor Max Lowenthal published his critical *The Federal Bureau of Investigation* before the Bureau had a chance to sabotage it, Nichols wailed, "Mr. Hoover, if I had known this book was going to be published, I'd have thrown by body between the presses and stopped it." I entered the FBI only a few months after Lowenthal's tome went on sale and witnessed what the Bureau did to dissuade readers. Agents dropped by bookstores, suggesting that the proprietors might not want to stock such a blasphemous volume, and went into libraries to take copies out of their Dewey decimal system order and scramble them in the stacks so no one could find them. Hoover sicced his conservative press dogs, Fulton Lewis, Jr., George Sokolsky and Walter Trohan, on the author, smearing him as a communist sympathizer. Then the House Un-American Activities Committee, which pulled out a hankie every time the FBI director sneezed, subjected Lowenthal and his publisher to a grilling on their political beliefs, as if no loyal citizen would criticize the FBI. The Bureau finished off Lowenthal by slapping a full-time surveillance on him as if he was engaged in subversion. He would never publish again.

Nichols's pioneering use of sympathetic congressional bodies to punish FBI critics continued after he left. In October 1962 segregationist Senator James O. Eastland of Mississippi unleashed his Senate Internal Security Subcommittee on a small radio network impetuous enough to broadcast programs debunking the FBI. The debunker was an ex-agent named Jack Levine, who loosed a broadside of charges ranging from deliberate sloth in pursuing civil rights cases to punitive personnel policies; his views were aired over WBAI, the New York affiliate of the Pacifica Network. When the Bureau marginalized him as a one-year agent who didn't know what he was talking about, Levine asked me to back him up. I did, going on WBAI's sister station, KPFA, in Berkeley.

The twin broadcasts began to kick up a fuss in the press. On October 23, *The New York Times*, the *Boston Herald* and the *Chicago Daily News* called for answers to the questions raised. But the Cuban Missile Crisis had begun the day before, and for two weeks it would eclipse all other news. In its aftermath Hoover's beadledom was forgotten in the general concern over how narrowly nuclear annihilation had been averted. Suddenly Eastland announced a "Red Probe," as the newspapers called it, of the Pacifica Network, subpoenaing seven officers to closed-door hearings. Although Eastland said he was troubled that a communist functionary had been allowed on the air, the only fresh fact to emerge was that the voices of George Lincoln Rockwell, the American Nazi fuhrer, and John Birch Society zealots had also been heard. But the cost of defending itself nearly bankrupted listener-supported Pacifica. As for Jack Levine, he joined a prominent Phoenix law firm and applied for admission to the Arizona bar. He was turned down on the basis of a letter from Hoover that he had made false accusations against the FBI. But the Arizona Supreme Court ordered him admitted to practice, opining that holding views contrary to Hoover's did not amount to poor character.

It was Nichols who perfected the practice of muzzling FBI critics on Capitol Hill through blackmail. A Niagara Falls of incriminating material on public officials cascaded into Crime Records from the field offices. The flow was fed by tidbits from informants, surveillance photos and films, electronic eavesdropping tapes, seized evidence and police records and sources. Dossiers augmented by newspaper clips were built on members of Congress and the executive branch. I recall as an agent the murmurs about the high-security room in the printing section of Crime Records where these materials were safeguarded. The preferred method for utilizing them was for a Crime Records agent to show up at an official's office and say, for example, "We came on this information about your wife in the course of an investigation, and, although we have no intention of doing anything with it, just thought you'd like to know." Rare indeed was the official—even one who was not approached but assumed the Bureau had a dossier—who didn't toe the line.

Nichols was equally adept at painting a glowing portrait of the Bureau. Agents on his staff churned out articles on how the FBI always got its man (or woman in the cases of Kathryn Kelly and Ma Barker), which were run unedited by publications under the bylines of one of their own writers. Radio programs conforming with the image filled the airwaves: "The FBI in Peace and War," "I Was a Communist for the FBI," and "This Is Your FBI" were three. Nichols's grand feat was a 1956 book, *The FBI Story*, written by wire service reporter Don White-head with the editorial oversight of Crime Records to ensure that the mystique of the G-men remained intact. The book became a motion picture starring Jimmy Stewart and Vera Miles, with an FBI agent in a director's chair during shooting to guarantee that the filming conformed with the script. In a publicity gimmick, theaters admitted FBI agents who exhibited their credentials for free, but the film was so maudlin and stilted that I cringed in my seat. It won no Academy Awards but did seal the reputation of the Bureau as the world's premier law enforcement agency. *The FBI Story* was followed by a pair of ideological tracts, *Masters of Deceit* and *A Study of Communism*, which carried Hoover as the author but were, in fact, ghosted in Crime Records. They were so boringly didactic that there was no sales sizzle. But Lewis Rosenstiel, the head of Schenley Liquors, bought up thousands of copies through his J. Edgar Hoover Foundation and distributed them to educational institutions, where they presumably enjoyed a long shelf life. Nichols left the FBI in 1957 but didn't need a personnel service to find another job—he moved seamlessly over to Schenley, where he became director of public relations, exploiting his list of FBI congressional contacts to lobby for liquor tax relief.

Nichols's successor in Crime Records was Deke DeLoach, who had so maniacally defended the Bureau's record on organized crime at my Civil Service hearing. DeLoach was known to the agents as a cutthroat operator, an evaluation justified by his methods in defaming Congressman Cornelius Gallagher of New Jersey in 1968. Gallagher proposed to deliver a speech on the House floor denouncing the FBI's excessive surveillance of citizens. He pulled no punches and got a bit personal. "It has been called to my attention," the speech draft began, "that the Director of the FBI and the Deputy Director of the FBI [Clyde Tolson] have been living as man and wife for 28 years at the public's expense; as a member of Congress we have an oversight duty to make sure that the funds that go to the FBI are properly spent."

As recounted by Curt Gentry in *J. Edgar Hoover*, Gallagher took a false step by furnishing an advance copy of the draft to Roy Cohn, whom he and his wife had known for some time. "You'll be sorry," Cohn said. "I know how they work." Cohn informed Hoover, who activated DeLoach. He leaked selective data gleaned from wiretaps, which seemed to suggest that the congressman was schmoozing with Mafia figures, to *Life* magazine, whose reporters had long received confidential information from Bureau files under the table in return for FBI-friendly articles. After the *Life* article ran, DeLoach told Cohn, "If you still know that guy, you had better get him to resign from Congress." If he didn't resign, Deloach warned, a story would be circulated that a minor mob figure in the *Life* article had died of a seizure while making love to Gallagher's wife, and in fact, the Bureau was already floating the smear in Washington political circles. An outraged Gallagher took to the floor of the House to perorate, "I doubt if even Goebbels [the Nazi propaganda minister] had the terrible capacity of a DeLoach to spread the big lie, nor could Goebbels exceed the filthy mind of a DeLoach." The lie sickened even Cohn, who, in 1986 while dying of AIDS complications, signed a statement substantiating Gallagher's version of the entire episode.

The FBI's unscrupulous tactics of intimidation and the use of journalistic collaborators were neatly illustrated in articles I submitted to *Playboy*. At the time, the so-called girlie magazines were one of the few mass-circulation homes for controversial investigative reporting. In early 1963, I proposed a piece on Hoover's strange reluctance to go after organized crime. No sooner had the proposal landed on the desk of editor Murray Fisher than, in his words, "we were visited by a pair of J. Edgar's finest to inquire into our plans, of which they had somehow gotten wind." Publisher Hugh Hefner turned it down, saying Robert Kennedy had finally gotten the Bureau involved.

Two years later, when the FBI relapsed into inaction following the death of President Kennedy, I sent Fisher a manuscript spelling out Hoover's priorities: "Senior FBI agents moved up and down the ranks of automobiles in the parking lot of the Seattle-Tacoma International Airport, occasionally jotting down a license number. Their mission was part of a nationwide drive, but it wasn't aimed at organized crime. The agents were recording out-of-state license numbers on the random chance of finding a stolen car that had been taken interstate. If one was found, they would be able to claim a double statistic: one car recovered, plus the recovery value of the car. . . . It would go into the statistical hopper that enables Hoover each year to boast of 'new peaks of achievement.'"

Playboy loved the article, entitled "Crime Is Too Big for the FBI," and offered $1,000 for it. But Fisher felt it needed some rearrangement for emphasis, and proposed bringing in crime reporter Sandy Smith of the *Chicago Sun-Times*. Smith accepted the assignment, but within days of being handed the manuscript he informed Fisher that it "was filled with inaccuracies and errors," and he "didn't feel that there was enough in it to salvage." Based on Smith's "general criticism," *Playboy* killed the article. It was not until I obtained my FBI file under FOIA years later that Sandy Smith was exposed as a Bureau stooge. When he had left *Playboy* with my manuscript in hand, he made a beeline for the Chicago FBI office. He was not a stranger there. A March 16, 1965, communique from the Chicago SAC to Deke DeLoach advised that Smith was, as DeLoach knew, "a great admirer of the Director and a very strong backer of the Bureau," and that "we have utilized Smith on many different occasions and his value to the Bureau and the Chicago Office is inestimable."

Smith had shown up at the FBI office with a great sense of urgency, saying *Playboy* had attempted to hire him for $500 to rewrite the article, but, although he "had absolutely no intention of doing this assignment," he saw "an opportunity to get the article . . . so that we could take a look at it." The communique said that Smith intended "to tell Fisher that he wants no part of this article as it is completely ridiculous, inaccurate and not worth the paper it is written on." A few days later, DeLoach was able to gloat that *Playboy* "turned it down based on Smith's objection and advice."

In the end, "Crime Is Too Big for the FBI" was published on November 8, 1965, by the much smaller *The Nation*, which paid $75, and was republished in the mainstream journal *Pageant*, which paid nothing. Although Hoover could do nothing about the pesky *The Nation*, whose editor Carey McWilliams believed he put his pants on one leg at a time, he recriminated against *Pageant* by ordering, "See that *Pageant* is not on any of our mailing lists and is given no assistance of any kind." Sandy Smith, who begged the FBI not to do anything that might unmask his role in savaging my article because it had been given to him in the strictest of confidence and his reputation was at stake, went on to bigger and better things. He became one of *Life*'s stable of reporters specializing in the underworld, where the FBI continued to feed him information from its files so that he could authoritatively quote "Justice Department sources." He and DeLoach kept using each other. In 1968 Smith helped prepare the *Life* article that vilified Congressman Gallagher and his wife.

When the FBI was unable to block publication, it looked at the possibility of smothering sales. This is what happened to my book, *The Police Establishment*. The book evolved from a 1966 discussion around a party punchbowl with John Dodds, the vice president of G. P. Putnam's Sons, who commissioned it off an outline. I had hardly begun a research trip when the FBI received a tip that the book was in the works. FOIA releases show that DeLoach dispatched "an ardent friend and admirer of the Bureau" who was close to Putnam's publisher, Walter Minton, to find out if the tip was accurate. Dodds later identified the "ardent friend" as Robin "Curly" Harris, a member of the Hearst press close to Hoover's sidekick, Walter Winchell. Harris relayed the bad news that it was indeed true, but felt he could "pull the rug out from under" the book if the Bureau fed him "some off-the-record public source data that he could bring to Walter Minton's attention which would show what a low character Turner is." Harris reported that as a personal favor, Minton promised to give him a copy of my manuscript as soon as it arrived.

When the draft manuscript arrived in FBI hands, it was reviewed by

Crime Records, which distorted the message by calling it an "attack upon the law enforcement profession" that contained "vicious references to the Director and the FBI." But Dodds saw it differently, writing, "It is very impressive. The tone is excellent and generally you are on the right track." In fact, Dodds was so impressed that when next we met he asked if I would consider coauthoring a book with Gary Francis Powers, the U-2 CIA spy plane pilot who had been shot down over the Soviet Union in May 1960 and repatriated a year later. The advance against royalties would be $35,000, a princely sum that was ten times the advance I had received for *The Police Establishment*, with the lion's share of the original payment going to me as the writer.

"John, I would love to do it," I said, "but I have one question. Will the CIA be allowed to censor the manuscript?"

Dodds nodded affirmatively. "It's in the agreement between the CIA and Powers," he explained.

"Well, I can't live with that," I declared. (Curt Gentry became the writer of the book, titled *Operation Overflight*.)

In the meantime Harris stepped up the pressure to convince Minton to abandon *The Police Establishment*. He slipped the publisher the inflammatory review from Crime Records, commenting that he strongly doubted the book "is the type that Putnam's Sons wants to be associated with." He trash-talked me as a "thoroughly unreliable character" engaged in "rotten activities." But Minton said he was inclined to go ahead with the book because it was under contract.

The Police Establishment was published in June 1968 to auspicious reviews, especially in *Newsweek* and the *Washington Post Book World*, where crime specialist Nicholas Pileggi saw it as "a comprehensive, well-written book about the entire police system in the United States." He particularly liked one passage: "Although the police did not create hard-core poverty, they physically contain it, the poor are prone to believe, with exaggerated zeal. The police enforce a white middle-class morality that is alien to broad segments of our population." Everything was in place for sales to take off. Some months earlier, the trade journal *Publishers Weekly* had reported that Putnam's intended to back the

book with heavy "advertising in cities where police conduct is an issue," and arrange a national media tour. But there was no advertising,
no media tour (the "Joe Pyne Show" appearance happened on my own
initiative and at my expense). Putnam's let the book die a natural death.

At the same time, DeLoach was trying to get a handle on another
book I had in progress, *Hoover's FBI: The Men and the Myth*, which
was based largely on my personal experiences. The flack man had been
alerted to the book as early as 1962, when it was in the conceptual stage
and I casually mentioned it on the Pacifica Network broadcast. As a
result of the Max Lowenthal contretemps, in which Louis Nichols found
out about the book too late to "stop the presses," the Bureau took measures to assure that it would never happen again. "After this," William
Sullivan told Gentry, "we developed informants in the publishing
houses." Notable among them were Bennett Cerf of Random House,
who had published *The FBI Story*, and Henry Holt, whose house did
Masters of Deceit. But the roster of insiders extended to copy editors,
publicity directors and virtually anyone in a position to know. Upon
hearing of my intentions, DeLoach tapped his sources at, according to
his handwritten notes, "Random House, Holt Co., Harpers, et al," but
came up dry. Several months later, however, after my literary agent
had submitted a draft manuscript to several publishers, one of them
sent a copy to the FBI, which wrote a chapter-by-chapter rebuttal.

For seven years, *Hoover's FBI* made the rounds of New York publishing houses, who were at once fascinated and fearful. Doubleday
hung on to it for an unconscionable year trying to muster the courage
to go ahead. Finally, in 1970, my agent placed it with the small Los
Angeles house Sherbourne Press, and it hit the bookstores. The FBI,
having been forewarned by an announcement in the trade press several months before, was ready. The strategy orchestrated by Hoover
was to ignore it initially in the hope that, since the publisher had limited promotional and distribution resources, it would not catch on.

But just in case, an internal memo stated, all divisions in the Bureau were ordered to conduct "a review of major identifiable allegations and investigations in captioned book for the purpose of exposing

factual inaccuracies worthy of refutation." It had to be one of the most exhaustive, most expensive—and most quibbling— book reviews ever written. For example, in Chapter Eleven I asserted that police across the nation griped that "the Bureau tends to be overly secretive with information it collects on criminals—in other words, exchange of information with the FBI is something of a 'one-way' street.'" This charge was so well known that it should have been a matter of judicial notice, and Hoover justified it because, he said, some police were corrupt. As an agent, I was so embarrassed by the policy that when dealing with detectives I would leave an FBI report on the table while I went to the bathroom. To combat my charge, the Training, General Investigative, Special Investigative, Administrative and Crime Records divisions joined together in the usual numbers game: "The FBI disseminated 305,545 items of criminal intelligence information to other law enforcement agencies during the fiscal year 1969, an increase of over 5,000 above the 1968 total." But only a small percentage of those "items" aided in the solution of crimes. Most were more fit for a gossip column or consisted of information obtained from one police department and turned over to another.

But when *Hoover's FBI* started getting salutatory reviews in the *San Francisco Chronicle*, the *Denver Post* and *Playboy* ("Fascinating, frightening, devastating"), Hoover decided enough was enough. He handed Jeremiah O'Leary of the *Washington Evening Star*, a "quite friendly" reporter who had helped the Bureau identify another reporter's sources, a review written by Crime Records that fragged the book. O'Leary ran it virtually unchanged—under his name. Hoover sent him a laudatory letter, at the same time authorizing the reprinting of a thousand copies of the review for distribution around the country. Nor did Hoover spare Sherbourne Press, spreading the allegation that the publisher was a pornographer, neglecting to mention that a 1965 obscenity charge had been dismissed.

To discredit me, there was an anonymous letter, nasty in tone, that the Bureau infiltrated into media libraries around the country, where it could be used in any story about me. Among other distortions, it stated that I had been fired by Hoover, but it didn't disclose that the Civil Service appeal had been rigged. It launched the canard that I was "a dedicated enemy of law enforcement." It claimed I lacked character because I changed my position on the JFK assassination, omitting that most Americans had come to believe there was a conspiracy (Hoover, ever paranoid, was sure I switched sides solely to find another platform from which to attack him). A copy of the letter was given to me by Bob Walters, a *Washington Evening Star* reporter who deplored his colleague O'Leary's conduct.

When I went on the media circuit to thump *Hoover's FBI*, strange things happened. I was invited by NBC to do an interview for the network's "Monitor" program, but this was quickly canceled because Deke DeLoach was a frequent guest. When I arrived at the studios of KYW-TV in Philadelphia, host Tom Snyder said in greeting, "We even knew what color suit you'd be wearing." An FBI man named Larson had been in touch with Snyder's producer, confiding that I had been under surveillance since an earlier stop in Cincinnati. Snyder had a call-in format, and one of the callers claimed to be a citizen who had just picked a book off his home library shelf by the Overstreets, an aged couple who stood out as reactionaries in the liberal field of education. The Overstreets had devoted a full chapter to roasting me for contesting Hoover, and the caller recited quotes from the text. In the background I heard the familiar sound of typewriters clacking away in an FBI steno pool—the setting was no home library. This was later confirmed by a FOIA document in which the Philadelphia SAC boasted to DeLoach, "A pretext call was made by a Supervisor of the Phila. Division" during which "the fact that [I] was a liar was drawn out." This self-delusion was music to Hoover's ears.

Although practically every show invited the FBI to send a representative to debate the issues face to face, it preferred to act underhandedly. In Pittsburgh I appeared on the "Contact" program on KDKA-TV hosted by Marie Torre. Bureau documents reveal that Torre was considered "quite pro-FBI" and friendly with the local SAC, but she had no control over the selection of guests. When the producer, Mike

Fields, called the FBI to offer a place on the show, he was advised that "There was a very simple solution to this—not to have Turner on." Fields countered that the topic of the FBI was of national interest and my book addressed issues. With that, Crime Records ordered The Letter to be hand delivered to Fields to assist Torre "in defending the FBI against this unwarranted criticism by this completely discredited ex-Agent." When I showed up, Fields, disturbed that the Bureau would not behave in a forthright manner, gave me a copy. To her credit, Torre, although mildly siding with the FBI, used none of the letter's gratuitous material. Typical of the call-ins was a woman who said she had been an FBI fan, "but now that I see you and listen to you, I am changing my mind." But if the Bureau's tactics backfired in Pittsburgh, they evidently succeeded at several other bookings on the tour, which were canceled without explanation.

Sales of *Hoover's FBI* were modest, and Hoover held in abeyance the all-out counterattack the Crime Records staff had so laboriously readied. But what goes around comes around: Dell published a paperback edition with a great cover of a sour-looking Hoover against a background of the FBI seal framed in red like a *Time* magazine cover. The paperback went into two printings, but when a third was on order, Hoover suddenly died.

The attempted suppression of *Hoover's FBI* was one of DeLoach's last acts as Crime Records chief. In June 1970 he unexpectedly resigned, only two months short of his thirtieth anniversary in the organization. Officially, he was leaving to accept the position of vice president at Pepsico tendered by its top executive, Donald Kendall, a close friend of Nixon whom DeLoach knew as the FBI's White House liaison. It was no secret that DeLoach aspired to replace Hoover, and some insiders thought he was "on tap" at Pepsico until the old man was gone. Even the conservative columnists Rowland Evans and Robert Novak were moved to observe, on June 14, 1970, that had "DeLoach ever succeeded Hoover (as seemed quite probable a few years ago), charges against him of right-wing bias and blatant opportunism would have racked and possibly wrecked the FBI." The columnists might have been aware that reporter Jack Nelson of the *Los Angeles Times* had been probing rumors of corruption on the part of high Bureau officials, including DeLoach. According to Curt Gentry, Nelson's story never saw print because a deal was struck between the *Times*'s management and the FBI: the newspaper would abort its probe in return for DeLoach's leaving the government. In 1995, DeLoach produced a book whitewashing the FBI's role in the assassinations of JFK and Martin Luther King and Hoover's blackmailing of Congress, among other controversies. Its title: *Hoover's FBI.*

When L. Patrick Gray took over as director, following Hoover's demise, he lost no time in ousting Thomas Bishop, DeLoach's successor, and paring Crime Records down to size, scattering staffers, whom he didn't trust, all over the country. But the mindset didn't change. When Clarence Kelley subsequently was named director, he brought with him his press aide, William Ellingsworth, from the Kansas City Police Department. Ellingsworth found himself ostracized and subjected to a whispering campaign. He resigned with a blast at the Hoover loyalists, saying, "They wanted a public relations program. I wanted a public information program."

Today, Crime Records has morphed into the Public Affairs Office, a much tidier operation. Although it doesn't behave as high-handedly and abusively as Crime Records under Nichols and DeLoach, the tendency to control the image never wavered. Producers of the 1960s television series "The FBI," starring Efrem Zimbalist, Jr., as Inspector Erskine, yielded artistic control in return for Hoover's seal of approval. There was an FBI agent on the set to edit out material that might not square with the legend. The very conservative actor continued as a front man for the FBI. On May 25, 1971, I appeared on the Public Broadcasting Service program "The Advocates" to debate whether the Director, who was growing controversial, should be replaced. Taking the pro side, along with columnist Jack Anderson, I argued that not only was Hoover derelict himself, but that he "used his tremendous influence to shoot down efforts to create an agency that would cope with organized crime." Zimbalist, the star of the con side, proved the aphorism that when under fire, the FBI just makes another movie. He narrated a Bureau-produced highlight film that glamorized the agency's history under Hoover, starting with the shoot-'em-up days of the 1930s. But when asked, "That wasn't really 'Baby Face' Nelson being shot down, was it?" Zimbalist had to admit, "I didn't make the film. I don't know." More recently, the producers of ABC-TV's "FBI: The Untold Stories" also gave the Bureau veto power over content. When the producers wanted to air the story of FBI agent Mark Putnam, who murdered a female informant for whom he had a fatal attraction, that power was exercised.

During the Hoover era, the FBI, alone among the federal agencies, was a power unto itself, above criticism, above the law. This phenomenon was in great measure the work of Crime Records, which mowed down its critics with machine gun rapidity, incessantly self-promoted, and hid flaws and illegalities behind a newsprint curtain. It is no exaggeration to say that under Hoover the country came perilously close to a de facto police state, where dissident thought was crushed. In a democracy, the manner in which a public agency, especially a law enforcement one, discharges its public trust should be subjected to the utmost scrutiny. That can't happen when an agency becomes infatuated with its own press clippings, and the blaring of its publicity horn drowns out all other sounds.

7

THE *FAREWELL AMERICA* PLOT

It had to be one of the most intrigue-ridden publishing ventures ever, more so than Che Guevara's diary or the memoirs of Stalin's daughter Svetlana. The story of *Farewell America* may have begun with a visit to the KGB in Mexico City; it progressed to the office of French President Charles de Gaulle in Paris. And it most certainly was aimed at advancing the 1968 presidential campaign of Robert F. Kennedy in America. In the doing, *l'affaire Farewell*, which was so convoluted it seemed borrowed from a John Le Carré novel, somehow liberated the famous Zapruder film from the *Life* magazine vault in which it had been sequestered.

My involvement in this international adventure was set up when I shifted from being a student of the Warren Commission Report to a critic. The more I learned, the more obvious it became that there was more to the JFK assassination than Lee Harvey Oswald, who allegedly had occupied a sniper's perch in the Texas School Book Depository building. Remembering that Dallas police officer Welcome Eugene Barnett had told me a woman ran up to him to report a shot from the now-famous grassy knoll, I found that, despite the FBI's attempts to keep the wraps on, there were scores of spectators in Dealey Plaza who heard at least one shot from the knoll (including, it came out years later, Kennedy aides Kenneth O'Donnell and David Powers). I was particularly swayed by the fact that a dermal nitrate test on Oswald's cheek by the police detected no blowback of nitrate residues as would be expected if he fired a rifle (although residues were found on his right hand, which suggested he fired the handgun that killed Officer J. D. Tippit). Testifying before the Warren Commission, an FBI ballistics technician had explained the absence of cheek residues as the result of a tightly sealed chamber on the old Italian Army rifle supposedly fired by Oswald, which didn't sound right. I called Dr. Vincent Guinn, head of the General Atomics project in San Diego, which had developed an ultrasensitive process called nuclear activation analysis (NAA). He and Raymond Pinker, director of the Los Angeles Police Department crime lab at the time, also had been puzzled by the technician's explanation. As I wrote in *Invisible Witness: The Use and Abuse of the New Technology of Crime Investigation* in 1968, the pair "ordered an Italian Carcano rifle such as Oswald supposedly fired from the same mail order house in Chicago. They fired the obsolete weapon a number of times—some gun experts think it is likely to blow up—and tested their cheeks by NAA. Nitrates were present in abundance." Nor could the Carcano be put in Oswald's hands that day by fingerprints—none were found on the weapon.

Flaws in the official version kept piling up. Jack Ruby's mob ties and gunrunning operations belied his assertion that he had shot Oswald to spare Jacqueline Kennedy the ordeal of a trial. I found suspicious the fate of the Zapruder film taken by a spectator standing on the grassy knoll, which showed the entire assassination sequence. *Life* bought it from Abraham Zapruder and, instead of putting it to commercial use, squirreled it away. Not even Warren Commission members viewed it as a motion picture. The magazine published staggered still frames in a cover story endorsing the Warren Report when it was issued in September 1964, putting captions under each frame. The caption under frame 313, where Kennedy's head explodes, said it was from a shot from the front. But that meant Oswald couldn't have fired it. When *Life* realized its "error," it stopped the presses and rewrote the caption as a shot from the rear. The film also graphically demonstrated that the president and Texas Governor John Connally, sitting in the jump seat in front of him, were struck by bullets within three-quarters of a second of each other, dictating two weapons. The Warren Commission disposed of this quandary by inventing the Magic Bullet Theory, which held that one bullet zig-zagged completely through the president and the governor, smashing bones, emerging unmutilated. The theory was absurd, and over the years John and Nellie Connally, who also were in the limousine, insisted that there were two bullets (although, as political creatures, they didn't think this meant a conspiracy).

In February 1967 I received a call from Jim Garrison, the New Orleans District Attorney, whose probe into the JFK assassination had broken into the news a few weeks earlier. "Bill, I need your help," he said. "The paramilitary right and Cuban exiles are figuring prominently in the investigation." He had pegged me as an expert on the subject after reading a *Ramparts* article I had done on the Minutemen, a forerunner of today's ultraright militia units. I had interviewed the national leader of the Minutemen, Robert B. DePugh, in his Missouri redoubt, venturing there with some trepidation since a California unit had warned that time was short for *Ramparts* editors to "change our nefarious ways." But DePugh was surprisingly cordial. He boasted, "We have the most sophisticated and best-equipped underground army movement this world has ever seen." His membership harbored specialists not only in firearms but electronics, demolition, and chemical and biological warfare. And he added, out of the blue, that he suspected a couple of his members were on the shooting team at Dallas, using ammo encased in plastic sleeves so it could be fired from a larger caliber weapon without being matched to that weapon. DePugh knew that in 1962 one of his "patriots" named John Morris cooked up a plot to assassinate Senator J. William Fulbright because he wasn't "voting American" (he opposed the Vietnam War). When DePugh got wind of it, after money had actually changed hands, he squelched it, he said, in order to head off a massive federal probe of his organization. In researching the article, I picked up information that a Minutemen cell in Dallas threatened to "snuff" Stanley Marcus of the upscale Nieman-Marcus department store chain because he was Jewish and liberal (I called Marcus to inform him of the danger).

When Garrison phoned, I was familiar with him through the legal press, for which I wrote forensic science articles. Such was his reputation in the law enforcement field that he had been asked to write the foreword to *Crime, Law and Corrections*, a collection of criminology essays. It was haunting. As an army officer, Garrison had helped liberate the Nazi concentration camp at Dachau, and he had witnessed its horrors. Allegorizing on an extraterrestrial being descending onto a self-desolated world, he asks, "What happened to your disinterested millions? Your uncommitted and uninvolved, your preoccupied and bored? Where today are their private horizons and their mirrored worlds of self? Where is their splendid indifference now?"

In conferring with Garrison on the boilerplate of his investigation, it occurred to me that the Russian KGB probably had a thick file on Lee Harvey Oswald, who remained an enigma as to which side he was on. He had resided in the Soviet Union from 1959 to 1962 as an ostensible defector, staging a bit of guerrilla theater by slashing his wrists to persuade the Russians to allow him to stay. The KGB perforce would have been intensely curious about this ex-Marine radar expert who had been stationed at Atsugi, Japan, where there was a U-2 spy plane base.

After repatriating from the U.S.S.R., Oswald found work at a Dallas photographic and graphic arts firm, where he conversed in Russian with a fellow employee, Charles Ofstein. As Ofstein testified before the Warren Commission, Oswald disclosed, "All the time I was in Minsk I never saw a vapor trail," a suggestion that he was watching for high-flying aircraft such as the U-2. Oswald also talked about the dispersion of Russian military units, saying "they didn't intermingle their armored divisions and infantry divisions and various units the way we do in the United States, and they would have all of their aircraft in one geographical location and their tanks in another geographical location, and their infantry in another. . . ." The putative defector went out of his way at some risk to pick up intelligence on the Soviet armed forces. He told Ofstein that he journeyed from Minsk to Moscow one May Day to observe the huge parade of military units. On one occasion Oswald asked Ofstein to enlarge a photo that he explained was of "some military headquarters and that the guards stationed there . . . had orders to shoot any trespassers." Oswald displayed a more than casual interest in analyzing the Russian military.

But how to approach the Russians? As I told Garrison, "The press wolves out there would never stop howling if they caught us asking the time of day of the KGB." I thought of a plan. I would act as cut-out, isolating the DA's office from a third man who would make the contact. The person I had in mind was an ex-CIA contract pilot who had flown bombing raids against Cuba from Guatemala. He was tall and angular, with tousled sandy hair, cobalt eyes and a magnetic personality. He had appeared on the doorstep of Stanley Scheinbaum after the Michigan State University exposé appeared in *Ramparts*, offering to do "volunteer work" to redeem himself for his checkered stint with the Agency. Scheinbaum turned him over to me.

When I first met with him in January 1966, he was clutching a clipping from the *Fresno Bee* of March 7, 1965, from which he had carefully excised his name with a razor blade. It was in a way an obituary. It quoted Dr. Orlando Bosch, chief of the anti-Castro action group Insurrectional Movement for the Recovery of the Revolution (MIRR) in Miami, as saying, "His B-26 fighter-bomber was last seen by one of our patrol boats in flames. He was on his way back from a fire bombing mission in the Pinar Del Rio Province in western Cuba. The last radio transmission was that he was too low to bail out and could not maintain altitude." Bosch disclosed that the missing-in-action pilot "was first introduced to us as a reserve pilot for the Bay of Pigs invasion. He has done volunteer work for our organization and other anti-Communist organizations since 1959." In fact, he had bailed out of the anti-Castro movement, forcing the CIA-backed Bosch to kill off his identity. I gave him the nom de paix Jim Rose because it was the Rose Bowl time of year. Rose was the ideal candidate to approach the KGB—they would understand each other perfectly.

They did. I squeezed some travel money from a bemused Warren Hinckle, bought an airline ticket in cash so it could not be traced, and dispatched Rose to the Russian embassy in Mexico City, which was preferable to the one in Washington, the home turf of the CIA and the FBI. I instructed him to walk straight in and ask for the third secretary, usually a KGB *rezidentura*. Before long he was shaking hands with an owlish man with horn-rim glasses whom he would later identify from photos as Valery V. Kostikov, a KGB officer the CIA considered implicated in "wet affairs" (assassinations). Although Rose had no way of knowing it at the time, Kostikov was one of two KGB men who interviewed Lee Harvey Oswald when, in September 1963, he had desperately tried to secure a quick visa to reenter Russia via Cuba.

Kostikov asked Rose to turn over the camera dangling on a strap around his neck as a tourist prop; the KGB officer might have considered it something else, since the CIA laboratory had perfected camera guns that were aimed through the viewfinder. "I got it back later in better working order than when I gave it to him," Rose recounted. Rose explained the Garrison investigation to Kostikov and how there was a question of Oswald's true affiliation as well as increasing evidence of Cuban exile involvement with elements of the CIA in the assassination. Would it be possible, Rose delicately inquired, to obtain a "sanitized" version of the dossier on Oswald and whatever else might assist the investigation? "It will be necessary for you to stay in Mexico City for a few days," the Russian temporized. He asked the name of Rose's hotel, suggesting he stick close to it.

Rose was tailed from the embassy to his hotel, and remained under surveillance. He assumed it was the KGB, and that they were protecting him. That night at dinner, he observed a burly Russian-looking man sitting at a table across the room watching him without pretending to do anything else. Rose sent him a vodka neat, which prompted a smile and a salute. "They used a tail on a tail," Rose said. "It was very professional."

On the third day, one of his tails asked that he visit the embassy again. Kostikov was waiting. "What you request is not impossible," he said, choosing his words carefully. "But it is not necessary that it will happen. The only way that it could possibly occur is in a way that would be most unexpected, and untraceable to its source. Something might be left in your hands, for instance, by a visitor to your country." After this guarded answer, which Rose guessed came from Moscow, Kostikov changed the subject. "Do you like books?" he asked. He handed Rose two Soviet books, *West-East Inseparable Twain* and *USSR Today and Tomorrow*, apologizing that they were on the only ones translated into English. As a further gesture, he invited Rose and me to be guests at the forthcoming fiftieth-anniversary Red Army Ball at the embassy. Neither of us owned a tuxedo, so we didn't attend.

Eight months later, in April 1968, Jim Garrison phoned to report that he might have the Russian response (he always insisted that I go to a "neutral" phone to discuss sensitive matters). He had just received a call from New York from someone identifying himself as a representative of Frontiers Publishing Company of Geneva, Switzerland. The representative said his firm had an important work in progress on the Kennedy assassination that would soon be published in Europe, and he wondered if Garrison would be interested in taking a look. Within days the DA's mailbag brought three black-bound volumes of manuscript specklessly typed on an IBM machine. It was titled simply *The Plot*. Garrison dispatched a copy to me via courier.

The Plot manuscript, which would eventually be brought out as *Farewell America*, had a note attached saying that a fourth volume was being written. The author of record was James Hepburn, whose name was not to be found in the *Writer's Directory*. A brief biography stated he had attended the London School of Economics and the Institute of Political Studies in Paris, "where he prepared for the public service." It claimed that Hepburn had lived for a short time in the United States, making the acquaintance of Jacqueline Bouvier (Kennedy) and Senator John Kennedy. The text was sprinkled with European metaphors, such as the description of the Kennedy limousine swinging into

Dealey Plaza: "Then the leaves began to fall, and soon the traces disappeared."

The immense breadth of knowledge contained in the manuscript dictated that Hepburn, whoever he was, was the beneficiary of a network of sources. Although borrowing liberally from published critics of the Warren Report, the manuscript displayed tremendous scope in the sections about the roots of the Cold War, the interlinkage between the large American corporate and banking interests and the ever-growing U.S. intelligence apparatus, and the international petroleum cartels. Brought alive by sinister portraits of CIA spymaster Allen Dulles, the cantankerous Dallas oilman H. L. Hunt, Roy Cohn and a bevy of military brass and Mafia chieftains, it advanced the theory that JFK was killed by an ad hoc amalgam of powerful interests, public and private, which had nightmares about a Kennedy dynasty that might extend through a Teddy presidency. The amalgam was called The Committee. It sponsored and carried out the assassination of JFK at both the supervisory level and the "gun" level—possibly recruiting professional assassins from the ranks of Cuban exiles embittered by Kennedy's failure to supervene with military force at the Bay of Pigs and to invade Cuba during the missile crisis. The bottom line was that JFK's enemies, collaborating with the CIA and other interested parties, moved to exorcise the Kennedy curse.

The manuscript bristled with such restricted information on the CIA that it could only have come from an inside source, and the author ventured cryptically, "In the domain of pure intelligence, the KGB is superior to the CIA." The social side of the Kennedys did not escape notice. One of the early chapters, entitled simply "King," dealt with the elegance of John and Jackie's White House. The gossips, it noted, complained that "the Kennedys spent $2000 on the food for one of their parties, neglecting to add (or perhaps they didn't know) that the President donated his entire salary to charity." Just how close to the White House the book's creators got is revealed in a paragraph about JFK's love life: "The President was discriminating in his affairs. . . . There were models of all nationalities, local beauty queens, society girls and, when he was really in a hurry, call girls. A Secret Service agent whose code name was 'Dentist' was in charge of the President's pleasures." The manuscript went on to lecture about sitting in judgment on such matters: "Puritanism is so widespread in this world, and hypocrisy so strong, that some readers will be shocked by these passages. . . . Why should a nation tolerate a President who is politically corrupt, but not one who is physiologically normal?" This was scabrous stuff for the time, when there was a gentlemen's agreement in the media not to bare the sex life of public officials. But it didn't survive *Farewell America*'s publication, having been scissored out by some phantom censor.

Before long, Jim Garrison called to say, "You know that fourth volume? It just walked in the door." But the messenger from Frontiers Publishing didn't have the final volume with him—a representative would have to be sent to Geneva to read it. I couldn't go because I was tied up with a political campaign, so the DA sent one of his corps of volunteer investigators, Steve Jaffe, a professional photographer. Jaffe went to the given address of Frontiers in Geneva, only to find that it was the office of a large law firm, Fiduciaire Wanner, specializing in Swiss banks. Frontiers was incorporated in Liechtenstein, he was told, but its editorial suite was in Paris. In the City of Light he again found himself in Fiduciaire Wanner offices, but this time his visit produced a man who gave his name as Hervé Lamarr, the publisher of *Farewell America*, née *The Plot*. Regretfully, Lamarr said, the author, James Hepburn, was not available. In fact, the Frenchman confessed over Pernods, Hepburn didn't exist as such. Lamarr had concocted the name out of flaming admiration of Audrey Hepburn. The James had come from *j'aime*—I love. A nice French touch.

As they bistro hopped, Jaffe discovered that Lamarr's background was every bit as exotic as his taste in actresses. He had been in the French army, attended Harvard, edited a women's magazine, served in the French diplomatic corps in Indochina—and was connected to French intelligence. This last item was confirmed when Lamarr took Jaffe to the Elysée Palace to see André Ducret, the chief of the secret service, whose office adjoined that of General Charles de Gaulle, the president. Ducret told the young American how vital his mission and Garrison's investigation were, and how France appreciated their efforts. He disclosed that his secret service had indeed furnished information for certain parts of *Farewell America*. Then he ducked into de Gaulle's office and returned with the general's personal calling card, on which he inscribed, *"Je suis très sensible à la confiance que vous m'exprimez."* (I am very moved by the confidence you have expressed in me.) The book now bore the imprimature of the highest councils of the French government, which was not too surprising. The haughty president of the republic had very much admired Kennedy's style, and never believed that Oswald was a "lone nut." "You're kidding me!" he scoffed to an interviewer when apprised of the Warren Commission's verdict. "Cowboys and Indians!" he concluded. De Gaulle himself had been the target of a conspiracy of military officers a year before Dallas; the conspirators, known as the Secret Army Organization and opposed to de Gaulle's pullout from Algeria, set up a cross fire ambush of his car, but he narrowly escaped when his driver sharply accelerated.

When Jaffe pressed for the book's principal sources, Lamarr named, among others, Ducret; Interpol, the international police clearing house; and Philippe Vosjoly, the chief French petroleum espionage agent in the United States, who assertedly infiltrated the CIA, the Texas oil industry, and anti-Castro action groups in South Florida. Vosjoly, Lamarr said, had interviewed a member of the paramilitary ambush team in Dealey Plaza, a Cuban exile, in Mexico City. And there was another source: Daniel Patrick Moynihan, an assistant secretary of labor in the Kennedy administration (later a senator from New York). Lamarr confided that on the day after the assassination, Robert Kennedy called in Moynihan, one of the family's most trusted aides, and instructed him to quietly assemble a small staff to explore two possibilities: that mortal enemy Jimmy Hoffa was behind it, or that the Secret Service had been bought off. In due time, Moynihan handed RFK a confidential report that there was no evidence of Hoffa's involvement or of Secret Service culpability. Through "personal friendships" with Kennedy insiders,

Lamarr said, the report was delivered into the hands of French intelligence.

This pretty well accounted for a cryptic passage in a *Farewell America* chapter called "Secret Service" that went, "Only Daniel P. Moynihan, a former longshoreman, had some idea of such things." The chapter detailed the "glaring errors" of the president's guards, even to the number of bourbons and water they downed the night before. But it also credited the Secret Service agents with professionalism in recognizing the work of professionals on the other side. "They were the first in the President's entourage to realize that the assassination was a well-organized plot," the chapter said. "They discussed it at Parkland Hospital and later during the plane ride back to Washington. They mentioned it in their personal reports to Secret Service Chief James Rowley that night. Ten hours after the assassination, Rowley knew that there had been three gunmen, and perhaps four, at Dallas that day, and later, on the telephone, Jerry Behn (head of the White House detail) remarked to Forrest Sorrels (head of the Dallas Secret Service), 'It's a plot.' 'Of course,' was Rowley's reply. Robert Kennedy . . . learned that evening from Rowley that the Secret Service believed the President had been the victim of a powerful organization."

As for Oswald, *Farewell America* portrayed him as a CIA contract agent who had been sent to the Soviet Union to exploit his particular knowledge of the U-2 spy plane—he had been trained for the mission, learning both the Russian language and U-2 technology at the U-2 base in Atsugi. This was solid information, Lamarr assured Jaffe, which came from a French intelligence agent in Japan, Richard Savitt, who had known the Marine during his hitch there. After "defecting" in Moscow, Oswald made his way to Minsk, which was under the path of U-2 overflights between Turkey and Finland. There, *Farewell* matter-of-factly declared, he "was in regular contact with the CIA through its Moscow station at the American Embassy. As a U-2 specialist, he may have used a special radio transmitter broadcasting on a 30-inch wavelength, which is undetectable on the ground but can be picked up at 70,000 feet by a U-2, which is equipped with an ultra-high-frequency recording system (5,000 words in 7 seconds)." Upon Oswald's repatriation to the United States, the book reported, the CIA would have entertained the possibility that he had been converted to a double agent by the Soviets.

Who was the real author? Lamarr promised Jaffe that his identity would be divulged upon publication of an American edition of the book. In the meantime the author was limned as one man—not famous, not an aide of Kennedy—but an established American writer. Not long after Jaffe left Paris, *Farewell* was published in France as *L'Amerique Brule* (America Burns). *L'Express*, the country's foremost news magazine, termed it "the hope of one America against another," and it sold briskly. German and Italian editions followed, and *Bild*, Germany's largest daily, serialized it with the teaser "explosive as a bomb." At the same time, Frontiers Publishing, in the person of Lamarr, was searching for an American publisher. Warren Hinckle was tempted, puckishly foreseeing a *Ramparts* cover story, "Who Killed Kennedy, by the KGB." But first he wanted to see that elusive fourth volume that hadn't been included in the European editions. Surely it would pack a punch, perhaps name players. While in New York, Hinckle decided to brace Patrick Moynihan about his report on Hoffa and the Secret Service. At first the amiable Irishman refused to talk, but a second call to his Cambridge home, in which the subject under review was broached, brought him rushing to Manhattan. Hinckle and Bob Scheer, who also was present, briefed him on what the French were saying. Although he denied knowing Lamarr, he did not deny his secret mission for RFK. Nor did he confirm it. Clearly on edge, he wanted to make some private phone calls. "I have to ask some people," he said. Some twenty minutes later, he emerged more composed to announce that he had nothing to say on the matter.

By this time, a one-page sequel had been added to the *Farewell* manuscript, which was headed "The Man of November 5th." It began, "The choice made by the people of the United States on November 5th, 1968, will have profound and far-reaching consequences for the life, liberty and happiness of the universe. The peoples of the earth are awaiting new decisions." The entire tone, mirroring the angst Europeans felt regarding Pax Americana, conveyed the hope that Bobby Kennedy would be successful in his presidential run that year. But then, as if the clack of the typewriter had been interrupted by a news bulletin, the text lapsed into the past tense.

> There was another funeral. Once again the stars and stripes flew at half-mast. On an evening in June, Robert Kennedy joined his brother beneath the hill at Arlington, and those who pass by can bring them flowers. The tombs are splendid, but the scores have not been settled. Who killed them? And why?

When Bobby Kennedy was shot, the *Farewell* project seemed to die with him, as if its sole purpose had been to boost his candidacy. Three months later, Hervé Lamarr called long distance, saying he had to see me. He would be in San Francisco the following day and would be staying at the Fairmont Hotel on Nob Hill. I told him I had to catch a plane to New York but could stop by for an hour on the way to the airport. Lamarr was slight and fidgety, with a wispy mustache and fingertips yellowed by countless Gitanes. The conversation went nowhere, and I wondered what the great urgency was. The Frenchman talked aimlessly, deflecting questions about the project. Jim Rose was with me and drove me to the airport.

The punch line came that night when Lamarr called Jim Rose and said, "You're both professionals. There's an important package I want you to have." It could be picked up at the St. Francis Hotel, at the bottom of Nob Hill. Rose approached the bell captain, gave a password, and was handed a sealed film can. When I returned from New York we screened what turned out to be a motion picture rendition of *Farewell*. As a sonorous narrator chronicled John Kennedy's political career, still photos of the president with kings and kids, pols and everyday people rolled along with shots of his grim-faced enemies: Dallas right-wing oilman H. L. Hunt; the pro-Blue General Edwin A. Walker, whom Kennedy had cashiered; the Big Steel executives forced to rescind price hikes; J. Edgar Hoover, who considered Camelot subversive; Richard Nixon; and on and on. There were also digressive interludes, such as one in which Frank Sinatra was heard singing "It's the Wrong Face" while visuals suggested secret *amours*. Then the music turned dirgeful as actual footage showed John and Jacqueline Kennedy boarding Air Force 1 in Fort Worth for the short hop to Dallas. There was the motorcade to downtown spliced together from the home movies of spectators lining the route. And then . . . the Zapruder film.

I was not prepared for how horrifyingly graphic the film was in moving form. After his limousine slows at a sharp turn, Kennedy clutches his throat in reaction to the first shot. He slowly slumps forward. Then his head literally explodes, creating a halo of blood mist. The force of the hit knocks him backward so violently into the rear seat cushion that it is compressed. He rebounds forward as Jackie grabs for him. There is no mistaking that the kill shot was fired from a frontal zone, somewhere on the grassy knoll. The Texas School Book Depository was to the rear.

With the film can in hand, I flew to Los Angeles to try to verify that it was the genuine article. A colleague, CBS television newsman Pete Noyes, had the network's film expert thoroughly examine it. Noting that the frames were in perfect order, that the coloring was consistent, and that there were no signs of tampering or editing, the expert pronounced the film a genuine second-generation print. I offered it to CBS to show nationally, and the Los Angeles executives who watched a studio screening were excited at the prospect. But top executives in New York scotched it on grounds that *Life* held the property rights and would sue. ABC and NBC also declined. It was left to a small Los Angeles UHF channel to air the Zapruder film for the first time.

How the French laid hands on the film was possibly explained by Richard Lubic, a member of RFK's California campaign who was with him in the pantry the night he was shot at the Ambassador Hotel in Los Angeles. Lubic told me that very early in 1968, when he was a staffer at *Life*'s companion publication, *Time*, in Time-Life headquarters in New York, the film was missing from its vault for several days. When the absence was discovered, there was quite a stir. The FBI and the CIA investigated, and even Mayor John Lindsay came by to ensure that the New York police gave it their best Kojak try. Although it was patently an inside job, no suspect was ever fingered.

When an American edition of *Farewell* was finally printed, an afterword was a bit coy as to the method of purloining. "We were fortunate enough to obtain two copies of this film, from two different sources in the United States," it read. "One is a poor copy, the other of excellent quality." Pointing out that the stills *Life* had run when the Warren Report came out were retouched, the afterword stated, "The unedited version of this very moving film utterly demolishes the official version of the assassination put out by the Warren Commission. The Zapruder movie belongs to history and to men everywhere."

The American edition of *Farewell* was never displayed in the windows of Brentano's and Doubleday. At the Fairmont Hotel session, Lamarr had casually answered "Sure" when I asked him if there would be one. A few weeks later, a notice arrived from a freight forwarder that a consignment of books from a Montreal warehouse was ready to be picked up. The shipping bill of $282 had not been prepaid, but the money to settle it was on deposit in a Swiss bank branch in San Francisco. To the end Lamarr was playing at foreign intrigue. Frontiers Publishing vanished as suddenly as it had sprung up, and Lamarr slipped back into the intelligence shadows.

It was left to me to settle the historical account. There were six cartons of some one hundred hardcover books each, printed in Belgium, in the shipment, and I distributed them all to researchers, college bookstores and institutions. The Los Angeles public library has five, the Australian embassy one. The Library of Congress catalog card number is 68-57391.

I also took to the hustings to show the Zapruder film to groups across the country, mostly on college campuses. While the overwhelming majority of audience members gasped at the head snap and agreed that it was convincing evidence of a shot from the front, an occasional hand would be raised to ask about theories put forth by Warren Report supporters that Kennedy's head jumped towards Oswald's rifle due either to a neurological reaction or jet propulsion effect. When I showed the film to an SRO crowd at Texas A & M University, an ROTC cadet called my attention to an article in a medical journal by Dr. John Lattimer advancing the jet propulsion theory. By this time I had had enough of the fanciful hypothesis. "Dr. Cyril Wecht, the forensic pathologist who is coroner of Pittsburgh and has seen countless gunshot wounds, concludes the shot came from the front," I replied testily. "Dr. Lattimer's medical specialty is urology, and I am tempted to ask: isn't that a pisser?"

I also pointed out to the doubting cadet that the windshield of a motorcycle cop riding to the immediate left rear of the limousine was splattered with brain and bone debris, which substantiated that the fatal head shot was fired from the right front—the grassy knoll zone. In any case, the repeated showing of the Zapruder film placed it in the public domain, where it belonged in the first place. *Life* eventually returned the original to the Zapruder family, which in 1978 gave it to the National Archives for "storage." When Congress created the JFK Assassination Records Review Board in response to heightened public awareness of a conspiracy as a result of Oliver Stone's 1991 motion picture *JFK*, in which the Zapruder film was shown (I lent Stone my copy), the board accomplished a legal "taking" of the original to put it "in the custody of the American people." In 1999 an arbitration panel set the value of the original at $16 million, to be paid to the family.

After Frontiers Publishing vanished without a trace, questions lingered. Did Jim Rose's August 1967 visit to the Russian embassy in Mexico City trigger the *Farewell America* project? Valery Kostikov said that any response would be "in a way that would be most unexpected, and untraceable," as for example "Something might be left in your hands by a visitor to your country." That is what happened, but it leaves the puzzling question, how could the Russians have set French intelligence in motion? It was an open secret that the French foreign espionage agency, SDECE, was so penetrated by the KGB that in intelligence circles it was quipped that the SDECE drank more vodka than wine. Although the KGB connection remains ambiguous, the stamp of the fleur de lis is unmistakable, as evidenced by the project's endorsement by de Gaulle and Ducret. This suggests, as Lamarr indicated, that there was witting collaboration by members of the Kennedy inner circle, because it is doubtful that de Gaulle would have proceeded without it. Although the family consistently held the public position that the Warren Report was the final answer, privately Bobby Kennedy expressed a different opinion by words and action. Charging Daniel Moynihan with forming a task force to look into whether Hoffa was implicated and the Secret Service was bribed demonstrates that he was skeptical from the start. The Moynihan report found its way to French intelligence, with some of its findings appearing in *Farewell*. A decade ago, Toronto bookseller Al Navis, who had just stumbled upon boxes of *Farewell America* collecting dust in a Montreal warehouse, queried David Powers, the Kennedy adjutant who was curator of the John F. Kennedy Museum, about the book. "I can't confirm or deny the European connection," Powers replied, "but Bobby definitely didn't believe the Warren Report." RFK's press secretary, Frank Mankiewicz, recently confirmed that RFK was engrossed in the Garrison case. "When the Garrison investigation started," Mankiewicz told author Gus Russo, "Bobby asked me if he had anything. I said I didn't know. He asked me to learn everything I could about it. He said to me, 'I may need it in the future.'" In May 1968 RFK's California campaign aide, Richard Lubic, tracked me down by phone in Garrison's office to advise, "After he's elected, Bobby's going to go. He's going to reopen the investigation." On June 3, two days before he was shot, RFK said, "I now fully realize that only the powers of the presidency will reveal the secrets of my brother's death." Ever pragmatic, he understood that only by becoming president and controlling the Justice Department could he realistically undertake a new probe.

The most likely exegesis of *Farewell America* is that it was a clandestine project by the "European connection," aided by access to the Kennedy group, to independently promote RFK's presidential bid, at the same time setting the stage for a fresh investigation once he was in the White House. Probably the riddle of *Farewell America* will never be fully solved. But in its brief life span the project produced a vital legacy. As the book hopefully put it, "The Zapruder movie belongs to history and to men everywhere." That desire has now been realized.

8

THE GARRISON COMMISSION

The address Minutemen defector Jerry Milton Brooks had cited, 531 Lafayette Place, turned out to be the side entrance to a weatherbeaten three-story building at the corner of Camp Street on the fringe of downtown New Orleans. In conjunction with my *Ramparts* article on the Minutemen, Brooks, who possessed a photoretentive memory, reeled off the names, addresses and license plate numbers of key members in cities from Kansas City to Miami. Brooks had acquired this mental Rolodex of the organization from his days as a Minutemen aide de camp, which ended in 1965 when he had a falling out with Robert DePugh. One of those named was W. Guy Banister, a former FBI official. The name was familiar: when I was an FBI agent Banister, the Special Agent in Charge of the Chicago office, had a reputation for being outspoken, his most memorable line being "the Bureau [headquarters] and the field have been divorced for years and are living in adultery." Since speaking out was not appreciated in Hoover's FBI, I was curious about what had happened to this most unusual SAC.

It was my first visit to Jim Garrison's office after he asked for help. During a break, I walked over to 531 Lafayette Place. There was no inscription on the door denoting it as Banister's business, only a realtor's shingle and a sticker of the then-nascent Republican Party of Louisiana. The door opened to stairs leading to a second-floor space that was unoccupied. Diagonally across the space was a second set of stairs, which led down to a door on Camp Street. The number over the door read "544." 544 Camp Street was the return address Lee Harvey Oswald had stamped on the first batch of pro-Castro literature he handed out on the streets of the Crescent City in August 1963. Subsequent batches bore a post office box number, suggesting that the use of the street address had been a lapse. What was Oswald's connection to Banister?

When I reported the Camp Street discovery to Garrison, I recommended that we assign priority to interviewing Banister. Too late, he said, Banister had been found dead in bed in June 1964, his pearl-handled, monogrammed .357 Magnum revolver at his side. Although there was no autopsy, his demise was attributed to a heart attack. But Brooks, who had done some clipping and filing for Banister in 1962, had identified his deputy, Hugh F. Ward, as also belonging to the Minutemen as well as an outfit called the Anti-Communism League of the Caribbean, which was headed by Banister after he came to New Orleans in 1955. Brooks credited the ACLC with helping the CIA overthrow the leftist Arbenz government in Guatemala, opening the way for a succession of rightist strongmen. The ACLC continued to act as an intermediary between the CIA and right-wing insurgency movements in the Caribbean, including Cuba after Castro gained power. There was a chance that Ward would be willing to talk, but it turned out he was gone as well. On May 23, 1965, he was at the controls of a Piper Aztec chartered by former New Orleans mayor DeLessups Morrison when the craft, engines sputtering, crashed on a fog-shrouded hill near Ciudad Victoria, Mexico, killing all on board. That left Maurice Brooks Gatlin, Sr., an attorney associated with Banister, on Brooks's list of key Minutemen in Louisiana. According to Brooks, Gatlin served as legal counsel to the ACLC. In fact, Brooks had been a kind of protégé of Gatlin. The attorney's passport was stamped with visas of countries around the world. In Brooks's estimation, he was a "transporter" for the CIA. On one occasion Gatlin bodaciously told Brooks, "I have pretty good connections. Stick with me—I'll give you a license to kill." Brooks became a firm believer in 1962 when Gatlin displayed a thick wad of bills, saying he had $100,000 of CIA money earmarked for a French reactionary clique planning to assassinate General de Gaulle. Shortly thereafter Gatlin flew to Paris, and shortly after that came the Secret Army Organization's abortive ambush of the French president. But Gatlin as well was beyond Garrison's reach. In 1964 he fell or was pushed from the sixth floor of the Panama Hotel in Panama, dying instantly.

As I sat in Garrison's office discussing the fates of Banister, Ward and Gatlin, my mind flashed back to the previous November when *Ramparts* had run a story on the "mysterious deaths" theory of doughty Texas editor Penn Jones, Jr. With David Welsh, I had gone down to Midlothian, a dusty cotton market town south of Dallas, to meet with Jones on his front porch. He had compiled a list of an unlucky thirteen people who were witnesses to the assassination or somehow touched by it and had died violently or questionably inside of three years, which he saw as a highly excessive actuarial rate. One on the list was Tom Howard, Jack Ruby's initial attorney, who concocted the story that the mobster killed Oswald to spare Jacqueline Kennedy the ordeal of a trial (he died of a supposed heart attack). Another was Lee Bowers, who was sitting in a railroad tower behind the grassy knoll and spotted two strange men behind the picket fence on the knoll just as the presidential limousine passed and a flash and commotion ensued (he was involved in a one-car accident). A third was Earlene Roberts, the boarding house manager who stated that Oswald rushed into his room for a few minutes shortly after the shooting in Dealey Plaza, during which a Dallas police car stopped in front and honked twice as if to signal (she was struck by a presumed heart attack). The mysterious-deaths article so fascinated Walter Cronkite that he sent a film crew to Midlothian for a CBS News series on Jones. Although the theory caught on as "evidence" of a conspiracy, I was bemusedly skeptical.

But the untimely deaths of Banister, Ward and Gatlin gave me pause that there might in fact have been systematic elimination of people who knew too much. Two months earlier there had been a fourth curious mortality in this set: David William Ferrie, an investigator for the ex-FBI official's private detective agency, Guy Banister & Associates. Garrison's interest in Ferrie dated back to the morning after the assassination, when he summoned his staff to the office for a "brainstorming" session to explore the possibility that Oswald had accomplices in New Orleans.

Although it would not be known until after the Warren Report was published, on that same Saturday morning the Secret Service was checking out the return address of 544 Camp Street that the accused assassin had rubber-stamped on some of his handouts promoting a rump chapter of the Fair Play for Cuba Committee. The agents asked the building manager if Oswald "had occupied office space" but learned instead that "Cuban revolutionaries had been tenants until recently." They talked to an exile accountant who revealed that "those Cubans were members of organizations known as 'Crusade to Free Cuba Committee' and 'Cuban Revolutionary Council,'" which had been headed by Sergio Arcacha Smith, a former Batista diplomat. The agents reported that they had been unable to find any trace of the Fair Play for Cuba Committee, evincing no curiosity over why pro-Castro literature would bear the address of anti-Castro groups.

On Monday, the Warren Report later disclosed, the FBI's Ernest C. Wall, Jr., a Spanish-speaking agent who liaisoned with the exile groups, called Guy Banister to inquire about Arcacha Smith. According to Wall's single-paragraph report, Banister responded that Arcacha Smith had been the head of the Cuban Revolutionary Council and "some time ago had told him on one occasion that he, Smith, had an office in the building located at 544 Camp Street." Nothing about Banister and the Cuban Revolutionary Council, created by the CIA as an umbrella group for the Bay of Pigs invasion, being under the same roof. As a limited hangout, it was a classic. The Warren Report dutifully stated that "investigation has indicated that neither the Fair Play for Cuba Committee nor Lee Oswald ever maintained an office at that address."

Following the Saturday meeting, Garrison's men had put out feelers to the city's netherworld, and it was Assistant DA Frank Klein who registered the first feedback. It came from a slight, furtive, sometime private eye named Jack S. Martin, whose most recent employer was Guy Banister. Martin had reason to be angry with his boss. The previous afternoon, after the news from Dallas, the two went to the Katzenjammer Bar next door and downed a number of bourbons. Then they went up to Banister's office, where an argument erupted. Banister pulled out his revolver and savagely pistol-whipped Martin, who was rushed to Baptist Hospital and treated for head injuries. But Martin refused to press charges. He told the police that the older man was like a father to him and that they had simply argued over "politics and other things."

By the time he met with Klein the next day, however, a sober Martin was in no mood to protect Banister and talked about "the other things." He suspected Banister and David Ferrie of being implicated in the assassination. He knew Ferrie well, although there was bad blood between them. Both were affiliated with the Apostolic Orthodox Old Catholic Church, a breakaway sect steeped in theological anticommunism. An exceptionally skilled pilot, Ferrie had been dismissed from Eastern Airlines the previous year due to publicity about homosexual activities. Banister had traveled to Miami to testify on his behalf at an appeals hearing. According to Martin, Ferrie had commanded a Civil Air Patrol squadron to which Oswald belonged during his high school days in New Orleans. He taught Oswald to shoot with a telescopic sight, and had been involved in an assassination plot. Less than two weeks before JFK's visit to Dallas, Ferrie made a trip there. His assigned role, Martin alleged, was to fly the escaping conspirators over the border to Matamoros, Mexico. What caused Klein to straighten up was Martin's casual mention that on the afternoon of the assassination, Ferrie drove off on a sudden trip to Texas.

On that morning, the DA's men soon verified, Ferrie had been in the federal courthouse for the windup of the criminal trial of Mafia chieftain Carlos Marcello. As a Banister investigator, he had been assigned to the case by defense attorney C. Wray Gill, and had met personally with the Mafioso. Marcello was charged with illegal entry into the United States after he had been summarily deported to Guatemala by Bobby Kennedy, and there was talk that Ferrie had flown him back across the border. At noon a verdict of not guilty was handed down, and the courthouse emptied. Shortly after, the news from Dallas was broadcast.

When Ferrie returned from the whirlwind trip on Monday, he was interrogated by Klein, with attorney Gill present. Ferrie insisted his trip had been arranged "on the spur of the moment." With two companions, he had driven straight through to Houston on Friday night. On Saturday afternoon the trio skated at an ice rink; that evening they made the short jaunt to Galveston and hunted geese on Sunday. Garrison was unconvinced by the account. An all-night dash through the worst rainstorm in years on a mercurial junket of a thousand miles for impromptu recreational purposes was too much to swallow. "It was a curious trip to a curious place at a curious time," Garrison told me in retrospect. He booked Ferrie as a "fugitive from Texas" and turned him over to the FBI. He was questioned by Ernest Wall, the same agent who earlier that day had made the less-than-inquisitive call to Banister, and released.

So the Ferrie file was closed. For three years Garrison carried on with business as usual, an unusual DA. During World War II he had flown a tiny Piper Cub as an artillery spotter during the Allied sweep into Germany, coming upon the Dachau concentration camp horrors that were etched so deeply in his conscience. With a diploma from Tulane Law School, he briefly tried the life of an FBI agent, and then a stint with a corporate law firm, which proved equally unrewarding. After a second tour of Army duty, this time in the Korean War, he signed on as an assistant DA in New Orleans and began his public career. Following two failed tries at elective office, he pulled an upset in the 1961 district attorney race. Bucking the Democratic machine and backed only by five young attorneys known as the "Nothing Group" because of their dearth of money and prestige, he took to television. Six and a half feet tall with a vibrant baritone voice, his presence filled the studio. Like Jack Kennedy, whom he greatly admired, Garrison projected a youthful vigor and enthusiasm that was missing in his conventional opponents.

The maverick DA displayed no reluctance to tangle with the established order. Turning down a mob offer that would have netted him $3,000 a week as his share of slot machine receipts, he proceeded to raid Bourbon Street clip joints, crack down on prostitution, and eliminate the bail bond rackets. The raids prompted the city's eight criminal judges, fearful of the effect on tourism, to block his source of funds, a fines and forfeitures pool. The running dispute that ensued was the talk of the town. At a luncheon of the Temple Sinai Brotherhood, Garrison likened the judges to the "sacred cows of India." On another occasion he accused them of goldbricking by taking 206 holidays, "not counting legal holidays like All Saint's Day, Long's Birthday, and St. Winterbottom's Day." Outraged, the judges filed criminal defamation charges (groused one, "People holler 'Moo' at me"). The case escalated to the U.S. Supreme Court, which gave a landmark decision upholding the DA's right to criticize other public officials. Garrison's show of independence delighted the voters, who in 1965 returned him to office by a two-to-one margin—the first New Orleans DA to be reelected in thirty years.

Garrison's political philosophy defied categorization—the closest I could come was to term him a Bayou populist. He subscribed in part to Ayn Rand's libertarian dogma, but was too much of a traditional democrat to accept its inevitable elitism. He was friendly with segregationists and archconservatives but bristled at mention of the Ku Klux Klan. Black leaders had no quarrel with his conduct of office, and he appointed blacks as assistant DAs, a rare move in the Deep South in those days. When the police vice squad tried to sweep James Baldwin's *Another Country* from bookstore shelves, he refused to prosecute ("How do you define obscenity?") and denounced the censorship in stinging terms, thus incurring the wrath of the White Citizens Council. After starting his assassination probe, some of his views on other issues changed. "A year ago I was a mild hawk on Vietnam," he told me. "But no more. I've discovered the government has told so many lies in this case it can't be believed on anything."

Garrison was by far the most intellectual law enforcement official I ever met. He avidly devoured history (as reflected in his metaphor, "Honorable men did in Caesar," apropos Kennedy's slaying) and quoted a wide variety of sources—from Graham Greene and Lewis Carroll to Shakespeare. He especially liked to recite Polonius's advice to Laertes. He was a chess master. But he was not exactly a square. Once known as a Bourbon Street swinger, he remained a familiar sight in several night spots, where he held forth on the piano while crooning a basso profundo rendition of tunes popular half a generation earlier. His imbibing was moderate—two Tanqueray martinis. He had a wry sense of humor. Once, when a file entrusted to a volunteer helper suspected of inform-ing to the FBI disappeared, he quipped, "Well, would you ask a rabbit to deliver a carrot?" He was sensitive about others' feelings. On several occasions I watched him sit fretfully listening to a visitor give him worth-less information but give the departing person the impression that it had immeasurably aided the investigation. Although he was accused of using the Kennedy case to advance his political ambitions, in pri-vate moments he talked wistfully about going back to private practice as a defense attorney. He saw no virtue in capital punishment, nor in guns. Once he handed me a photo of Dallas police holding aloft a rifle in front of the Texas School Book Depository building moments after the assassination in the hope that I could identify the model.

"I can't," I said. "And besides, I hate guns."

"So do I," he chuckled. "The Bureau had to give me special training so I could just qualify on the range."

What rekindled Garrison's interest in the JFK assassination was a conversation in November 1966 with Louisiana Senator Russell B. Long as they flew to New York. The previous week Long had remarked in the course of a press conference that he doubted the findings of the Warren Commission. Garrison wanted to know why, and bombarded the senator with questions in the manner, he recalled, "of a prosecutor cross-examining a witness." Long insisted that there were grievous flaws

and unexplored territory in the Warren Report. He considered it unlikely that a gunman of Oswald's "mediocre skill" could have fired
with pinpoint accuracy within a time constraint barely sufficient "for a
man to get off two shots from a bolt-action rifle, much less three." Long
saw Oswald as a "fall guy," a decoy to draw attention "while another
man fired the fatal shot." Long's surety caused Garrison to wonder how
perceptive the FBI had been in dismissing Ferrie as a suspect. Back in
New Orleans, he went into virtual seclusion in his study at home,
lucubrating over the twenty-six volumes of the Warren Report. The
indexes contained the name "Farrie," probably meaning David Ferrie.
There was a rumor that a New Orleans library card belonging to "Farrie"
had been in Oswald's possession when apprehended.

Quietly, Garrison opened an investigation and refocused on Ferrie,
who on December 15, 1966, was brought in for further questioning.
When asked details of the strange trip to Texas, he begged off, citing a
lack of memory, and referred his questioners to FBI agent Wall. What
about the goose hunting? "We did in fact get to where the geese were
and there were thousands," he flippantly retorted. "But you couldn't
approach them. They were a wise bunch of birds." Pressed for details
of what took place at the ice rink, Ferrie snapped, "Ice skate—what do
you think?" It didn't take long for the DA's men to poke holes in Ferrie's
story. Melvin Coffey, one of his young companions on the trip, deposed that the Texas junket was not "on the spur of the moment," as
Ferrie had contended, but had been arranged "a couple of days" before. As for the goose hunting, no one had brought along a shotgun. At
the National Archives, DA researchers found forty pages of FBI reports
on Ferrie, but only one that was unclassified. It was an FBI report of a
1963 interview of Chuck Rolland, proprietor of the Winterland Skating Rink in Houston, who stated that Ferrie had called on November
22 to ask the rink's schedule, since he wanted to do some skating while
in Houston. Ferrie showed up the following afternoon with two companions and "carried on a short general conversation" with Rolland.
But when Garrison's investigators backtracked to the rink in early 1967,
Rolland made a vital disclosure that wasn't in the FBI report. None of

the three men in the Ferrie party skated, Rolland was sure. Ferrie spent the entire two hours he was at the rink standing by a pay telephone, waiting for a call, which ultimately came.

At this point, Garrison knew the trip had been no wild goose chase and that Ferrie was lying through his teeth. The DA decided to wait him out. The pilot became a nervous wreck, subsisting on endless cigarettes, bottomless cups of coffee and enough tranquilizer pills to pacify an army. In the meantime, the depth of Ferrie's hostility toward Kennedy became clear. In 1961, a speech he was giving before the Military Order of World Wars turned into a diatribe against the president for a "double cross" of the Bay of Pigs invasion force; several in the audience walked out, and the chairman abruptly adjourned the meeting. At other times he ranted against Kennedy's failure to commit U.S. military force against Cuba, using such pejoratives as he "ought to be shot."

On February 22, 1967, David Ferrie suddenly died at age forty-eight. Although he left notes suggestive of suicide, coroner Nicholas Chetta ruled that the cause of death was an embolism at the base of the brain. Bobby Kennedy, who was closely following the Garrison case, called Chetta at home to find out what happened. Nine days later, on March 3, columnist Jack Anderson broke a story that the possible reason RFK was "tormented by more than natural grief" in the period after his brother's death was that he approved plots by Mafia figures to assassinate Castro, which boomeranged. What rendered this Fidel-did-it scenario highly improbable was the claim by Anderson's unnamed source that the CIA-Mafia team sent on the kill-Castro mission was captured by Castro, converted to his cause, and exfiltrated back into the United States to do in JFK. It later turned out that the source was the dapper Mafia lieutenant Johnny Roselli, who indeed ran assassination operations out of secluded Point Mary near Miami. But Roselli had a personal reason for "dropping an H-Bomb," as Anderson put it, for he was under threat of deportation after being convicted of fraud, and wanted to show he was a true patriot by trying to get rid of an enemy of America.

But the real significance of the Anderson column was that for the first time the cover was stripped from the CIA's most jealously held secret: its devil's pact with the Mafia to assassinate a foreign head of state, which in turn might lead to an Agency role in the Kennedy affair. The story could have been a CIA plant to deflect attention from its own culpability, which was the direction Garrison was taking, and onto Castro. It originated with Robert Maheu, who acted as the CIA's intermediary with the Mafia. Maheu handed it to Edward P. Morgan, a fellow FBI alumnus and capital lawyer regarded as a skillful power broker. In turn, Morgan passed it on to Anderson, who might have thought he had a legitimate scoop.

Unwittingly, Garrison was on a trail that would lead to a Castro assassination plotter. At the very moment Ferrie died, a DA investigator was in Miami looking for one of his associates in the anti-Castro movement, Eladio "Yito" del Valle, as a possible suspect in the Kennedy assassination. The Cuban had been a congressman from Havana under the corrupt dictator Fulgencio Batista, who amassed a small fortune smuggling cigarettes and contraband into the island. His partner in many of these crimes was Santos Trafficante, the Tampa capo who belonged to Carlos Marcello's Sunbelt Mafia and whose gaming casino in Cuba had been shut down by Castro. Although Garrison didn't know it at the time, Trafficante was involved in the CIA-Mafia hit schemes.

What Garrison did know was that as early as 1960 Ferrie moonlighted from his Eastern Airlines job to fly missions against Cuba for del Valle, whose Miami storefront served as a cover for, as journalist Diego Gonzales Tendedera, who knew del Valle from Cuba, put it, "gathering freedom fighters and procuring guns, grenades, bombs and sabotage equipment." According to Gonzales, Ferrie took off "two or three times a week in del Valle's twin-engine Apache to drop incendiaries on strategic targets and rescue anti-Communist Cubans who wanted to escape." He was paid $1,000 to $1,500 per flight, depending on how dangerous it was. Cadets in Ferrie's New Orleans Civil Air Patrol squadron told the DA that Ferrie had boasted he had trained exile pilots for the Bay of Pigs, and was "working for the CIA rescuing Cubans out of Castro's prisons." He proudly flashed a diagonal scar across his stomach, which he said was the deed of a Castro militiaman who intercepted him when he landed on a road and was nearly captured. On one occasion, Ferrie said, he was called to Miami so the CIA "could test him to see if he was the type of person who told his business to anybody."

Eladio del Valle's body was found in a Miami parking lot twelve hours after Ferrie's was discovered in New Orleans. The DA investigator who was searching for del Valle, Bernardo De Torres, turned out to be a suspicious character in his own right. A veteran of the Bay of Pigs, De Torres showed up on Garrison's doorstep early in the probe, saying he was a private detective from Miami who wanted to help, and dropping the name of Miami DA Richard Gerstein, a friend of Garrison's, as an opener.* In retrospect, Garrison remembered that every lead De Torres developed ended up in a box canyon. He also learned that De Torres was forwarding reports on his investigation to the Miami CIA station. In 1977 the House Select Committee on Assassinations (HSCA) came to believe that De Torres might have played a role in Dallas. "De Torres has pictures of Dealey Plaza in a safe-deposit box," a HSCA report states. "These pictures were taken during the assassination of JFK." When hauled before the committee, De Torres denied any implication.

As for del Valle, he had been shot in the heart point-blank, and his skull had been split. As Garrison's chief investigator, Louis Ivon, pointed out in an internal memo dated February 26, 1967, "his body was left in

---

*Gerstein believed in the legitimacy of Garrison's probe. In 1968 he agreed to act as an intermediary for $25,000 donated to Garrison's investigative fund by wealthy industrialist and philanthrophist Louis E. Wolfson. It was arranged that Wolfson would hand checks in increments of $5,000 to Larry King, now the CNN celebrity interviewer, who at the time dealt with Wolfson on a business level through his Royalty Enterprises, in which Hearst columnist Jim Bishop was a partner. In turn, King would pass on the checks to Gerstein, who would hand them to Garrison when he saw him. By the end of 1968 Wolfson had given King five $5,000 checks, completing his pledge. But Garrison had not received the full amount. According to court documents (case number 71-10512 in re the *State of Florida vs. Larry King*), King "admitted that he failed to deliver $5,000." Pressed to repay the sum, he "failed to do so, but was able to forestall prosecution." King was finally arrested and booked on December 20, 1971, and charged with grand larceny, but by that time the two-year statute of limitations had tolled and the charge was dropped.

the vicinity of Bernardo De Torres's apartment." The murder was never solved, although Miami police speculated that drug dealing was involved. What has come out since then points in a different direction. Del Valle was a gunrunner, bag man and hit man tied in with Batista-regime exiles. He boasted that he had a military force inside Cuba and one on standby in Central America. According to a recently declassified document dated November 2, 1960, Senator George Smathers of Florida, a CIA contact, asked the Agency to support del Valle, which it did. Smathers had been dubbed "the senator from Cuba" because of his unwavering praise for Batista. Smathers was a bon vivant of Kennedyesque stature, and the president savored wining and dining with him. But Kennedy eventually grew exasperated at Smathers's incessant advocacy of knocking off Castro. Finally, at a White House supper *à deux*, he became so angry at the table talk that he broke a plate with his fork. In 1978 Tony Cuesta, a member of the Alpha 66 action group in Miami, testified before the HSCA that del Valle and an individual named Luis Castillo were involved in the JFK plot. Recently, Cuban counterintelligence director General Fabian Escalante disclosed that one of his double agents in Florida quoted del Valle as saying that JFK "had to be killed to solve the Cuba problem."

But in 1967 Garrison considered it significant that del Valle headed the Florida chapter of the Committee to Free Cuba, which was set up by the CIA in early 1963 to succeed the Cuban Revolutionary Council, whose cover had been blown by the Bay of Pigs. It exemplified the sinuosity of the anti-Castro movement. Subsidized by the Agency, it was also used as a front for operations. In New Orleans it was quartered at 544 Camp Street, where Sergio Arcacha Smith altered its name to the Crusade to Free Cuba. What caused Garrison to snap to attention was Dallas DA Henry Wade's comment at a press conference the night of the assassination, "Oswald is a member of the Free Cuba Committee," only to be corrected by Jack Ruby, "No, he is a member of the Fair Play for Cuba Committee." Wade had it right . . . almost. The following day Deputy Sheriff Buddy Walthers, catching up on his paperwork, wrote an urgent memo saying he had informed the Secret

Service "that for the past few months at a house at 31228 Harlandale, some Cubans had been having meetings on the weekend and were possably [sic] connected with the 'Freedom for Cuba Party' of which Oswald was a member." Three days later, Walthers plaintively added, "I don't know what action the Secret Service has taken but I learned today that sometime between seven days before the president was shot and the day after he was shot these Cubans moved from this house. My informant stated that subject Oswald had been to this house before." The house on Harlandale was in the Oak Cliff section, not far from where Oswald roomed under the alias O. H. Lee.

Garrison sent investigators to Dallas to interview Arcacha Smith, who had moved there after the assassination, but he ducked them. However, recently released documents show that 31228 Harlandale had been rented in June 1963 by one Manuel O. Rodriguez in the name of the Committee to Free Cuba. Rodriguez had been requested to do so by Andres Sargen of Miami, a top gun in Alpha 66, which was under the Committee to Free Cuba umbrella. A Dallas FBI memo dated the day after the assassination stated that, according to an informant, Rodriguez "was known to be violently anti-President Kennedy," so much so that the Secret Service had him in its Protective Research file of potential threats to the president. The Warren Commission was advised that Rodriguez, a survivor of the Bay of Pigs invasion, "was attempting to purchase arms in Dallas for Alpha 66. Rodriguez is also a member of the DRE." DRE stood for Student Revolutionary Directorate, another die-hard action group aligned with Alpha 66. In the months leading up to the assassination, agent Frank Ellsworth of the Alcohol, Tobacco and Firearms Division (ATF) in Dallas was looking into a gun shop owner, John Thomas Masen, for firearms violations. Ellsworth reported that Masen, whom he characterized as "an ardent member of the Minutemen," admitted that Rodriguez "was attempting to buy arms—machine guns, bazookas, and other heavy equipment"—to be used in a second invasion of Cuba mounted by the DRE. But on November 8, two weeks before the assassination, Ted Shackley, the CIA chief of station in Miami, the nerve center of operations against Cuba, signaled Langley that he disapproved of the DRE's invasion plan. He argued that the plan called for too long a supply line for a covert operation, and that the DRE hotspurs on the Agency's payroll were too unruly.

Garrison knew nothing about the aborted DRE invasion, only that Oswald had tried to infiltrate the DRE in New Orleans in the summer of 1963, offering his Marine Corps skills as an inducement. He also was aware that the FBI had been forewarned that an exile action group intended to assassinate the president. A former security clerk in the Bureau's New Orleans office, William S. Walter, stepped forward to tell Garrison that he had reconstructed an urgent teletype from headquarters which had been sent at 1:45 A.M. on November 17, five days before the assassination. It read:

INFO HAS BEEN RECEIVED BY THE BUREAU THAT A CUBAN FACTION MILITANT REVOLUTIONARY GROUP MAY ATTEMPT TO ASSASSINATE PRESIDENT KENNEDY ON HIS PROPOSED TRIP TO DALLAS TEXAS NOVEMBER TWENTY-TWO DASH TWENTY THREE.

Offices receiving the teletype were instructed to contact their informants to seek substantiation of any of the information, but the wire did not specifically identify the DRE as the revolutionary group.

What began to tie all this together, Garrison noted, was a New Orleans newspaper banner on August 1, 1963: "Explosives Cache Home Lent to Cuban, Says Owner's Wife." The FBI had raided a paramilitary training site and arms cache on the north shore of Lake Pontchartrain, seizing more than a ton of dynamite, twenty 100-pound bomb casings, fuses, napalm ingredients and other war materiel. But no arrests were announced, and the wife of the property owner, Mrs. William J. McLaney, avowed that the premises had been loaned to a newly arrived Cuban. William McLaney and his brother Michael, who lived in Miami, had owned the gambling casino in the Hotel Nacional during the Batista regime. The story of the bust had a one-day roll.

At the time, the FBI, under terms of the missile crisis settlement the previous October, was cracking down under the Neutrality Act on unauthorized anti-Castro actions while looking the other way from those carried out under CIA auspices. Evidently the FBI got its wires crossed with the CIA's, for it developed that although Michael McLaney was bankrolling bombing raids against Havana refineries and at least one air strike to kill Castro, he cleared them with the Agency (when I asked McLaney for comment years later, all he would say was, "Have a drink. They have long memories up in Washington and might not recognize that the statute of limitations has run out"). As it turned out, the FBI had briefly detained eleven men who were on the site. This was revealed in a February 14, 1967, memo by Garrison investigator William Gurvich, who learned it from a U.S. Customs contact. On the list: Sam Benton, a minor mobster and McLaney factotem; Richard Lauchli, Jr., a Minutemen cofounder from Illinois, who was a major arms supplier to the action groups; John Kock Gene, a DRE officer from Miami, and several of his paramilitaries; and Victor Espinosa Hernandez, an exile paymaster who had purchased the munitions from Lauchli.

But who tipped off the FBI to the Lake Pontchartrain Eleven? At the time, no one had a clue. But information that has come to light in the interim points to Victor Espinosa, the paymaster. Espinosa was a lifelong *amigo* of Rolando Cubela, a founding father of the DRE in Cuba in 1958, when it competed with Castro's forces to defeat Batista and form a new government. Shunted to a minor post in the Castro regime, the ambitious Cubela notified the CIA in 1963 that he wanted to "eliminate" him. Espinosa spilled the beans to the Immigration and Naturalization Service that Cubela, now code-named AM/LASH, was scheming with the CIA to assassinate the Cuban *caudillo*, suggesting a link between the AM/LASH plot and the ongoing ones by the CIA-Mafia apparatus. The INS passed on his compromising news to the FBI, which in turn bumped it over to the Agency. But Desmond FitzGerald, the CIA official handling Cubela, was not dissuaded: On November 22 one of his agents passed a poison pen to Cubela in Paris with which to inject Castro. When they emerged onto the street that night, they heard the bulletin that JFK had been shot. Three years went by. Then, according to Evan Thomas in *The Very Best Men*, "A

Cuban exile, Eladio del Valle, tipped the CIA that Cubela was secretly in league with [Santos] Trafficante." Shortly thereafter, del Valle was murdered, even as Garrison was looking for him.

The timing seems exquisite that only six days after the raid, on August 5, Lee Harvey Oswald tried to infiltrate the DRE. He walked into the store of Carlos Bringuier, head of the New Orleans chapter of the DRE, despite the fact that the DRE presence at the Lake Pontchartrain site had not appeared in the newspapers. Displaying a Marine manual, Oswald bragged "that he had been in the Marine Corps and was willing to train Cubans to fight Castro," Bringuier recalled. He returned the next day with the same pitch. A friend of Bringuier's who heard the conversation quoted Oswald as saying he knew "a few things about guerrilla warfare. . . . He said the thing he liked best of all was learning how to blow up the Huey P. Long Bridge." So the DRE leader could hardly believe his eyes four days later when he spotted Oswald on the street dispensing his pro-Castro literature.

Garrison felt that the answer to this riddle lay in the Camp Street connection. The DA had known Guy Banister when, after leaving the FBI, he was deputy superintendent of the New Orleans police. They would occasionally have lunch and swap stories about the Bureau. But after Banister was cashiered by the police department for brandishing his pistol in a French Quarter bar, Garrison lost track of him. It wasn't until he began his JFK probe and Oswald's tether to 544 Camp Street came to light that he focused on his now-dead friend as at least a material witness. A man who knew Banister well told the DA that he was tied in with the Office of Naval Intelligence through Guy Johnson, an ONI reserve officer and the first attorney to represent Clay Shaw, a foreign trade official, after he was charged in the assassination. Among office papers Garrison obtained from Banister's widow, Mary, was a memo to Johnson that stated, "We apparently have cut across a CIA operation in the Taca affair," Taca being a Central American airline.

But Banister was more heavily involved with the CIA. One of his associates disclosed, "Guy participated in every important anti-Communist South and Central American revolution which came along, acting as key liaison man for the U.S. Government-sponsored anti-Communist activities in Latin America." In Cuban affairs he worked hand in glove with his cotenant, Sergio Arcacha Smith of the Cuban Revolutionary Council and the Crusade to Free Cuba, whose office was a kind of Cuban Grand Central Station. With Banister as an incorporator, Arcacha also formed the Friends of Democratic Cuba shortly before the 1961 Bay of Pigs invasion to raise money. But Ronnie Caire, Arcacha's public relations coordinator, told Garrison that the Friends doubled as "an undercover operation in conjunction with the CIA and FBI which involved the shipment and transportation of individuals and supplies in and out of Cuba." As an integral part of the invasion, Arcacha and Banister arranged the transshipment of munitions for a diversionary strike and provocation near the Guantánamo Naval Base. After the invasion flopped, the talk turned to assassinating Castro. An Arcacha associate, Ricardo Davis, brought to the attention of DA investigators that he sat in on a conversation between Banister and Colonel Orlando Piedra, formerly the chief of Batista's secret police, in which they batted about "putting poison in the air-conditioning ducts in the Havana Presidential Palace and killing all occupants."

What Garrison found out is that Oswald's name was exploited by the Camp Street crowd while he lived in the Soviet Union. Buried in the volumes of the Warren Report was an FBI interview of Oscar W. Deslatte, assistant manager of the Bolton Ford Truck Center in New Orleans, two days after Dallas. The FBI report said that on January 20, 1961, two men identifying themselves as Friends of Democratic Cuba wanted to purchase ten trucks. Their spokesman, Joseph Moore, "said that he thought they should get the trucks for no profit for his organization. Moore then told [Deslatte] that he should change the name on the bid form from Moore to Oswald; no first name given. The individual with Moore said that was his name and it should go on the form as he was the man with the money and would pay for the trucks, if they were purchased." Deslatte, who had remembered the name Oswald, gave the FBI agents a copy. But the purchase form was missing from the National Archives. Garrison was curious, and located Bolton Ford's former manager, Fred A. Sewell, who happened to be present when Moore and "Oswald" came calling. Sewell recalled that the second man also gave the first name of Lee, but did not use Harvey. He was a "thin man with his hair a little long, who looked like he might need a meal," Sewell deposed. Joseph Moore was actually a Latino, perhaps Cuban, and seemed more technical and educated than "Oswald." But Sewell perceived "Oswald" as the "overseer," speaking up, "I'm the man handling the money. You ought to have my name too." Sewell gave the DA a copy of the bid form, which, in Deslatte's precise handwriting, shows Joseph Moore crossed out and Oswald substituted.

How Oswald was swept into the Banister operation so early was a mystery. The possibility existed that it was through David Ferrie, in whose Falcon Civil Air Patrol squadron Oswald had enlisted while in high school, or through his uncle, Charles "Dutch" Murret, a minor functionary in the Carlos Marcello crime organization, which contributed to Arcacha's Cuban Revolutionary Council. Garrison tried to resolve this question by subpoenaing agent Regis Kennedy, who was the FBI's liaison to Banister, before the grand jury. Informants who had worked for Banister reported that Kennedy, who trivialized Marcello as a "tomato paste salesman," was in Banister's office at least once a day, forwarding a daily report on sensitive matters directly to John Mohr at FBI headquarters. However, before the grand jury, Kennedy invoked executive privilege and never testified.

Others close to Banister were not so recalcitrant. His widow told Garrison's men that she found among her husband's effects in a storeroom at 544 Camp Street a supply of "Hands Off Cuba!" leaflets, exactly what Oswald had been handing out on the streets. George Higgenbotham disclosed that he had been one of a stable of young men employed by Banister to infiltrate college campuses and report on leftist activity. He recalled that when he kidded his boss about people papering the streets with leftist literature, Banister snapped, "Cool it—one of them is mine." Banister's longtime secretary, Delphine Roberts, refused to talk to Garrison, but in 1978, when the House Select Committee on Assassinations looked her up, she relented, saying she had

kept quiet because she believed her boss and David Ferrie were murdered and feared for her own life. She acknowledged that she "saw
Oswald in Banister's office on several occasions, the first being when
he was interviewed for a job during the summer of 1963." She knew
that Banister received CIA funding and that he ran a network of young
agents. When Oswald showed up, filled out an "agent" form, and went
into a long closed-door session with Banister, she gathered that the two
already knew each other. After that, Oswald appeared frequently, using a vacant office. He accompanied David Ferrie to a training camp
north of Lake Pontchartrain "to train with rifles." It therefore came as a
shock when Roberts saw Oswald on the sidewalk handing out pro-Castro
leaflets.

"He's with us," Banister calmed her. "He's with the office."

"I knew there were such things as counterspies, spies and counterspies," she said, "and the importance of such things."

It is virtually certain that Banister was using Oswald to posture as a
Castro partisan in what is known in intelligence circles as a dangle
operation, trying to lure leftists and pro-Castroites to the bait so that
their profiles could be entered in Banister's huge file collection. Roberts was instructed to maintain a file on Oswald, but not to read it for
her own safety. According to the House Select Committee on Assassinations, "Banister advised her that she should not talk to anyone about
Oswald or any activity that she might have heard about anti-Castro
action such as gunrunning."

That Banister coupled Oswald with anti-Castro gunrunning tended
to confirm a concept that Garrison and I discussed: Oswald was an FBI
informant, which would have been reason enough to withhold his name
from the Secret Service as a potential threat to the president. As mentioned earlier, shortly after the assassination I had received information from a source close to the Dallas FBI that Oswald had been contacted by two agents there, James Hosty and W. Harlan Brown, and
that Oswald was a security informant for the office. Hoover had denied
to the Warren Commission that Hosty had met with Oswald ten days
before the assassination, which the commission's report duly disposed

of under the heading "Rumors and Speculation." Yet the commission was troubled by the discovery that Hosty's name, which had been entered in the accused assassin's address book, was excised from a typed copy furnished to the commission by the Bureau (it wasn't even a convincing omission: the page number was misplaced, and the margins weren't the same). Still, the commission had no way of rebutting Hoover's letter of denial. "Lee Harvey Oswald was never used by this Bureau in an informant capacity," he wrote. "He was never paid any money for furnishing information and he most certainly was not an informant of the Federal Bureau of Investigation." I was struck by how nuanced this disclaimer was. There were two levels of informants. The first was a potential security informant (PSI) or potential criminal informant (PCI), who was in a position to furnish information. PSIs or PCIs (Jack Ruby had been a PCI years earlier) were informants in a trial stage. If they furnished information of value over a considerable period of time, they were eligible to become full-fledged security informants (SIs) or criminal informants (CIs), approved by headquarters and provided with regular renumeration. Hoover did not specifically deny that Oswald was a PSI.

There was every indication that Oswald was enlisted as a PSI in New Orleans in the summer of 1963. William Walter, the Bureau security clerk on duty when the warning teletype about a radical Cuban group came in, thought so. Four days after making contact with the DRE's Carlos Bringuier in the wake of the Lake Pontchartrain raid, Oswald was distributing his pro-Castro literature on the street when a surprised Bringuier accosted him and they scuffled. Both were arrested for disturbing the peace, and in jail Oswald asked to see an FBI agent. John Quigley, who was on call that Saturday, obliged, and they conversed for an hour and a half. Although the police claimed Oswald wanted to explain his Fair Play for Cuba promotion, what actually was said has never been revealed. Walter happened to be on duty that day, and he recalled that when Quigley returned to the office, he asked Walter to check the indexes on Oswald. He located an index card denoting two cases: one was a "105" classification, presumably a routine check stemming from Oswald's residency in the Soviet Union, the other a "134," which was the designation for a PSI or SI. This informant file was assigned to agent Warren deBrueys, who monitored activities for and against Castro. When Garrison subpoenaed deBrueys before the grand jury, he, like Regis Kennedy, stood on executive privilege. But Delphine Roberts told the House Select Committee that Banister "also believed that Oswald was working for the FBI at the time that he was in N.O. [New Orleans]."

So Oswald appears to have been trolling for Castroites on Banister's behalf while at the same time trying to penetrate the DRE for the FBI. The street encounter with Bringuier blew his cover. A month later, after the enigmatic trip to Mexico City, Oswald wound up in Dallas. Both Hosty and Harlan Brown were on FBI Squad 4, which was responsible for Neutrality Act enforcement in the Texas city. But they did not crack down on everyone: In a February 28, 1968, memorandum to Garrison, I reported that Loran Eugene Hall, an anti-Castro commando, said that when he was detained by Dallas police in mid-October 1963 driving to Florida with a trailer load of arms, "Agent Harlan Brown of the FBI took him to another room in the jail, told him the Bureau had no charges against him, and he was released." In an interview with author Mary La Fontaine, Hosty acknowledged he was probing gunrunning: in particular, "the investigation of mostly right-wing subversives, like Minutemen." This assignment brought Minutemen arms dealer Masen, from whom the DRE was ordering weapons, into his sights. And it may have inspired Hosty to dub Oswald a PSI and insinuate him into the Dallas DRE contingent harbored in the house on Harlandale. When the Cubans suddenly decamped only days before the assassination, had they found out that Oswald had simultaneously worked for Banister and the FBI in New Orleans? Had Banister set him up, knowing that Oswald's leftist charade would cast suspicion on Castro and the Russians? After being jailed for the Kennedy assassination, Oswald desperately proclaimed, "I'm just a patsy." Banister himself knew more than he admitted. As Delphine Roberts put it, "Banister stated many times that the truth would not come out in the Warren Report and he believed that a conspiracy took place." Conceivably, he was an accessory before the fact. "It appears that quite possibly Banister had foreknowledge of the assassination," House Select Committee investigator S. Jonathan Blackmer wrote on September 1, 1977, "and in some part participated in a cover up that prevented significant information from coming to the attention of the FBI and the Warren Commission."

In the January 1968 issue of *Ramparts*, I wrote the cover story titled "The Garrison Commission on the Assassination of President Kennedy," which chronicled the investigation. "For the past nine months, I have worked closely with the DA and his staff, hoping to contribute to their investigation," I prefaced. "In my opinion there is no question that they have uncovered a conspiracy." On the day after Christmas 1967, Garrison and I appeared at a press conference in the Monteleone Hotel in New Orleans to announce the forthcoming piece. When it was over, I went up to my room to fetch some documents out of my briefcase. The door wouldn't open—someone had jammed a chair under the inside doorknob. Through a crack I caught a glimpse of the back of a man in a business suit clambering out the open window onto the fire escape. I yelled to Lou Ivon, the chief DA investigator, who was following me, to get outside to the bottom of the fire escape. But by the time he got there, the man had disappeared.

"We must be getting close, Lou," I said. "Someone out there wants very badly to know what we know."

9

THE MEDIA'S CIRCUS

"We're going to let the chips fall where they may. I've been assured of that," promised CBS News field producer Robert Richter in the spring of 1967 in trying to convince me to be a talking head on a documentary special, "The Warren Report." The special had been in the works even before news of the Garrison investigation broke, inspired by a spate of books and articles ripping the Warren Commission's methodology, reasoning and assumptions, which had reduced public acceptance of its conclusions to a mere 35 percent. But I was aware that CBS's editorial position, led by Dan Rather, had been to ratify the Warren Report, and it was doubtful that the network would reverse itself. Nevertheless, I accepted Richter's assurance. The early returns were auspicious: CBS correspondent Bill Stout confidentially reported that seven out of the eight teams sent into the field came back with a conclusion of conspiracy.

It was therefore with considerable revulsion that I watched "The Warren Report" when it aired in June 1967. It struggled to validate that Oswald could have fired three shots from the old bolt-action Carcano within the time constraint of 5.6 seconds (FBI firearms instructor Gene

Jones, who tried the feat, said, "No way," but he was left off the panel of experts). It brought on a military doctor who had been a consultant to the Warren Commission to simulate, using blocks of gelatin separated by Masonite moldings end to end, how the "magic bullet penetrated through Kennedy and Governor Connally," but in all four tests the bullet failed to penetrate Connally's thigh; undaunted, the doctor proposed that "it would have taken very little more velocity to have caused a similar wound." Then CBS put on a physicist employed by a defense contractor to rebut the notion that the killing head shot came from a frontal zone rather than the Texas School Book Depository building. It was all due to a "spalling" effect, the physicist flatly declared. Even Walter Cronkite, who was narrating, was befuddled. "That is one explanation from a physicist as to how a head could move backwards after being struck from behind," he intoned. What was broadcast of my interview concerned Dealey Plaza as an ideal ambush site and included my opinion that "the massive head shot, where the President's head was literally blown apart, came from a quartering angle on the grassy knoll." This was not an off-the-wall remark: I had been to Dallas and surveyed Dealey Plaza. Not only did the grassy knoll, with its picket fence and trees, provide perfect cover, but it made a perfect firing platform. I was sure I could take a .357 Magnum revolver with an eight-inch barrel, rest the barrel in a notch of the fence, and not miss. This wiped out Cronkite's earlier argument that no dropped rifle or empty cartridge shells were found behind the picket fence.

"Number one," I said, "using a revolver or pistol, the shells do not eject. The shooters don't even have to bother to pick up their discharged shells. Number two, they can slip the gun under their coat. . . . Very simple. In fact, it's so simple that it probably happened that way." It was too simple for Cronkite, who pontificated that "it's difficult to take such versions seriously. But unquestionably there are those who will do so, and it is their privilege."

In fact there was photographic evidence of a shooter hidden on the grassy knoll. It was a Polaroid shapshot taken by spectator Mary Moorman, who was facing the knoll when the shots were fired. Her companion, Jean L. Hill, testified to the Warren Commission, "I very frankly thought they were coming from the knoll." When CBS was preparing its special, researcher Raymond Marcus gave a blowup of the Moorman photograph to producer Richter, who said he strongly believed he discerned a man. But executive producer Leslie Midgley, who had the last word, didn't agree, and viewers saw a quick-flash of the photograph with a dismissive voice-over: "If there are men up there, they definitely can't be seen with the naked eye." But Marcus persisted, doing what CBS should have done. He asked a dozen experts in the fields of commercial and technical photography to examine Moorman's photograph. To preserve objectivity, they were not told that it was connected to the assassination.

One of the experts, a photo analyst with an aerospace firm, commented, "You don't need an expert to tell you what's there — it's a man." Nine of the others concluded that there was a man, assigning degrees of certainty ranging from "probable" to "positive." Benjamin F. Poole, coordinator of the Massachusetts Institute of Technology's graphic art services, declared he was positive the image was a man with "light hair or partially bald, most likely with glasses on, as indicated by reflections which appear as black dots." Robert C. Lyon, a veteran commercial photographer affiliated with MIT, identified a man of "slight to medium build, holding what appears to be a straight, highlighted object between his hands." Lyon noted that the man's "right arm cocked upwards," and that he seemed to have dark eye sockets or be wearing sunglasses. Howard E. Tribe, an expert in technical photography at UCLA, saw the upper half of a man with "his hands held above the waistline." Richard T. Hefferan, an MIT graphic arts supervisor, saw the "image of a man," sketching a figure with receding hairline, open-throat shirt, and cocked right arm.

Jim Garrison fared no better, his lengthy interview cut to thirty seconds of air time. "This gave me just about enough time to be a discordant bleep in the network's massive four-hour tribute to the Warren Commission," he cracked.

Since I had ten more years of law enforcement experience than

Cronkite, I felt his dismissive attitude was one more example of the intellectual dishonesty that dominated the special. It was epitomized by Dan Rather's summation:

> I'm content with the basic findings of the Warren Commission, that the evidence is overwhelming that Oswald fired at the President, and that Oswald probably killed President Kennedy alone. I am not content with the findings on Oswald's possible connections with government agencies, particularly with the CIA. I'm not totally convinced that at some earlier time, unconnected with the assassination, Oswald may have had more connections than we've been told about, or that have been shown. I'm not totally convinced about the single bullet theory. But I don't think it's absolutely necessary to the final conclusion of the Warren Commission Report.

Oswald's past connections, perhaps to the CIA, irrelevant? The single-bullet theory not indispensable to the integrity of the Warren Report? Rather's tortured reasoning convinced me that he was conforming to a pre-set bias.

This was confirmed when Robert Richter called to apologize, saying he had not misled me in our initial let-the-chips-fall conversation. "The project started out as an objective look at the criticism and as a search for fresh evidence," he elaborated. "But somewhere along the line the whole tone was changed so as to completely reinforce the Warren Report." The change came, he observed, after a phone call from Washington to CBS President Frank Stanton. The caller was a high government official, possibly Lyndon Johnson. His journalistic integrity violated, Richter resigned from CBS.

Another media manipulation was the defection of William Gurvich, the Garrison aide who had discovered the identities of the Lake Pontchartrain Eleven. The son of an FBI agent, Gurvich and his two brothers ran a security guard service and detective agency. Shortly before Christmas 1966, when the DA's investigation was still under wraps, Gurvich showed up and said he had heard about it and wanted to volunteer his services gratis. Badly understaffed, Garrison readily accepted. Gurvich plunged in with enthusiasm. He wanted to make the trip to

Dallas to serve witness papers on Sergio Arcacha Smith so he could quip, "I've gotcha, Arcacha." He announced the arrest of suspect Clay Shaw after he was indicted. He pretended that he was the chief investigator, although Lou Ivon actually was.

I first met Bill Gurvich on March 6, 1967, when I delivered some research materials to the DA's office. We talked for two hours, and I gained the impression that either he was being cozy with me or didn't really know the case. As Garrison later put it, "Bill had never completely read the Warren Report and its twenty-six volumes, and we didn't assign him leads demanding a solid background in the case. But he was an expert photographer, and did fine work for us in this area." On the walls of Garrison's office hung huge blowups of Dealey Plaza, a tribute to Gurvich's photographic skills. Following our introductory meeting, I talked with Gurvich a number of times by phone. He complained that the FBI undoubtedly was monitoring the lines, and when NBC reporters started interviewing jail inmates he charged that the network was out to get Garrison. "NBC went to the right place," he told me. "Jim put those convicts there and they're liable to say anything against him."

Because his knowledge of the case was sketchy, however, Gurvich was not being cut in on all phases. When he groused that he could not do a proper job without full briefings, Lou Ivon became suspicious and isolated him even more. Apparently his diminished status got the best of him. He began seeing Walter Sheridan, who headed the NBC crew in town, telling Ivon he was trying to pry details from him that would assist the DA. This didn't satisfy Ivon, who knew Sheridan had been on Bobby Kennedy's "Get Hoffa" squad and had arrived in New Orleans on a "Get Garrison" assignment. Ivon had his man measured. On June 22, on a trip arranged by Sheridan, Gurvich flew to New York to meet with Senator Kennedy, telling him that Garrison had nothing that would lead to a solution of his brother's death. Although both declined comment afterwards, NBC News immediately reported that the DA's "chief aide" had skewered him.

That Sunday Gurvich sent Garrison a telegram that it was most urgent they meet the following morning in his office to discuss the investigation. What there was to discuss remains unclear. But Gurvich was surprised when, at the appointed hour of 10:30, he was met not by Garrison but by me.

"What are you doing here?" he demanded.

I told him Garrison had asked me to come down for more consultation.

"I don't care what happened at Dealey Plaza," he cried. "All I care about is the character assassination going on right here in Orleans Parish."

I sat astonished as the normally cool detective ranted on. He was perspiring freely and looked deathly pale.

"I'm sick," he moaned. "I caught the flu in New York."

But I sensed that his anguish was more mental than physical, that the decision to betray Garrison had been a torturous one. Lou Ivon firmly escorted him out of the office and into the swirl of a waiting press.

Gurvich had agonized too long over his decision to defect to appear on the NBC special produced by Sheridan, which had been broadcast the previous week. But CBS preempted time on its four-part "The Warren Report" special the night after our meeting to put Gurvich on live. He asserted that he "saw no reason for the investigation" and felt that "Mr. Shaw should never have been arrested." He had personally conveyed this sentiment to RFK, who seemed "to be rather disgusted to think that someone was exploiting his brother's death." Gurvich contended that the DA had brought the CIA into his investigation because he could say anything he wanted about it without fear of reply. He alleged that Garrison had engaged in illegal and unethical practices, but when asked to specify, he begged off that he would prefer to save it for the grand jury. He got his chance the following day, when the grand jury gave him a full hearing. But the panel also heard from me and Ross Yancey, a veteran reporter covering the investigation for the *New Orleans States-Item*. We refuted Gurvich's claim that Garrison had no case and that he had been repulsed by the investigation as early as Clay

Shaw's arrest. Grand jury foreman Albert V. LaBiche announced that after considering "the many charges claimed by many principals in the news media," the jury had decided "no new evidence had been produced to confirm any of the allegations." But CBS didn't see fit, in the interest of fairness, to break into its final installment of "The Warren Report" that night to report that the grand jury had rejected Gurvich's accusations of the night before.

At least CBS put Garrison on the program, where he held his own under a when-did-you-stop-beating-your-wife interrogation by Mike Wallace. NBC didn't allow Garrison his say in its "White Paper" special, but attacked him with such unremitting hostility that the Federal Communications Commission ordered that he be allowed a half hour of network time in rebuttal under the Fairness Doctrine. It was obvious that Walter Sheridan, the producer, had left New York with a contract on Garrison. Boyish-looking with closely cropped sandy hair, Sheridan was first an FBI agent, then joined the supersecret National Security Agency before becoming RFK's point man in the crusade against Hoffa. There was also a whiff of the CIA. Author Jim Hougan in his landmark book *Spooks* revealed that while attached to the White House, Sheridan presided "over the personnel and currency of whole units of the Central Intelligence Agency." This was hardly surprising since in 1956 Sheridan had completed the Agency's Basic Orientation Course for employees. After RFK was elected a senator, Sheridan turned down a staff position in order to go with NBC News. There is the possibility that the senator, chary that the DA might strip the cover from the CIA secret war against Cuba that he had waged as his brother's attorney general, dispatched Sheridan to put a halt to it (in 1967 Operation Mongoose was still a secret). Zachary "Red" Strate, a New Orleans builder convicted with Hoffa, testified in federal court that "Walter Sheridan offered me evidence of government bugging so I could get a new trial at my hearing in Chicago, in exchange for helping to discredit District Attorney Jim Garrison. . . . I gather Sheridan was working for Robert Kennedy. He said he was interested in stopping the probe of the Kennedy assassination in New Orleans." It is equally plausible that the initiative to smear the DA came from NBC's New Orleans affiliate, WDSU. The station was owned by Edith and Edgar Stern, longtime social friends of Shaw, whom they viewed as a civic leader. After Shaw was indicted, WDSU missed no opportunity to snipe at Garrison. A recently released CIA memo from a high official to the Deputy Director for Plans (the covert action side) affirms that NBC was out to get Garrison. Citing Walter Sheridan as his source, the official advised that "NBC plans to do a derogatory TV special on Garrison and his probe of the Kennedy assassination, that NBC regards Garrison as a menace to the country and means to destroy him."

In New Orleans, Sheridan teamed up with a journeyman journalist named James Phelan, who had a strange obsession with deconstructing the DA's case. I first met Phelan in 1962, when *True* magazine assigned him to do a story on my FBI career, including the debunking of Hoover. Although he interviewed me extensively, the article was never written. I found out why when I picked up the September 25, 1965, issue of *The Saturday Evening Post.* The cover story was "Hoover's FBI" by Phelan, which could only be described as a puff piece. In introducing the author, the magazine imparted: "James Phelan has worked closely with the FBI on many occasions during his 25 years as an investigative reporter." When next I saw him, Phelan rather sheepishly explained, "I went into the interview with Hoover with a list of twelve questions. I left with twelve unanswered and eleven unasked." But I knew that no journalist got an interview with Hoover unless his loyalty to the Bureau's point of view was proven. Phelan's symbiotic relationship with the FBI continued. According to a recently declassified document, on April 3, 1967, against all journalistic canons, he appeared at FBI headquarters and "furnished data he had obtained" concerning the Garrison probe, including a copy "of an interview of Perry Raymond Russo by one of Garrison's investigators, Andrew J. Sciambra, which occurred 2-25-67."

Perry Russo was the state's key witness in the prosecution of Shaw. A clean-cut graduate of Loyola University, who in 1964 had campaigned for Republican Barry Goldwater, he was a salesman for the Equitable Life Insurance Company. Russo contacted the DA's office three days after David Ferrie passed away, and Sciambra talked to him at once. Garrison considered Russo's account so significant that he brought him into the office to thoroughly test whether he was telling the truth. Russo recounted that when Ferrie's picture was shown on television following his death, he recognized him as the leader of a Civil Air Patrol squadron whom he had met in 1960 through a young friend who was a member. The friend, Al Landry, boasted that he was being trained by Ferrie in jungle warfare "to help bring about a more democratic government" in Cuba. Landry's parents asked Russo to help "break Ferrie's hold on their son." Ferrie became enraged at Russo's efforts and threatened to kill him, but there was a reconciliation, and they resumed a copacetic relationship.

In September 1963, Russo continued, he dropped in on Ferrie, "and there seemed to be some sort of a party in progress." Among the eight or nine guests were two men in fatigues who could have been Cuban. When the party broke up, two men remained in addition to Ferrie. One Russo knew as Leon Oswald, whom he had encountered previously in the apartment and assumed was one of Ferrie's revolving door of roommates. The other was an older, tall man introduced as Clem Bertrand. Russo stayed on because he didn't have a ride home. Oswald glared at Russo and demanded, "What the hell is he doing here?" Ferrie replied that Russo was "alright—he doesn't know anything." The pilot then took the initiative and, gesticulating animatedly, poured out a plan for the ambush shooting of Kennedy. He referred repeatedly to "triangulation," each time thrusting three fingers into the air. There would be a diversionary shot, the direct hit, and a "scapegoat." Leon Oswald listened impassively. So did Clem Bertrand, who with his short, silvery hair and natty, maroon jacket seemed out of place with his carelessly dressed companions in the clutter of the apartment. During the discussion, everyone expressed intense dislike not only of Kennedy but Fidel Castro. Bertrand argued that it would be too difficult to assassinate Castro inside Cuba.

The talk switched to escape, Russo said. Ferrie favored a flight to Brazil with a refueling stop in Mexico, or a riskier shortcut under the

Cuban radar screen. Bertrand disagreed on grounds that the flight would be too long.

"Shut up and leave him alone," interjected Oswald. "He's the pilot."

"A washed-up pilot," Bertrand shot back in apparent reference to Ferrie's termination from Eastern Airlines.

From the conversation, Russo gathered that none of the three intended to be at the scene when the assassination came down. Ferrie declared that he would be giving a speech at Southwestern Louisiana State College. Bertrand said he would be on the West Coast on business. Oswald said nothing. Ferrie drove Russo home.

When Sciambra displayed a photo lineup, Russo picked out Clay Shaw as Clem Bertrand. At first, Russo could not positively identify a photo of Lee Harvey Oswald as Leon Oswald, but when a police artist added hair touches he nodded. Garrison then called on Dr. Chetta, the coroner, to administer a sodium pentothal test, and Dr. Esmond Fatter, an expert in hypnosis and memory, to coordinate the examination. Sodium pentothal, commonly called truth serum, acts as a kind of chemical lie detector, while hypnosis can enhance the memory and is often used in criminal cases to, say, help a witness recall a license plate number. Russo passed with flying colors.

At this point, Jim Phelan and Walter Sheridan went to work on Russo. At a time when other reporters were queued up outside the DA's office hoping for an interview, Phelan was on the inside because in 1963 he had written a complimentary account of Garrison's cleanup of Bourbon Street, "The Vice Man Cometh," in the *Saturday Evening Post*. Phelan spent time with the DA's staff and visited his home. In the course of their conversations, the open-handed Garrison would thrust a document or two at the journalist to substantiate a point. One of the documents so casually proffered was the Sciambra memorandum on his interview of Perry Russo, the one Phelan would turn over to the FBI.

Phelan noticed that the brief memo was silent about the party at David Ferrie's, Clay Bertrand and the assassination talk, which suggested that Russo didn't disclose this crucial information in the original interview. In his subsequent article, "Rush to Judgment in New Orleans," in the *Saturday Evening Post* of May 6, 1967, Phelan quoted Sciambra as saying, "Maybe I forgot to put it in." In fact, Sciambra had arranged for Phelan to talk with Russo, who confirmed that he had recounted it in their first meeting. And Russo had given his complete narrative of the fateful Ferrie party to the Baton Rouge press before Sciambra met with him. Sciambra elaborated to me that he had dictated his memo in snatches while trying to keep up with the flood of work engulfing the office. He estimated that he was half finished with the memo when his boss handed it to Phelan.

Later Mark Lane asked Phelan why he had omitted from his article the crucial fact that Russo told him he had given the entire story on the first interview. Phelan complained, Lane said, that he was bucking a tight deadline, that the magazine's editors had virtually locked him in an office to grind out the article. Naturally, a point or two might have been missed. In fact, it was an outright hit piece. In it Phelan stated that the memorandum was incomplete because Russo didn't mention anything to Sciambra about Ferrie's party—that story "was elicited from him under hypnosis." Phelan had not a shred of evidence that the highly regarded Dr. Fatter had planted the story in Russo's mind, yet that did not deter him from contending that Russo testified at Shaw's preliminary hearing, in which a judge found sufficient evidence to hold him for trial, under posthypnotic suggestion.

Phelan's "Rush" story was yellow journalism at its worst, but it developed "legs" as newspapers picked up on it and Walter Sheridan, who had put Phelan on the NBC payroll, used it as the centerpiece of his documentary. Sheridan's production was noteworthy for the absence of Perry Russo, which denied viewers an opportunity to judge his credibility for themselves. Sheridan and Phelan had visited him four times to try to turn him against Garrison and change his testimony. They promised to set him up in California, protect his job with Equitable, get him an attorney, and shield him from extradition back to Louisiana. But Russo was made of sterner stuff and flatly refused. So Sheridan falsely reported on the television special that the state's star witness had flunked a polygraph test.

I have always been puzzled why Phelan was so single-mindedly antagonistic when it came to Garrison, whom he had lionized earlier as a crusading DA. I entertained the notion that it wasn't Garrison himself but the touchiness of an assassination conspiracy that set him in motion. There was his you-scratch-my-back relationship with the FBI, which was dead set against the DA's investigation. There was also his closeness to Robert Maheu, the former FBI agent who had brokered the CIA-Mafia alliance to kill Castro and performed other on-call services for the Agency (when Garrison gave him the Sciambra memo, Phelan hustled over to Maheu's Las Vegas office to photocopy it). Phelan's connection to Maheu stemmed from his journalistic fascination with Howard Hughes, for whom Maheu fronted during his Las Vegas period. It was not beyond reason that the CIA, alarmed that in pursuing his probe Garrison might uncover anti-Castro black operations and Shaw's CIA links, used Maheu to point Phelan against the DA.

Whatever his motivation, Phelan continued to be consumed beyond journalistic interest with Garrison, as if he were a man on a mission that he could not allow to fail. He bombarded Garrison with phone calls and letters, pleading with him to reconsider prosecuting Shaw on the strength of Russo's story. And he showed up in the most unlikely places to plead his case. "I couldn't believe it," Garrison recalled. "I went up to Monticello, New York to give a speech and there was Phelan—with the same pitch." When I wrote an article in *Ramparts* rebutting Phelan's *Post* effort, he met with me and sounded aggrieved. He insisted he had not been handed a "slant" by his editors but had written it as he saw it. The way I saw it, I said, he was dead wrong. But he kept at it. In 1982, he wrote a thin memoir titled *Scandals, Scamps and Scoundrels*, which devoted an entire chapter to placing Garrison in the scoundrel category. As late as 1993 he was still wrestling with the wraith, calling to say he was contemplating an article on the thirtieth anniversary of the assassination and wondering if I had changed my mind about Garrison (I hadn't). He sounded a bit desperate. By that time, Oliver Stone's motion picture *JFK* had vindicated Garrison, and public opinion in support of the conspiracy theory had reached a stratospheric height.

Joining Phelan and Sheridan in the anti-Garrison campaign was *Newsweek*'s Hugh Aynesworth, whose background was equally provocative. At the time of the assassination, Aynesworth was a conservative reporter for the *Dallas Morning News* who befriended Marina Oswald and helped her sell her husband's address book to the newspaper for $50,000, from which he received a commission. He fed information to the Warren Commission and received tidbits in return. Although not on the regular staff, Aynesworth wrote a lurid article in *Newsweek*, May 15, 1967, that accused Garrison of improprieties and lampooned the many permutations of the prosecution, saying that his suspect was equal parts "Oswald, homosexual, rightwing extremist, FBI agent, Cosa Nostra hood, CIA operative and Russian double-agent." A document in the Lyndon B. Johnson Library reveals that Aynesworth had submitted a rough draft to the White House, noting that "I intend to make a complete report of my knowledge available to the FBI, as I have done in the past." It is probable that Aynesworth's reports helped flesh out Hoover's daily abstracts, "Progress of the Garrison Investigation," sent over to the White House.

Nor was Aynesworth, like Phelan and Sheridan, above tampering with a witness. His name was Darrell Garner, and he had been a boyfriend of Nancy Jane Mooney, an entertainer in Jack Ruby's nightclub who committed suicide. Garrison had been looking for Garner, who, it turned out, happened to be in New Orleans. Aynesworth got to him first. As Garner subsequently told the DA's office, the journalist urged "me to get out of New Orleans because Garrison would hang me by the balls, but he also said that the paper [*Newsweek*] was representing Clay Shaw." Aynesworth guaranteed Garner that if he went to Dallas, he would be provided with an attorney. Instead, Garner went to a local attorney, who advised him, he said, that "the Newsweekly [sic] is sponsoring Clay Shaw for attorneys and they are going to send you to Dallas and you wouldn't live a week there." So Garner walked into the DA's office and gave a statement, passing a polygraph test. He recounted that he became involved with people who "said that Kennedy had to be killed." He was promised "some money, big money," and was told by Jack Ruby that "they had some deal they had to work out, and I was given a gun." But Garner got cold feet, hocked the gun, and fled to Las Vegas, where he was when the assassination came down.

For a time it looked as if *Life* was going to be the lone major exception to the pack attack on Garrison. In its issue of November 25, 1966, the magazine published several still frames of the Zapruder film, elicited a statement from Governor Connally that he was struck by a separate bullet from the one that struck the president, and editorialized, "One conclusion is inescapable: the national interest deserves clear resolution of the doubts. A new investigative body should be set up, perhaps at the initiation of Congress." When news of Garrison's inquiry broke, associate editor Richard Billings and Miami bureau reporter Miguel Acoca showed up in his office. On June 25, 1967, I met them there. Both were knowledgeable about the Cuban exile action groups, and when Acoca came to California to run out leads, I was able to help him. It was clear that *Life* was putting together a piece that would portray Garrison in an objective light.

Then, some six weeks later, *Life* pulled a double cross. Billings brought in a staff writer who was the magazine's specialist on organized crime, Sandy Smith. It was the same Sandy Smith who, two years earlier, had underhandedly sabotaged my *Playboy* article on FBI inertia on the crime syndicate. At the time, the Bureau had characterized him as "a great admirer of the Director and a very strong backer of the Bureau" who had been "utilized" on "many different occasions." In 1966, after the FBI had been caught in *flagrante delicto* bugging Las Vegas hotels, Smith came to the rescue in a series in the *Chicago Sun-Times* justifying the action because of the casino "skims" that funneled big money into mob coffers around the land. Then he landed at *Life*, where the Bureau continued to feed him information, much of it gleaned from the bugs. Had I known Smith's true colors at the time, I of course would have warned off Garrison. I still don't know why the DA didn't kick him out the door when his hostile line of questioning began. Why, Smith demanded, had a racketeer named Frank Timphony been allowed to wax fat in his jurisdiction? Garrison patiently informed Smith that Timphony had flourished years earlier and in 1957, four years before he became DA, had retired and left New Orleans. What about his association with Sammy Marcello, a brother of Carlos Marcello? Garrison responded that the "association" consisted of bidding the time of day to Sammy at the New Orleans Athletic Club and Moran's Restaurant, a fashionable establishment in the French Quarter that hosted everyone who was anyone in the city. What about his several trips to Las Vegas, where his guest tabs had been picked up by the Sands Hotel, which was partially owned by Frank Sinatra, and on the last occasion by a former Marcello lieutenant named Mario Marino? Garrison pointed out that it was the policy of many hotels, the Sands among them, to pick up the tabs of public officials. One trip was for a convention of district attorneys, all of whom were afforded the same courtesy. The last visit was in March 1967, when Garrison, fatigued by the pressures of the JFK investigation and battling a stubborn bronchial condition, traveled there for some sun and rest. "It may interest you to know," he braced Smith, "that I paid $133 for phone calls and food. If I was a friend of the mob, as you seem to insinuate, and I knew the mob controlled the hotel, I would have told them to take the bill and shove it."

The *Life* story, entitled "Carlos Marcello: King Thug of Louisiana," ran September 7, 1967, under Smith's byline. A photo of Garrison was juxtapositioned with that of prominent mobsters so as to imply that he was one of them. It reported that he was comped by Marino, but made no mention that he had paid $133 in tabs. What Smith termed "links" to the mob were so diaphanous as to constitute guilt by minimal association. Anyone familiar with the peculiar culture of New Orleans would realize that the social lines were blurred and the criminal elite mingled easily (up to a point) with attorneys, judges and the business establishment. The city isn't called the Big Easy for nothing. One day after work, Garrison and I were having a drink at the New Orleans Athletic Club, discussing the efficacy of methadone, when Carlos Marcello's son, Anthony, and a bodyguard plunked themselves down at our table. After the hellos, Marcello invited Garrison to dinner that night, an invitation he declined on grounds of a previous engagement. "Maybe Bill would like to go," he offered, but I suddenly had a previous engagement. But Anthony's father didn't set foot in New Orleans. After Garrison was first elected and turned down a $3,000-a-week slice of the lucrative rackets, Carlos Marcello relocated to the Jefferson Parish side of the Mississippi River, beyond the DA's reach. I savored the irony of Smith labeling him the King Thug of Louisiana while the FBI's Regis Kennedy called him nothing more than a "tomato paste salesman."

In retrospect, it is obvious that the FBI played an obbligato to the "Get Garrison" melody of Phelan, Sheridan, Aynesworth and Smith. The smothering extent of the Bureau's role was not apparent until 1977 when former security clerk William Walter, by then a well-known banker, felt free to give Garrison an earful. There were ten to fifteen agents assigned to tail DA investigators, Walter said, to determine what leads they were checking out. Moreover, the DA's offices were wired. The Bureau monitored taps from the Technical Surveillance Room in its own office, and several former agents had been transferred to the telephone company's security office, "where he can patch anyone's phone line into the Bureau's local cable for self-activating recordings." This crew was under the supervision of Charles Carson, a retired FBI man employed by the Wackenhut Corporation, a nationwide security guard and detective agency (its founder, George Wackenhut, also ex-FBI, was such a lap dog that he kept a bust of Hoover on his desk). The Bureau's intense interest in Garrison belied its public stance that his investigation was invalid. Hoover probably ordered the surveillance to feed Lyndon Johnson's daily appetite for information. But there also may have been the ulterior motive of learning Garrison's moves in advance in order to counter them. Was the DA closing in on the Bureau's connection to Camp Street? Was he zeroing in on Marcello, the partner in crime of Hoover's shadow friend, Frank Costello? There was a host of compelling questions to which Hoover sought answers.

Garrison thought he finally had relief from the negative reporting when Edward Jay Epstein called to announce that he was on his way to New Orleans to do a summary for *The New Yorker* magazine. As a Cornell University graduate student, Epstein had interviewed members of the Warren Commission for his master's thesis, which he converted into a book called *Inquest*, which bared the inner workings of the Commission and the tortured logic used to dispel notions of a conspiracy. But I cautioned Garrison, "Be careful. Epstein stabbed the Commission in the back, and he'll stab you." Sure enough, he produced a 25,000-word screed that attacked the DA from every angle. He adopted uncritically Hugh Aynesworth's sensational tale that Garrison had tried to bribe one witness to falsify testimony and threatened to murder another witness. He scoffed at Professor Richard Popkin's article in the *New York Review of Books* of September 14, 1967 in praise of Garrison's discoveries. And he ridiculed Mark Lane and myself as volunteer "peripatetic demonologists" who were "attracted to Garrison like children of Hamelin to the Pied Piper," even though our investigative credentials totally eclipsed his. I asked Lou Ivon how painstaking Epstein's research in New Orleans had been. Not very, Lou laughed. He had spent some forty-eight hours in town, about three of them in the office, and Garrison dined with him at Broussard's that night. He hadn't been seen or heard from since — it was hit and run. Not long ago it came to light that the CIA immediately forwarded reprints of the Epstein article to its stations abroad to be used to counter any foreign wellspring of sentiment favoring Garrison. In 1974, when Epstein was doing a book on Oswald's double life called *Legend*, whose thesis was that he might have been a KGB asset, the Agency took the unique step of allowing him access to a KGB defector, Yuri Nosenko, who was being held under wraps (after the Soviet Union collapsed, KGB records showed that, in fact, Oswald was under tight surveillance in Russia as a suspected CIA plant).

The smearing of Garrison went so far as to portray him as on the cusp of craziness. In early 1968, I was discussing the status of the case on KHJ-TV in Los Angeles when the host, Stan Bohrman, patched in a surprise phone caller: Jerry Friedheim, the military correspondent for the *Chicago Tribune* (who later became the Pentagon's chief spokesman). Friedheim announced that Garrison's Army medical jacket documented that he had been discharged for mental illness. He sounded taken back when I retorted that the DA had reenlisted in the Army during the Korean War, contracted disabling amoebic dysentery and was given a medical discharge. What Friedheim considered a mental illness was a mild temporary depression secondary to the dysentery. Garrison later became an officer in the Louisiana National Guard and a member of the active reserve. "Jerry," I said, "if you want to perform a genuine public service, use your government contacts to get a look at those assassination documents that are locked in the archives for seventy-five years." But the damage had been done: the canard that Garrison was clinically demented gained wide currency.

Although the media ganged up on Garrison, it must be said that he fed them lunch through his lack of understanding of their appetite. It was obvious from the start that he should have had a press relations officer speaking for him, since he didn't have a clue how to handle pesky reporters and all too often painted himself into a corner as he tried to explain things. One of his first encounters with the fourth estate was a disaster. After working all night on the case, he was accosted by a gaggle of reporters demanding to know what progress he was making, to which he replied, "No comment." On the elevator going down, one reporter persisted, "When are the arrests going to be made?" Garrison had previously stated that everyone implicated would eventually be arrested, but that event might be a long way off. Fearful that the reporter had misinterpreted his confidence that the case would in time be solved, he reiterated, "Of course there will be arrests." The reporter escalated the question by asking, "You mean you've solved the case?" "Of course. We solved it weeks ago in the essentials," Garrison shot back defensively. As it came out in the local newspapers, there was an old photo of the DA grinning with the caption, "CASE SOLVED,

SAYS GARRISON." The story was flashed over the wires to the rest of the world.

On another occasion, when Garrison told reporters, "The key to the whole case is through the looking glass. Black is white, white is black. I don't want to be cryptic, but that's the way it is." The media sneered that his case was straight out of Alice in Wonderland. Actually, he was metaphorically describing an intelligence operation, which in essence the assassination was. And when he described David Ferrie, after his strange death, as "one of history's most important individuals," the media mocked him again. In fact, Ferrie was a key figure unlocking the answer to the crime of the century. What Garrison seemed unable to get across to reporters was that Ferrie was, in his estimation, at the operational level of the conspiracy, and Garrison considered it more important to track down those at the sponsorship level. As the Turkish police inspector put it in Eric Ambler's A Coffin for Demitrius, "The important thing to know about assassinations is not who fired the gun but who paid for the bullet." It was Garrison's belief that the CIA had paid for the bullet.

Although the Shaw trial was first set for October 1967, defense attorneys stalled it until February 1969. During this interregnum the media assault on Garrison continued, while the defense attorneys were aided by the FBI and the CIA—and the House Un-American Activities Committee. The Bureau supplied skinnies on me, other DA investigators, and witnesses. The Shaw attorneys asked Louisiana Congressman F. Edward Hebert to contact the HUAC as a former member and seek derogatory information on me and Mark Lane; Hebert regretfully reported that HUAC could find no files tying me to "organizations or publications which have been cited as subversive by the Committee," but he linked Lane to the National Lawyers Guild and several other leftist groups. At the same time, the CIA was up to its own mischief. According to Victor Marchetti, who was a staff assistant to Director Richard Helms, Helms acknowledged that Clay Shaw was associated with the Agency, and instructed his top aides to "do all we can to help Shaw." CIA General Counsel Lawrence Houston assured Helms that the Agency was "on top of the situation." Not long ago it was revealed that Garrison's staff was penetrated by nine CIA agents. His files on Shaw were copied wholesale and turned over to the defense. So by the time Shaw came to trial it was Garrison who had been tried in the press.

Garrison's first hurdle was to overcome skepticism on the part of the jury that the tall, courtly Shaw, who carried impeccable credentials as a social lion and patron of the arts and projected a detached, aristocratic manner, could conspire to assassinate a president. Born dirt poor in 1913 in a scrub pine area of Louisiana, he got no farther than the eleventh grade. As a supply officer in World War II, he performed with distinction and earned a Bronze Star. Upon his return to civilian life, he was named the first managing director of the International Trade Mart, which promoted world global commerce. Fluent in French and Spanish, Shaw traveled extensively to Europe and Latin America as the Mart's signature salesman. A first nighter at Crescent City musical and artistic events, he was himself a playwright, whose most notable effort was *Submerged*, about men trapped at the bottom of the sea in a submarine, which was made into a motion picture called *Men Without Women*. He lived in a meticulously restored Vieux Carré carriage house and was active in preserving the eighteenth-century architecture of the section. After his arrest in the JFK case, incidental to which sadomasochist paraphernalia was found in his house, he made bail and held a convivial press conference in the home of his lead attorney, Edward Wegmann. As a butler served drinks and canapes, Shaw amiably expounded on topics ranging from things gustatory to world politics. He preferred martinis on the rocks, and considered himself an "old-fashioned liberal of the Wilson-Roosevelt persuasion."

It was Shaw's secret life that put Garrison on his trail. Within days of the assassination, attorney Dean A. Andrews had tipped the FBI about a link between Oswald and Shaw, who was using the pseudonym Clay Bertrand (the same surname Perry Russo recalled). Andrews, a Falstaffian figure with a flair for hip language, later told the Warren

Autographed photograph of Hoover, dated November 26, 1952. Catering to the Director's vanity was considered a requisite for getting ahead.

George "Machine Gun" Kelly and his wife, Kathryn, photographed in the federal courtroom at Oklahoma city October 12, 1935, as they heard Judge Edgar S. Vaught sentence them to life imprisonment. They were found guilty in connection with the kidnaping of Charles F. Urschel. Hoover withheld evidence exonerating Kathryn.

The author (right) with four other G-men at a St. Louis indoor pistol range, 1952. Hoover remained locked into the shoot-'em-up 1930s, leaving organized crime untouched.

The author (right) with Special Agent Edward Garbers in 1957 on the Seattle waterfront. The Japanese training ship *Nippon Maru* is in the background. Weeks later, the author participated in a burglary of the Japanese consulate in Seattle.

UNITED STATES DEPARTMENT OF JUSTICE
FEDERAL BUREAU OF INVESTIGATION

WASHINGTON 25, D. C.

March 7, 1960

PERSONAL

Mr. William W. Turner
Federal Bureau of Investigation
Seattle, Washington

Dear Mr. Turner:

Your work in an operation of considerable value to the Bureau in the security field was of the highest caliber and I do not want the occasion to pass without thanking you.

The competent, resourceful and effective fashion in which you handled your responsibilities was indeed commendable and contributed materially to the successful handling of this delicate assignment. You demonstrated much skill and ability in this case and I want you to know of my appreciation.

Sincerely yours,

J. Edgar Hoover

A letter of commendation to the author from J. Edgar Hoover for a break-in to plant a bug in an espionage case.

A page from the FBI technical handbook showing simple bug installation. After the author published the page in 1966, Hoover wanted to prosecute him for violation of the espionage statute. Instead, the FBI chief called a halt to break-ins.

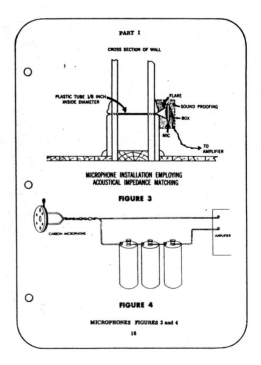

PART I

CROSS SECTION OF WALL

PLASTIC TUBE 1/8 INCH
INSIDE DIAMETER

FLARE
SOUND PROOFING
BOX
MIC
TO
AMPLIFIER

MICROPHONE INSTALLATION EMPLOYING
ACOUSTICAL IMPEDANCE MATCHING

FIGURE 3

CARBON MICROPHONE

AMPLIFIER

FIGURE 4

MICROPHONES FIGURES 3 and 4

16

President Kennedy and uniformed French President Charles de Gaulle braved Paris rain in an open car as they left the Arch of Triumph after ceremonies honoring France's Unknown Soldier, May 31, 1961. (Associated Press)

New Orleans DA Jim Garrison (right) holding a press conference with the author in New Orleans, December 26, 1967. Garrison charged that the FBI had prior knowledge of a conspiracy to kill JFK. At times he was too open with the media, painting himself into corners. (AP/Wide World Photos)

View from the grassy knoll to the roadway in Dealey Plaza, Dallas, where President Kennedy was shot on November 22, 1963. When the author contended on the CBS special "The Warren Report" in June 1967 that it was an ideal ambush site, consistent with the Zapruder film's evidence of a shot from a frontal zone, Walter Cronkite scoffed, "It's difficult to take such versions seriously."

The Newman Building in New Orleans, which housed ex-FBI agent Guy Banister's second-floor office. Banister was linked by Jerry Brooks to the delivery of $100,000 cash from the CIA to French officers plotting to assassinate President de Gaulle. The walk-up entrance on the right had the address 531 Lafayette Place, while the one on the left had 544 Camp Street, an address Lee Harvey Oswald stamped on pro-Castro literature he handed out three months before the JFK assassination. He actually was conducting a dangle operation for Banister to identify Castro sympathizers. (William Turner)

Jerry Milton Brooks, defector from the paramilitary right Minutemen, Kansas City, 1966. Brooks identified a New Orleans member as a CIA "transporter" who in 1962 delivered $100,000 cash to the French officers plotting to assassinate de Gaulle. He linked the transporter to ex-FBI executive W. Guy Banister, whose office at 531 Lafayette Place, New Orleans, was a nerve center for CIA-directed anti-Castro actions. (Laird Wilcox)

Senator J. William Fulbright of Arkansas, chairman of the Senate Foreign Relations Committee, June 1967. Briefed by the author two months earlier on how the CIA was blackmailing foreign students into becoming spies, the senator despaired his inability to do anything about it. "I'm just a country boy," he cracked. "Guess I'll go back to Arkansas." (AP/Wide World Photos)

Warren Hinckle, the *enfant terrible* of 1960s journalism who edited the upstart *Ramparts* magazine, of which the author was a senior editor. When *Ramparts* exposed CIA clandestine penetration of American institutions, the Agency struck back with Operation CHAOS to put the magazine out of business. (Harvey Cohen)

Gerry Patrick Hemming, head of the anti-Castro paramilitary action group Interpen, at a training base on No Name Key, Florida, 1963. Interpen was allied with Watergate burglar Frank Sturgis's International Anti-Communist Brigade. It was Hemming who in 1973 first disclosed CIA-backed twin assassination plots against Fidel Castro during his October 1971 state visit to Chile. In 1975 these attempted hits were missed by the Church Committee, a U.S. Senate panel that probed the Mafia-CIA plots. (E. Carl McNabb)

Orlando Bosch—"Doctor Death"—the head of the terrorist group Cuban Power, in custody in Miami, October 11, 1968. Bosch was convicted of cannonading a Polish freighter. In 1976 he was jailed in Costa Rica for planning the bombing assassination of Secretary of State Henry Kissinger for relaxing U.S. relations with Cuba. The same year he was incarcerated in Venezuela for bombing a Cuban airliner that killed all 73 people on board. (AP/Wide World Photos)

General Fabian Escalante, former chief of Cuban State Security, Rio de Janeiro, Brazil, August 1995. He directed counterintelligence defenses against CIA-directed aggressions. Escalante told the author that in 1965 his ace wire-man bugged the Nicaraguan base of an exile action group and nipped a plot to simultaneously assassinate Fidel Castro, pull off a coup and land an amphibious force to take over the island. (Gordon Winslow)

Ex-CIA pilot Jim Rose with P-51 Mustang, Santa Barbara, 1967. A reserve pilot for the 1961 Bay of Pigs invasion, Rose flew raids on Cuba. In 1965 he recanted and volunteered to help the "good guys." One of his new missions, for New Orleans District Attorney Jim Garrison's JFK probe, was to contact the KGB in Mexico to get the Russian skinny on Oswald. (E. Carl McNabb)

Zenith Technical Enterprises, the dummy front for the CIA's Miami station, code-named JM/WAVE. By 1973 this building was the last vestige of the sprawling station created for Attorney General Robert Kennedy's post–Bay of Pigs secret war against Cuba, dubbed Operation Mongoose. Case officers controlled some three thousand agents and subagents under assorted cover companies, and JM/WAVE had its own camouflaged navy to transport them. (Gordon Winslow)

The CIA raider *Rex*, berthed at West Palm Beach, Florida. Disguised as a corporate oceanographic research vessel, the converted subchaser transported exile commando squads on assault missions. On the night of October 23, 1963, a year after the missile crisis with the Soviet Union, the *Rex* was ambushed by Castro's forces as it landed commandos to blow up a copper mine. Cuban MiGs and U.S. Phantom jets scrambled, but a second crisis was narrowly averted when JM/WAVE recalled the Phantom jets. (Gordon Winslow)

Attorney General Robert F. Kennedy (left) and President John F. Kennedy outside the White House, May 7, 1963. They were running on parallel tracks on Cuba. RFK was ramrodding a CIA secret war that was to culminate in a second invasion and internal coup. JFK was in the initial phase of secret negotiations with Castro to normalize relations. Both thrusts ended with JFK's assassination six months later. (John F. Kennedy Library)

Los Angeles Coroner Thomas Naguchi measuring two bullet holes in a wall panel in the hotel pantry where Robert F. Kennedy was fatally shot after claiming victory in the California Democratic primary, June 5, 1968. The two bullets were in addition to the eight fired by suspect Sirhan Sirhan, evidencing a second shooter. (Los Angeles County Coroner's Office)

Manson family prosecutor Vincent Bugliosi (left) with the author (right) and coinvestigator Jonn Christian, Beverly Hills, August 1975. After the tally of bullets fired in the pantry reached thirteen, Bugliosi joined the author and Christian in probing the case. "The time has come for us to start looking for the members of the firing squad that night," he said. (Diane Hull)

Irma and Joel Kaplan celebrating in the United States after he escaped by helicopter from a Mexican prison in August 1971. He had been framed by the CIA in 1961 for a murder that never happened because he aided the wrong side in the Bay of Pigs invasion.

The helicopter snatch scene from the 1975 film *Breakout,* starring Charles Bronson as the pilot and Robert Duvall as Joel Kaplan. The CIA pressured Columbia Pictures by proxy to reduce a politically significant story to an adventure potboiler.

Commission that he ran a kind of turnstile law practice in which he secured the release of "gay swishers" arrested by the police for violations of sumptuary laws. Most of these clients were steered to him by a "lawyer without a briefcase" who introduced himself as Clay Bertrand. He had met personally with Bertrand only once, Andrews said, and knew him mostly as "a voice on the phone." In the summer of 1963 Bertrand referred Oswald, who asked about getting his "yellow paper discharge" from the Marines rectified and his Russian wife's immigration status straightened out. Andrews was sure it was Oswald because he came by several times after that.

Continuing, Andrews mentioned that on the day after the assassination he was recovering from an illness in the Hotel Dieu Hospital when "the phone rang and a voice I recognized as Clay Bertrand asked me if I would go to Dallas" to defend Oswald. By Sunday Andrews had completed arrangements for a law partner to go to Dallas when the partner called, saying, "Don't worry about it. Your client just got shot." Although two employees of his law firm verified that Oswald had been in the office, Andrews could produce no client file. "My office was rifled shortly after I got out of the hospital and I talked with FBI people," he explained. Andrews had given the Bureau a description of Bertrand as tall, distinguished and well-dressed, but agents tried to convince the attorney that Clay Bertrand didn't exist. "You can tell when the steam is on," Andrews enlightened commission counsel Wesley Liebeler. "They never leave. They are like cancer. Eternal." After several unpleasant sessions, Andrews let the G-men put words in his mouth. "You finally came to the conclusion that Clay Bertrand was a figment of your imagination?" Liebeler rhetorically asked. "That's what the Feebees put on," Andrews replied. "Persuasion."

Although the commission discounted Andrews's statement, Garrison didn't. He knew Andrews, having gone to Tulane law school with him, and felt that behind the jive talk he was solid. So one of the first things he did when he reopened his JFK file in late 1967, before the media caught on, was to send his investigators into the French Quarter to seek out the elusive Bertrand. Back came the word: Clay Bertrand was the name Clay Shaw used in the Quarter, and one of his haunts was Cosimo's Bar, which Andrews had depicted to Liebeler as "a freaky little joint" where he once spotted Bertrand. Garrison took Andrews to lunch and braced him on the true identity of Bertrand. The once-cocksure attorney looked stricken; he pleaded that if he fingered Shaw as Bertrand "it's goodbye Dean Andrews . . . I mean, like a bullet in my head." Hailed before the grand jury, Andrews exuded equivocation. "I cannot say positively that [Clay Shaw] is Clay Bertrand or he is not . . . the voice I recall is somewhat similar to this cat's voice, but his voice has overtones . . . Clay Bertrand's is a deep, cultured. well-educated voice—he don't talk like me, he used the King's English." The jury felt Andrews could have done better and indicted him for perjury, of which he was convicted. Knowing the awful bind his classmate was in, Garrison interceded to keep him out of jail.

A possible explanation of Andrews's mortal fear of "a bullet in the head" if he put the hat on Shaw as Bertrand came when a hit man volunteered that he had been tendered a contract on Garrison's life by Shaw and Ferrie. Edward Whalen, a career criminal from Philadelphia, said Ferrie had called him through a mutual acquaintance and promised big money for a job. In New Orleans, Ferrie introduced him to Shaw as Clay Bertrand. In Ferrie's apartment, the same one on Louisiana Avenue Parkway where Perry Russo had listened to the assassination talk in 1963, the pilot and the executive laid out a plan. They wanted to eliminate a witness who could put Shaw away for a long time. Shaw would advance $10,000, and then pay another $15,000 more when the job was done. Shaw would provide Whalen with a forged passport, and Ferrie would fly him to Mexico. But when Whalen learned that the victim was to be the DA, he balked. So Shaw sweetened the offer, saying that he knew Whalen's daughter suffered from polio and that he would pay all of her medical expenses. While they were talking, a man Ferrie introduced as Dean Andrews, wearing his perpetual sunglasses, dropped by. It was Andrews, Ferrie said, who had tipped them to Garrison's budding investigation. But Whalen wanted nothing to do with knocking off a public official. Although Garrison wasn't sure whether to fully believe the ex-con, he nevertheless beefed up his personal security.

The problem facing Garrison at that point was proving Shaw was Bertrand. The terrified Andrews was in denial. Several French Quarter bartenders had readily admitted to DA investigators that Clay Bertrand was the pseudonym Shaw used to mask his true identity, but not one would sign a statement. For his part, Shaw, rather than put an innocent face on it, flatly repudiated the idea. But Garrison came up with two reputable witnesses who could produce evidence that Shaw was Bertrand. One was Jessie Parker, a hostess at the VIP room at the New Orleans Airport, which was so exclusive that a pass key was needed to gain entry. Parker stated that in 1966 she observed Shaw, tall and striking in appearance, sign the guest register "Clay Bertrand." A handwriting expert agreed that the signature on the register was that of Shaw. The other was police officer Aloysius Habighorst, who had booked Shaw following his arrest. After fingerprinting the suspect, Habighorst routinely asked if he had ever used an alias. Shaw, evidently not thinking clearly, replied, "Clay Bertrand," which Habighorst duly typed on the fingerprint card and had Shaw sign it.

In the meantime, a hot lead came in that Shaw, Ferrie and Oswald had been sighted together in the town of Clinton in late August 1963, about the time Oswald discontinued posturing on the streets of New Orleans as a Castro partisan. Clinton was a fading cotton center north of Baton Rouge distinguished at the time by a voter-registration drive organized by the Congress of Racial Equality (CORE). The streets were full of people—blacks to prevent intimidation, whites looking for outsiders who might roll into town in support of the drive.

So when a black limousine driven by a dignified-looking man with chiseled features and chalky hair pulled up to the curb with two passengers, all eyes were upon it. Concerned that the occupants might be federal officials in town to help the blacks register, the segregationist town marshal, John Manchester, asked the driver who he was. "I'm from the International Trade Mart," the man answered. Manchester ran a license check by radio, which verified that the vehicle was registered to the Trade Mart. CORE offical Cory Collins, edgy that the trio were FBI agents, watched intently. A young, ordinary-appearing man got out of the limousine and entered the town's barbershop. The third man, memorable for a homemade, red mohair wig and pasted-on eyebrows, remained in the vehicle. The DA investigators interviewed nearly three hundred townspeople. Despite the passage of three years, many identified photos of Shaw, Oswald and Ferrie.

The barber, Edwin McGhee, recalled that Oswald asked for a haircut, showed him a Marine Corps discharge card, and mentioned that he was looking for a job at the nearby state hospital in Jackson. McGhee suggested that he might have a better chance if he registered to vote in the parish and saw Reeves Morgan, the state representative. Morgan remembered that Oswald came to his home early that evening, seeking an electrician's job at the hospital. Morgan told the visitor that he had to take care of his constituents first and recommended that he register to vote in Clinton. The following morning, Oswald was the only white face in a long line of blacks. Registrar Henry Palmer asked him where he lived, to which Oswald replied, "At the state hospital," where he knew a Cuban doctor named Frank Silva. When a Garrison investigator checked, the hospital's personnel director produced an index card with Oswald's name on it, although the application form itself had disappeared, and confirmed that a Dr. Francisco Silva had been on staff in 1963. Silva was a Cuban exile.

Although the purpose behind this odd tableau was unclear, it did reinforce a relationship between Shaw, Ferrie and Oswald. Three months later, on November 22, Oswald was at Dealey Plaza, to be accused of killing the president. Ferrie, on the way back from his mad dash to Houston, stopped overnight at Southwest Louisiana State College, just as he said he would in front of Perry Russo. And Shaw, who said he would arrange to be on the West Coast on business, was. I spoke with J. Monroe Sullivan, director of the San Francisco World Trade Center, which in 1963 was the only sister organization to the New Orleans Trade Mart. Sullivan recalled that some three weeks before the assassination, Clay Shaw, whom he had never met, phoned to ask him to put on a luncheon for that date because he had a program to obtain tenants for the International House in New Orleans, an affiliate of the Trade Mart. Shaw would send out the invitations and pay for everything. According to Sullivan, Shaw arrived at the San Francisco World Trade Center around mid-morning on November 22. As they were conversing, there was a bulletin that Kennedy had been shot in Dallas. Sullivan was stunned, but Shaw exhibited no reaction. A few minutes later, when the news arrived that the president was dead, Sullivan asked Shaw if he wanted to continue with the luncheon. He did. Sullivan called for a moment of silence, then introduced Shaw, who made his pitch for the International House. Sullivan was struck by Shaw's seeming indifference to the president's death.

Despite his pretension of being "an old-fashioned liberal," Shaw was, under the surface, the polar opposite of Kennedy. The first indication of his real convictions came in early 1967, when the small leftist organ *Minority of One*, edited by Max Arnoni, reported that, according to an Italian daily, Shaw was on the board of a Rome organization called Centro Mondiale Commerciale (World Trade Center), which was run by European fascists and utilized by the CIA as a political intelligence source. I directed this cogent piece of intelligence to the DA's office in a memo dated March 17, 1967, suggesting further inquiries concerning Shaw's activities in California and abroad "because of Shaw's confirmed presence in the Bay Area Nov. 21–23, 1963, and in view of the Arnoni report from Italy." Unfortunately, I sent the memo to the attention of William Gurvich.

But if Gurvich shortstopped it, Garrison was given the same information by another source, British philosopher Bertrand Russell, an early Garrison supporter. Through his secretary, Ralph Schoenman, the Nobel Prize winner forwarded foreign newspaper clips on the Centro Mondiale Commerciale. According to the Italian newspaper *Paesa Sera*, the CMC was founded in Montreal in the late 1950s by Major L. M. Bloomfield, a former U.S. intelligence officer. In 1961 it relocated to a gleaming new building in the Italian capital. By that time, Clay Shaw had been sitting on the board of directors for three years. Among his fellow directors were the publisher of the neo-Nazi *National-Zeitung* of Germany; Prince Guitere de Spadaforo, an Italian industrialist related by marriage to Hitler's finance minister, Hjalmar Schacht; the secretary of the Italian Neo-Fascist Party; and Ference Nagy, the ex-premier of Hungary, who contributed heavily to fascist groups in Europe as well as the Secret Army Organization gunning for de Gaulle. The Canadian daily *Le Devoir* added that Nagy "maintains close ties with the C.I.A., which link him with the Miami Cuban colony." There was, in fact, conjecture that Nagy belonged to the Gehlen Organization, named after the World War II Nazi general who was recruited by the CIA after the war to run an anti-Soviet espionage network. By 1963 Nagy had emigrated to Dallas.

Paesa Sera went on about CMC: "Among its possible involvements (supported by the presence in directive posts of men deeply committed to organizations of the extreme right) . . . is that the Center was the creature of the C.I.A. . . . set up as a cover for the transfer of C.I.A. funds in Italy for illegal political-espionage activities." Barely a year after moving to Rome, CMC was ousted by Italian police because it was suspected of being a CIA front. A similar fate befell a sister company called Permindex, which had been created in Switzerland ostensibly to promote trade shows. But in tracing the money used to finance the 1962 attempt by the Secret Army Organization (OAS) of right-wing French army officers to assassinate de Gaulle, French intelligence discovered that some $200,000 had been deposited in Permindex bank accounts. Some of the money may have been deposited by Maurice Brooks Gatlin, the Banister associate who told informant Jerry Brooks he was a "CIA transporter" who delivered $100,000 to the Secret Army Organization. Upon being satisfied that Permindex was serving as a conduit for funds to the OAS, the Swiss government dissolved it. Permindex and CMC relocated to the more hospitable clime of apartheid South Africa.

All of this evoked the possibility that New Orleans was the money nexus for both the OAS's plot against de Gaulle and the JFK assassination a year later. What made it even more intriguing was that the FBI had picked up a report about OAS terrorist Jean Suetre being in Dallas when the assassinatiom came down; agents questioned a Dr. Alderson of Houston, who had been in the French army with Suetre, implying that his erstwhile comrade-in-arms was a suspect. It was conceivable that Permindex was used, through Shaw, in the Kennedy plot. But Gatlin, who might have known about it, was dead, and Garrison lacked the resources to carry out an investigation overseas to pin down the roles of Shaw, Permindex and the CIA. Ordinarily this would have been a job for the FBI, but it was obstructing the case.

Press clippings did not constitute legal proof—testimony and documentation did. On March 30, 1967, Assistant DA Andrew Sciambra interviewed Betty Parrott, who was in a social orbit with operatives of the Friends of Democratic Cuba, of which Guy Banister was an incorporator. This brought her in frequent contact with Regis Kennedy, the FBI liaison to the Friends. Parrott told Sciambra that "Regis Kennedy confirmed to her the fact that Clay Shaw is a former C.I.A. agent who did some work for the C.I.A. in Italy over a five-year span." But Parrott could only testify as to hearsay, and Regis Kennedy invoked executive privilege to remain silent when subpoenaed by Garrison. For his part, Shaw, through his attorneys, allowed only that he had joined the CMC board in 1958 at the insistence of his own International Trade Mart board of directors. Shaw always was supremely confident that Garrison couldn't convict him, an attitude affirmed recently by the declassification of an April 6, 1967, memo from the New Orleans CIA station chief to Langley. The document disclosed that Alberto Fowler, an exile veteran of the Bay of Pigs who had lived at Shaw's house on Dauphine Street for three months, told Carlos Bringuier, the DRE leader who scuffled with Oswald, that "he was impressed by the fact that Shaw, who is reported to be [sic] in intelligence work in World War II in the Army, is now quite calm and assured because he, Shaw, feels that high-ranking Government officials are involved and will see that no harm comes to him."

The trial finally began in January 1969. Although a grand jury and preliminary hearing had determined that Garrison had probable cause to bring the case to trial, Shaw had reason to be smug. Governor Connally refused to extradite as a witness Sergio Arcacha Smith, who could have connected Shaw with Ferrie and Guy Banister. The governor of Nebraska declined to extradite Sandra Moffit, a friend of Perry Russo, who could have corroborated his account of Ferrie's "party." The governor of Ohio failed to extradite Gordon Novel, who was involved in clandestine operations with Ferrie, Banister and Arcacha and could have tied them together. Nevertheless, the prosecution made its case. Russo held up admirably despite a searing cross-examination. The Clinton witnesses testified convincingly about seeing Shaw, Ferrie and Oswald in town. But the judge would not allow Officer Habighorst to attest that Shaw had given the alias Clay Bertrand, apparently confusing him with a black sheep relative.

Then Garrison committed an incredible blunder by putting on a witness whose bizarre answers sent a buzz through the court. This was Charles Spiesel, an accountant from New York, who said he was visiting his daughter at Louisiana State University in 1963 when he met Ferrie in a French Quarter bar. In turn, Ferrie introduced him to Shaw, and there was talk of shooting Kennedy with a high-powered rifle and Ferrie flying the assassins to safety. I had examined the Spiesel file before the trial and assumed he would not be called under any circumstances. He was the kind of psychological time bomb who is attracted to a major case like a moth to the candle. Since Shaw's attorneys had copies of Garrison's files, the cross-examination was a disaster. Spiesel claimed he had been hypnotized many times by the New York police, who tortured him to give up his accounting practice. Asked whether he fingerprinted his daughter, he replied that he did when she left for LSU and when she returned, just to make sure she was his daughter. The Spiesel testimony was to the Shaw trial what the gloves that didn't fit were to O. J. Simpson's.

Garrison recouped a bit when he made a case for conspiracy. He subpoenaed the Zapruder film from *Life* and screened it for the jury. He coupled that with the testimony of Dealey Plaza witnesses that at least one shot was fired from the grassy knoll. In the end, the jury decided that although there had been a conspiracy, the prosecution hadn't plugged Shaw into it beyond a reasonable doubt. In a plaintive letter to me, Garrison found a ray of solace in the fact that an alternative juror would have voted for conviction.

In an internal memorandum, dated September 1, 1977, the House Select Committee on Assassinations validated Garrison's case, which it studied in depth. "While the trial of Shaw took two years to bring about and did eventually end in acquittal," it stated, "the basis for the charges seems sound and the investigation and prosecution thorough, given the extraordinary nature of the charges and the times." And it appended: "We have reason to believe Shaw was heavily involved in the anti-Castro efforts in New Orleans in the 1960's and possibly one of the high level planners or 'cut out' to the planners of the assassination." Shaw died of cancer three years after the trial.

In 1991, Garrison was rehabilitated when Oliver Stone's motion picture *JFK*, based on the DA's probe, turned out to be a box office smash. On the day he signed Kevin Costner to play the lead, Stone asked me to come to his office.

"Bill, am I in any danger?" he wanted to know.

"Not physically, Oliver, although they killed a president," I answered. "But there are other ways to get you."

He swung in his chair and, deadpan, instructed his associate, Alex Ho, "Alex, for the duration of this project, no hiring of girls under eighteen."

The anticipated media blitz began, incredibly, months before *JFK* was released when the *Washington Post*, with a stolen shooting script in hand, nastily attacked Garrison and Stone. Perhaps significantly, the author was national security correspondent George Lardner, Jr., whose beat encompassed the CIA and who was the last person known to have seen David Ferrie alive. The *Post*'s companion, *Newsweek*, chimed in with an unsparingly hostile review, "The Twisted Truth of 'JFK,'" that was timed for the film's premiere. Rival *Time* followed suit with a captious tome. *The New York Times*, a charter cheerleader for the Warren Report, led other major dailies in the trashing. In marked contrast, the top-rated movie critics Gene Siskel and Roger Ebert gave *JFK* their coveted "two thumbs up," with Ebert going so far as to rank the film the best of the year.

The media pit bulls didn't fool the public—it believed *JFK*. A CBS poll taken after the dust settled found that 89 percent of Americans thought there was a conspiracy, 81 percent that there was a coverup, and 49 percent that the CIA was involved. Congress responded by passing the JFK Records Act, which pried loose hundreds of thousands of documents from the intelligence agencies (although many were heavily redacted). Despite the fact that no one expected a "smoking gun"—orders to kill are not reduced to paper—the releases tended to strengthen Garrison's case. Ultimately, when all of the pieces are fitted together, the full picture will be what the DA sketched so long go.

At a time when the media wonder why the public distrusts them and considers their reports slanted, they have only to look in the mirror. Their performance in the Garrison investigation resembled Tom Wolf's novel *The Bonfire of the Vanities,* in which no one even asks what the truth is. It does not matter. It has become totally irrelevant to the projection of images and egos. The media circus that swirled around Garrison was promoted, aided and abetted by federal agencies with much to hide. In the end, however, the DA walked tall. The American public trusted in him.

10

DEADLY SECRETS:
THE STEALTH WAR AGAINST CUBA

Little did I know, late one night in 1973 when I sat down in the back room of a small grocery store on Flagler Street in Miami's Little Havana district, that I was about to hear a story unlocking a Pandora's box of secrets of the recondite period following the abortive Bay of Pigs invasion. The narrator was a grizzled Cuban exile who gave the name Pepe. In researching a book on the U.S. secret war against Cuba in the 1960s, I had been brought to him by Martin X. Casey, regarded by the war's participants as its "archivist." Pepe's graphic account of a 1963 naval raid gone terribly wrong strongly suggested that the Bay of Pigs two years earlier was merely the end of the beginning. After the debacle, the campaign had been stepped up, and it was to be capped by a second invasion by exile forces. But what Pepe had to say also revealed how close John and Robert Kennedy came to precipitating a second superpower crisis with the Soviet Union.

On the night of October 21, 1963, Pepe was a crew member of the disguised raider *Rex* when it launched a sabotage attack on a shore installation in Pinar del Rio Province. It was a CIA operation. Under a bare light bulb hanging from the ceiling, Pepe diagrammed the attack with a thick pencil on a brown paper grocery sack.

The *Rex* was not listed in *Jane's Fighting Ships*. It was a World War II subchaser pulled out of the mothball fleet at Green Cove Springs, Florida. Painted a classy dark blue, the 174-foot vessel could cut through the waves at twenty knots. It flew the blue-and-white flag of Nicaragua, whose strongman, General Luis Somoza, had hosted the Bay of Pigs invasion brigade. Registration papers showed that it was owned by the Belcher Oil Company of Miami, which fueled cruise ships. In turn, Belcher leased it to Collins Radio International, a major defense contractor, for "electronic and oceanographic research." There were oversized searchlights, elaborate electronic gear that towered amidships, and a large crane on the aft deck capable or raising and lowering twenty-foot speedboats. When I asked Pepe what his rating was on this impressive craft, he replied "gunner's mate," the same rank he had enjoyed in Batista's navy. He explained that after the *Rex* put to sea, its guns were brought up from below decks and secured in their topside mounts: two 40-mm. naval cannon, a 57-mm. recoilless rifle, and two 20-mm. cannon.

According to Pepe, the forty seamen—all Cubans—were paid $300 a month by the CIA, but their checks were drawn on the cover account of a commercial fisheries company. They were subjected to periodic polygraph tests to ensure their political loyalty. They lived at home, commuting to the secret war. When a mission was scheduled, they received a phone call, then a nondescript CIA van picked them up and took them to the West Palm Beach berth where the *Rex* was tied up. The dockage fees were paid by a CIA front, Sea Key Shipping Company, which operated out of a postal box. When the *Rex* left port, it gave its destination as the Caicos Islands in the outer Bahamas, and when it returned it was "from the high seas." Customs and immigration clearances were waived.

On that October day in 1963 the vans deposited the crew at the berth in mid-afternoon. Captain Alejandro Brooks paced nervously on the bridge as he awaited the arrival of Gordon Campbell, the CIA's director of naval operations, to arrive with the orders for the night's mission.

As the wait stretched into hours, Brooks had to twice admonish the crew, which was chattering loudly in Spanish, to quiet down; only two months earlier President Kennedy had become furious when he found out that the *Rex* had been at its West Palm dock, only a stone's throw from the family compound, while he was vacationing there. It was dusk when a black Cadillac pulled up and Campbell emerged. A tall man with a military bearing, he carried a soft leather briefcase up the gangplank. "It will be a moonless night," the CIA official told the captain, handing him a sealed packet. After Campbell disembarked, the *Rex* cast off, quickly cleared the harbor, and swung south. Its lights were completely blacked out.

At this point, Pepe's voice became edgy. Brooks opened the packet and read the orders by flashlight. Normally he stood off the Cuban shore a mile and a half and sent in landing parties by launch. But this night the orders were different and dangerous: Go within a half mile of shore. The *Rex* slid by the bright lights of Miami and slowed to a crawl off isolated Elliott Key. Brooks strained to spot the rafts in the inky darkness: two black rubber rafts with six men each, wearing black, with black stocking masks. The men belonged to the Comandos Mambises, named after the guerrilla fighters in Cuba's war of liberation from Spain. The Mambises were the CIA's elite, the Green Berets of the secret war. They were led by Major Manuel Villafana, a spit-and-polish officer who had commanded the Bay of Pigs air force. Villafana insisted that his men be low paid because he wanted them driven by hate, not money. The target on this mission was the giant Matahambre copper mine near Cape Corriente on the bootheel of Pinar del Rio Province. By blowing it up, the Mambises would put a substantial dent in the Cuban economy.

Pepe recounted that when the *Rex* arrived at the landing zone, there was a sense of foreboding: the Cape Corriente light, normally flashing its warning to marine traffic, was dark. But Brooks decided not to abort the mission. As the vessel came to a stop, two specially designed fiberglass speedboats, called Moppies, slid down high-speed davits on the afterdeck. The commandos clambered into them with backpacks full of

C-4 explosives, and M-3 grease guns slung over their shoulders. The Moppies stopped at the mouth of a river, where the Mambises inflated their rubber rafts, hopped in, and signaled ashore with an infrared blinker. They were to link up with two commandos who had infiltrated a week earlier to reconnoiter the target. The answer came back in the wrong code; it was a trap. The commandos fired at the riverbank, only to be raked by return fire from heavy machine guns. One raft was torn apart by tracer bullets, spilling the dead and dying into the water. The remaining raft wheeled and tried to reach the Moppies, but they had fled. The commandos then turned toward shore, where Castro's militia awaited them. Then one of the escaping Moppies was framed in the searchlight of a Russian-built P-6 patrol craft; the *Rex* quartermaster piloting it surrendered. The other Moppie sped into international waters, fired a shot across the bow of a passing merchant ship, and was rescued.

When Captain Brooks saw the firefight erupt, he ordered the *Rex* to turn tail and make a run for it. He was under standing orders to avoid the raider's capture at all costs. Pepe was now moving his pencil furiously over the grocery bag. Brooks made a feint toward the open sea, then doubled back and hugged the coastline, hoping to elude radar detection. The move paid off. Minutes later, a pair of Cuban helicopters made a beeline for the zone a mile and a half offshore where the *Rex* ordinarily waited for the commandos to return. They dropped flares, illuminating a vast expanse of sea. Pepe's excitement rose as if he were reliving the moment. "As we cleared the head, I saw the running lights of a freighter," he said. "I knew right away what was going to happen. The freighter ran right into the light of the flares. The Cubans thought it was us. They opened up on her."

The ship was the 32,500-ton *J. Louis*, flying a Liberian flag of convenience but owned by American multimillionaire Daniel Ludwig. It was carrying a cargo of bauxite from Jamaica to Texas. Five Cuban MiGs began strafing and rocket-launching runs. Captain Gerhard Krause radioed an international distress call. At Key West, U.S. Navy Phantom jets took off and headed for the scene. But just before arriving, the Phantoms were called back. Pepe could only guess why.

The CIA base in Miami had a huge rhombic antenna that blanketed the Caribbean, and the controllers may have assumed from the jumble of radio traffic that it was actually the *Rex*, maintaining radio silence, that was under attack. If that were the case, the raider, which was "plausibly deniable" under its civilian cover, was expendable. Or the CIA controllers may have realized that the MiGs had the wrong vessel but wanted the attack to continue so that the *Rex* could slip away.

Escape it did. During more than an hour, the MiGs made fourteen passes on the *J. Louis*, and large-caliber bullets chewed holes in the deck and hull and fire broke out on the forecastle and superstructure. Miraculously, none of the crew was injured. But in the meantime the *Rex* slunk out of Cuban waters, breaking radio silence to report to the CIA command post that the Cubans had realized their mistake and had sent two gunboats in pursuit. "Do what you have to do," was the noncommittal response. Outgunned, Brooks opted to try a seventy-mile sprint for Mexican waters off Cozumel Island. He made it. For two days the gunboats played cat and mouse with the *Rex*, then withdrew. On October 26 the raider skulked into West Palm Beach, first making sure that JFK was not in residence.

While the sea chase was going on, the State Department seized the initiative by announcing, "We are investigating the facts in the case to see whether a U.S. protest will be made on the basis of this violation and the U.S. ownership of this vessel"—the *J. Louis*. But official Washington didn't know until the return of the *Rex* that crewmen and commandos were missing in action. Two days later, the other shoe dropped when Fidel Castro appeared on Havana television to describe the *Rex* down to its distinguishing electronic gear and blue paint. To cap his act, he brought on stage two of the missing men, *Rex* quartermaster Luis Montero Carranzana, who had piloted a Moppie, and Dr. Clemente Inclan Werner, a Mambise. Both disclosed that they had been recruited by the CIA, Montero at $250 a month, Inclan at $400. They described previous missions they had carried out. Said White House press secretary Pierre Salinger, "We have nothing to say."

I was researching a book because Warren Hinckle and I had received a contract from a major publisher to exploit the 1972 Watergate break-in. On the burglary team were CIA agent James McCord and four Miamians, Frank Sturgis, Eugenio Martinez, Bernie "Macho" Barker and Virgilio Gonzalez, all of whom had served in the secret war. Our book proposal was based in large measure upon the reminiscences of Jim Rose, who had been one of the volunteer corps driven by anticommunism to fight Castro for CIA-backed action groups. One of those groups—the most violent—was Dr. Orlando Bosch's Insurrection Movement for the Recovery of the Revolution. According to Rose, Bosch had a strategic alliance with Sturgis, who ran his own outfit, grandly called the International Anti-Communist Brigade. The two appeared to be loose cannons, and the story we envisioned would chronicle the adventures, misadventures and strange subculture of these Castrophobic commandos at whom the CIA had thrown bucks and encouragement while acting as traffic cops directing their escapades.

But when I heard Pepe's account of the *Rex* incident, all that changed. We were now dealing with a story whose sweep—and international impact—was obviously far more momentous. In October 1962, only a year before the *Rex* was ambushed, JFK had promised Russian Premier Nikita Khrushchev, as part of the missile crisis settlement, to prevent aggressions against Cuba mounted from American soil. And only six weeks before, after an Alpha 66 attack, the Soviet Union warned that it would "not tolerate" further raids on Cuba by exiles "armed and supplied with North American weapons." By continuing to authorize missions like that of the *Rex*, Kennedy was playing with matches in a Caribbean tinderbox.

So we began an expanded probe of the entire Cuba Project, as the CIA's secret war was generically labeled. I checked into the rundown Arrowhead Motel in Miami, where CIA handlers had met with their charges, to provide familiar surroundings for interview. One of the first I talked with there, on November 28, 1973, was Gerry Patrick Hemming, leader of the Intercontinental Penetration Force (Interpen), also aligned with Frank Sturgis's Brigade. When Hemming and his brother, both gargantuan men, showed up wearing trench coats, I thought for a moment that they were Miami detectives bent on escorting me out of town for nosing into state secrets.

I wound up interviewing scores of veterans of the secret war, some of whom were forthcoming, others who weren't. Grayston Lynch was a CIA paramilitary who, in defiance of orders that there not be a "white face" on the Bay of Pigs beachhead, led a squad of exile frogmen ashore to set up landing beacons. "I have been cleared by the Agency to talk about events up to and including the Bay of Pigs, but not beyond," Lynch said. Asked what might happen if he breached that *omerta*, he considered it possible that his pension checks would stop. As our investigation discovered, the Agency's touchiness about post–Bay of Pigs events was understandable. The CIA had conspired with the Mafia to assassinate Castro, broke the Neutrality Act with abandon by setting up a huge concealed base in Miami to prosecute the secret war ordered by Bobby Kennedy, and was poised to sponsor a second exile invasion when John Kennedy was killed.

A number of the people I sought to interview were reluctant because of the specter of violence hovering over those who talked, "Things are still going on," said one, "and too many people are getting blown away." But I was able to finagle interviews with a variety of persons who didn't see themselves violating a code of silence. One was Rolando Masferrer, a swarthy, roly-poly man known as "El Tigre" when he ruled Oriente Province in Cuba by pistol politics during the Batista regime. I interviewed him on December 5, 1973, in a dark hole-in-the-wall office in Little Havana, a bodyguard lurking in the background holding a cigar box, which, I was sure, contained a pistol. A curious mixture of Renaissance man and stone-cold killer, Masferrer affected silk scarves, wrote poetry and painted, and patronized classical music. He denied that his paramilitary band was a gang of thugs, claiming they only killed opponents who did "their opposition with guns, not ballots." When Batista fell, Masferrer fled to Miami and organized one of the first attempts on Castro's life. But he brought with him, in addition to valises full of cash, a reputation so loathsome that the CIA had him forcibly hospitalized during the Bay of Pigs invasion so he could not participate. But Masferrer was a "business" associate of Eladio del Valle, the CIA asset and Trafficante bagman who was murdered in Miami at virtually the same time that David Ferrie, the Garrison suspect, died in New Orleans. Masferrer shunned talking about the Kennedy assassination, preferring other subjects such as a 1966 scheme to invade Haiti as a springboard to Cuba paid for by CBS in return for filming rights (the expedition was cut off by U.S. Customs, acting on a tip, as it was about to shove off from Florida). Speaking of the ready availability of munitions and explosives in the wake of the secret war, Masferrer told me, "You can buy anything you want in Miami if you have the money, with the exception of the atom bomb . . . probably." Not long after I interviewed him, Masferrer stepped on the starter of his Ford Torino and was blown to bits. A note mailed before the murder, signed "Zero," asserted he had been executed because of his "systematic work in the destruction of the anti-Communist struggle."

Then there was William D. Pawley, organizer of the storied Flying Tigers in China during World War II, who established the bus system in Havana, became a millionaire, and served as Eisenhower's ambassador to Brazil and Peru. At first, Pawley balked at an interview, but when I stroked his ego by telling him his deep footprints were all over Latin America, he agreed, on November 27, 1973, to at least meet and shake hands. The greeting stretched into a long discussion. The picture of executive elegance, Pawley crowed that he had helped convince Eisenhower that Castro was a communist. "I had several conferences with the president," he said, "and finally he was convinced that the anticommunist Cubans in Florida should be armed and given every assistance to overthrow the communist regime." Pawley pitched Ike to personally take command of the operation, arguing that the CIA should be restricted to its mandated role of intelligence gathering, but in the end, CIA Director Allen Dulles prevailed.

Pawley remained a Daddy Warbucks of the counterrevolution. He paid out of pocket to recruit exiles for the Bay of Pigs, and, after a DRE speedboat shot up a Havana waterfront hotel gunning for Castro in 1962, he put the arm on some of his rich friends, including Claire Booth

Luce, wife of *Time-Life* publisher Henry Luce and Eisenhower's ambassador to Italy, to sponsor DRE assault craft. According to Pawley, a month later DRE infiltration teams discovered Russian missiles in Cuba, setting up the October missile crisis. But when I asked about the Flying Tiger affair, one of the strangest episodes of the secret war, Pawley went mute, thinking he had kept the lid on it. But Gerry Hemming and Frank Sturgis, who were in on the planning, had already briefed me. In early 1963, an exile commando named Eddie Bayo claimed he had received signals from the underground in Cuba that two Russian missile officers wanted to defect. This implied that all of the Soviet missiles had not been removed, as Khrushchev had promised. Hemming's Interpen relayed the information to a Kennedy confidant, financier Theodore Racussin, who contacted the White House. Initially, Bayo was promised help in getting the officers out, perhaps on the theory that the United States was not the only party breaching the missile crisis agreement. But then the White House, concerned over a backfire, pulled out.

At this point, the plan passed from the hands of Kennedy's friends to those of his foes. Pawley, an ardent JFK detractor, heard about it and volunteered the use of his 65-foot yacht, *Flying Tiger,* to tow Bayo's small boat to the Cuban coast off Baracoa, where the Russians supposedly were stationed. In Pawley's eyes it was an opportunity to embarrass Kennedy, whose commitment to anticommunism he perceived as only skin deep. The Soviet officers would be spirited to the Gettysburg farm of his friend Dwight Eisenhower, debriefed, and produced at a press conference to make JFK look like a gullible fool. Pawley obtained logistical support through his CIA contact at Langley, Deputy Director Marshall "Pat" Carter, a member of the Eisenhower retinue.

The passenger manifest of the *Flying Tiger* was, to say the least, eclectic. In addition to the impeccably dressed Pawley, there were William "Rip" Robertson, a prototypical CIA cowboy with rumpled clothes, a careless slouch, glasses tied behind his head with a string, baseball cap and a pulp novel sticking out of his back pocket (Robertson had, against orders, waded ashore at the Bay of Pigs with Grayston Lynch); Terrence

Spencer, a *Life* photographer; and John Martino, a mob technician. At the time, the CIA had detailed Robertson to Johnny Roselli, the Mafia lieutenant who, aided by Martino, was sending teams into Cuba to kill Castro. On June 8, 1963, the *Flying Tiger* arrived off Baracoa. As he climbed into his small boat with three exiles, Bayo asked Pawley for his watch, saying, "I'll be back with it the day after tomorrow." He and his men never returned (in 1995 ex-Cuban security chief General Fabian Escalante told me that Bayo's boat was found swamped near Baracoa, but there was no sign of its occupants). Loran Hall, an Interpen instructor who in 1959 had been imprisoned by Castro with Martino and his boss, Santos Trafficante, called me in 1976 to say that the Soviet missile officers story was a fiction his pal Bayo had concocted to cover his real intent. Hall reported that he sat in on a meeting in February 1963 in which Chicago Mafia chieftain Sam Giancana posted a bounty of $30,000 on Castro's head for Bayo and Martino, with half to be paid up front. The down payment was used by Bayo, Hall said, to buy a boat and explosives with detonators, which Martino, the technician, assembled. As Hall put it, "Bayo was going to blow all to hell" the Presidential Palace with Castro in it, and the Ministry of Agriculture building for good measure. In fact, Pawley had pleaded with Bayo not to overload his boat, since there was no apparent reason he needed explosives to rescue the Russian officers. But when I interviewed him, Pawley remained mum on the missing men. The sons of one of them, Luis Cantin, who had gone to war wearing a beat-up fedora, were badgering him for indemnification. The *Life* photos were locked in his desk drawer, but he wouldn't show them. The last thing Pawley wanted known was how he lost a watch.

It was through Louis Wolfson, the wealthy Florida businessman who supported Jim Garrison, that I was able to interview Carlos Prio Socarras, a former president of Cuba ousted by Batista in 1952. A courtly looking man wearing horn-rim glasses and a prim mustache, he met me for an interview on April 12, 1974, in his brother's Miami home. Prio was the éminence grise of the counterrevolution. He was a millionaire many times over, having set a new standard for ingeniously corrupt schemes while the island's chief executive. Yearning to regain power, he bought a boat, the *Granma*, for Castro, which he used in 1953 to land in Cuba and touch off the revolution. After Batista was ousted, Prio hustled to Havana, expecting Castro to reward him with the presidency. In anticipation, he took up residence at his Havana estate, La Chata. Prio recounted for me how Castro told him about his visit with Richard Nixon in the White House in April 1960, when he was trying to swing U.S. support. Nixon immediately exhibited FBI files he maintained identified communists in the neoteric Cuban government. Toward the end of the session, Nixon claimed that the United States wanted to aid Cuba because of the condition in which the country had been left. "And when would you send all this aid?" Castro asked. "As soon as you call general elections," the vice president replied, knowing that such a requirement had not been put on Batista. In the end, Prio was overlooked by Castro, perhaps because he helped the DRE, whose military units had tried to beat Castro's to Havana. He retreated to Miami and turned moneybags to the action groups, including those of Sturgis and Orlando Bosch. Prio was mob-connected from the Cuban gambling days, so it was no surprise that in 1963, when dispossessed casino owners set up their own umbrella group to overthrow Castro, the Junta of the Government of Cuba in Exile (JGCE), Prio was its nominee for president (JGCE disappeared shortly before JFK was shot). At the time I talked to him, Prio headed a coalition called Belligerent Cubans, whose stated aim was to "campaign against Castro" in league "with elements within Cuba and without CIA help." But the old pol's days were numbered: on April 5, 1977, he was found shot to death. The police assumed it was suicide, but in exile whisper circles the talk was that Prio, like Masferrer, was on the Zero death list for being more talk than action. But the timing might also have been revelatory: he died shortly after being placed on the interview list of the House Select Committee on Assassinations.

In the course of our research, Hinckle and I interviewed hundreds of persons at one level or another and vetted stacks of public and private documents. We also contacted the Cuban government for its version of the secret war events. In 1978, when Cuban diplomats were allowed to travel in the United States, Castro dispatched Rolando Salup, the third secretary of the Cuban mission to the United Nations, to meet with us. Salup set up a channel through Mexico City for us to obtain answers to questions as they arose. In 1981, upon publication of *The Fish Is Red: The Story of the Secret War Against Castro*, we appeared on the NBC "Today" show with Jane Pauley, and the reviews were auspicious. But the book didn't sell very well. According to Toronto bookseller Al Navis, writing in the June 1996 issue of *Firsts: The Book Collector's Magazine*, "the government convinced the publisher (Harper & Row) to recall the book from distributors; the FBI sent agents into bookstores to buy up whatever copies remained." In 1992, after two trips to Cuba and the opening of more doors at home, we produced an expanded volume entitled *Deadly Secrets: The CIA-Mafia War Against Castro and the Assassination of J.F.K.*, which was published by gutsy Thunder's Mouth Press. This edition found wide distribution and did well.

The grunt-level central character of any secret war chronicle has to be Frank Sturgis. Ruggedly handsome and silken in voice, Sturgis served thirteen months in jail for the Watergate burglary. He never understood why three presidents—Nixon, Ford and Carter—rejected his applications for a pardon. It was especially galling that Ford pardoned Tokyo Rose, an American citizen who taunted G.I.s over Radio Tokyo during World War II. As a teenage enlistee in the Marines, Sturgis had listened to Tokyo Rose's propaganda and had fought in battles across the Pacific. "The first man I killed, I almost cried," he said.

When he signed on for the secret war, Sturgis became a close buddy of Eugenio Martinez, a lanky, effusive exile who went on 350 boat missions against Cuba. When Watergate came down, CIA Director Richard Helms tried to trivialize Martinez's Agency role—he was still on the payroll—as that of a mere tipster, provoking Sturgis to fume, "In Miami, Martinez is a goddam hero today. There is not a Cuban shoeshine boy who'd accept a quarter from him; he's just a giant to them. A *tipster*!" One night I interviewed three of the Miami Four burglars, Sturgis, Martinez and the locksmith Virgilio Gonzalez—Bernie Barker, Howard Hunt's bagman, was in seclusion—in a suite high in the Eden Roc Hotel on the Miami Beach strip. As they looked out on the twinkling lights of Miami, once the secret war's swamp to the CIA alligator, I asked, "If the circumstances repeated themselves, would you do it again?" They looked at each other knowingly, then yelped in unison, "Yes!"

Sturgis's obsession with Cuba preceded the secret war. In 1955, in Miami, he watched a fiery revolutionary in a guayabera denounce the dictator Batista. His name was Fidel Castro, and Sturgis, later smuggled into his redoubt in the Sierra Maestra by Prio, trained his guerrilla forces. After the rebel victory on New Year's Day, 1959, a grateful Castro named Sturgis security chief of the air force and gambling czar. But Sturgis didn't stay on the job all that long. In April, four months after the victory, Castro was invited by newspaper editors to visit New York and Washington. He was greeted by admiring throngs everywhere. On NBC-TV's "Meet the Press" he voiced opposition to communism and declared he would side with the United States in any showdown with the Soviet Union. Although a visiting head of state, Castro was snubbed by President Eisenhower, who arranged to be golfing in North Carolina. He was handed off to Nixon, who, as soon as he was out the White House door, pronounced him as at least "under communist discipline." The CIA was not so sure, sizing up Castro as an "enigma" with whom "there may still be the possibility of a constructive relationship."* But

---

*This seems to have been the case. In *The Wall Street Journal* of January 19, 1982, U.S. Representative Charles O. Porter of Oregon told how, en route to a meeting with the editors, he assured Castro on behalf of the State Department that the United States was willing "to triple existing aid programs to keep his good will. All he wanted, he told me, was the U.S. to help in sending him the best expert on land reform, a suggestion I passed on but was never implemented." In front of the editors, the Cuban insisted that he wasn't a communist, that he would hold elections in the near future, and that he would abide by the Organization of American States (OAS) charter and welcome private investment. "I believe he meant what he said," Porter went on, "but that when the multinational oil companies cut him off because he confiscated their refineries, just as he confiscated every other business which had been paying off Batista, Castro had no choice but to make a deal with the Soviet Union for oil from the Baku fields and accept the ideological tie-in. The Cuban economy without oil would have gone belly up in three months."

the opportunity was lost. At this stage, Fidel was not a communist—he had belonged to the mildly liberal Ortodoxo Party—but his brother Raul had been a member of the Young Communist League and brought his comrades into the ruling council. This left flank pushed for an alignment with a superpower, and, since Fidel had been stiffed by the White House, which was isolating Cuba, only the Soviet Union was left. This version of how revolutionary Cuba went socialist was not challenged by Fidel. When I submitted draft sections of *The Fish Is Red* for comment, he left this one untouched but questioned others.

With a moist finger to the political wind, Frank Sturgis sensed that the regime was veering left and became a double agent for the CIA. He immediately scored a coup, recruiting Maria Lorenz, the daughter of a German ship captain who had jumped ship to become Fidel's lover. A smashing looker, Maria had become a woman scorned when she found out Fidel was playing the field. "I could kill the son of a bitch!" she fumed to Sturgis, who gave her the chance. He passed her a poison pill confected by the CIA laboratory's Dr. Strangelove, Joseph Scheider, with instructions to drop it in Fidel's coffee. Maria dropped it in his coffee, but in the pot, not his demitasse cup. "It diluted the damn poison," Sturgis recalled. "When Fidel and his bodyguards drank the poisoned coffee, everybody got sick. But it didn't kill anybody!" Before long Sturgis found out that his dual role wasn't a secret, so he hightailed it to Miami.

By this time, Richard Nixon, the White House action officer on Cuba, had ordered the CIA to prepare an invasion of Cuba by an exile force given the cover story that its sponsors were wealthy industrialists whose Cuban properties had been expropriated. The recruits, formed into Brigade 2506, were sequestered in Guatemala while the planning for Operation Pluto, as the invasion was code named, took shape. But it had not reached a "go" mode before the November 1960 presidential election. Early in the campaign, John Kennedy had styled Castro as "part of the legacy of Bolívar," and opined that had Eisenhower not made himself scarce when the Cuban leader came calling, relations between the two countries might have been more equitable. But as

Cuba drifted into the Soviet orbit, Kennedy out-hawked Nixon in calling for the removal of Castro. He squeezed out a narrow win.

William Pawley told me that Eisenhower was champing at the bit to launch the invasion before he left office in January. "I'd like to get this thing done in the time remaining," Pawley quoted him as saying. The problem was that there were less than 500 members of Brigade 2506 under arms in Guatemala, whereas the invasion blueprint called for at least 1,200. But Pawley figured that the lack of fighters could be filled by troops from South American countries, which would have the benefit of making it look like an all-Latin affair. Justification, he reasoned, lay in the charter of the Organization of American States, which sanctioned unilateral military action by member nations against an aggressor "extracontinental power." The villain of the piece would be the Soviet Union, whose arms shipments to Cuba were creating a military capability, in Pawley's words, "far larger than any army in Latin America." In December 1960, with Ike's blessing, Pawley, posing as a tourist, flew to Buenos Aires with his wife Edna for a prearranged meeting with President Arturo Frondizi. He proposed that Argentina commit a shipload of troops to reinforce Brigade 2506, citing the OAS authority. Pawley told me that Frondizi was enthusiastically receptive, saying, "You tell me how much and where. This is the first time the United States has used excellent judgment in dealing with a secret problem. You speak fluent Spanish and come here incognito." Pawley explained that for security reasons, no advance details could be given: the Argentine ship would have to stand off the Cuban coast at a designated time and place to await instructions from the invasion command. Pawley then skipped over the Andes to Peru, where he had served as U.S. ambassador. He had no trouble convincing President Manuel Prado to send a shipload of marines under the same conditions as Argentina.

But preparations for the invasion lagged, and Operation Pluto had to be handed off to John Kennedy. CIA Director Allen Dulles briefed the incoming president as soon as he took the oath of office. Kennedy was reluctant, fearing a blowback if the American hand was revealed, but Dulles countered that "dumping" Brigade 2506 back on the streets of Miami would have worse consequences. Pawley said his role ended with the departure of the Eisenhower administration, so he had no idea whether the Argentine-Peruvian commitment was passed on to Kennedy (there is no evidence that it was). Kennedy felt squeezed, but gave the green light. "I know everyone is grabbing their nuts on this one," he groused to aide Theodore Sorensen as D-Day, April 17, drew near.

The invasion was an Agency screwup from the start. A recently declassified section of an inquest conducted under General Maxwell Taylor reflects that the Soviets knew in advance the exact invasion date, although not its location, and that the Agency knew they knew some eight days beforehand but went ahead nonetheless. An agent on the FBI's Cuba Desk told me what happened when JFK visited the family compound in West Palm Beach a few days after the disaster. "You blew it!" Joseph P. Kennedy greeted his son. The patriarch had taken a hit in the wallet when the Coca-Cola franchise he owned in Havana with Irish tenor Morton Downey had gone the way of the revolution. "I know that outfit," he said of the CIA, "and I wouldn't pay them a hundred bucks a week." For his part, Allen Dulles alibied cryptically, "We were expecting something else to happen."

As my Miami interviews disclosed, Operation Pluto had two other moving parts that Kennedy probably didn't know about, either of which conceivably could have changed the outcome and account for the CIA's indifference to the Russian knowledge of the date. One was a diversionary strike with a twist that would "justify" sending in the Marines. Months before the invasion, Frank Sturgis and Gerry Hemming set up a training camp on the McLaney property north of New Orleans—the same camp that the FBI would mistakenly raid in 1963—where 168 exile troops belonging to the Movement for the Recovery of the Revolution (MRR) of Manuel Artime, a commander of Brigade 2506, bivouacked. The nerve center of the operation was the office of Guy Banister, then housed in the Balter Building, where crates of munitions—rifle grenades, land mines and small missiles—were stored before being loaded on board the *Santa Ana*, a peeling banana boat flying the

Costa Rican flag and leased by the CIA for $7,000 a month. A week before the Bay of Pigs landing, the *Santa Ana*, skippered by the MRR's Nino Diaz, cast off and headed for Baracoa, which was near the U.S. naval base at Guantánamo. Aboard were a CIA paramilitary advisor, Curley Sanchez, and the MRR troops. For three nights the *Santa Ana* stood off Baracoa, waiting for the Bay of Pigs landing before feigning a landing of its own to draw off Castro's forces. But a scouting party sent ashore reported intense military activity, leading Diaz to assume he had been found out. Over vigorous dissent by Sanchez, he received permission from the CIA command post to withdraw. But in 1978, a former CIA officer, James B. Wilcott, let on to Warren Hinckle that the *Santa Ana* mission was not a diversion at all but a provocation. It was conceived, he said, after it became clear to the planners that there would be no popular uprising in support of the Bay of Pigs invasion. "The original invasion plans were then changed to include the creation of an incident that would call for an all-out attack by the U.S. military," Wilcott expanded. "Kennedy was not to know of the change." The MRR troops, wearing uniforms of the Cuban army, would mount an attack on the Guantánamo naval base. The planners were convinced that JFK, confronted with evidence that Castro's forces were committing the aggression, would have no choice but to send in the Marines.

The second "something else" to be synchronized with the invasion was the assassination of Fidel Castro. The theory was that Cuba would be plunged into chaos by the death of its *caudillo*, leaving no one with the charisma to rally the armed forces. Although I had been able to draw a picture of the plot from the American side, General Escalante recently filled in details known only to the Cuban security services. It began when E. Howard Hunt, destined to become a Watergate figure, ran the idea of assassination past his boss, CIA Deputy Director Richard M. Bissell, Jr., the architect of the Bay of Pigs invasion. Bissell replied that it was already "in the hands of a special group." What Bissell didn't tell Hunt, since it was still highly confidential, was that the "special group" was the CIA-Mafia alliance. With Robert Maheu, the former FBI man on Howard Hughes's payroll, acting as cutout, the Agency teamed up with Chicago capo Sam Giancana and Santos Trafficante to knock off the vexatious Cuban and regain their lost casinos.

A key player brought into the plan was Manuel Antonio "Tony" de Varona, a corrupt prime minister of Cuba under Carlos Prio; the pair of *revanchistes* had interlocking financial interests with Meyer Lansky, and it was Lansky who turned Varona over to Trafficante. Varona's value was that he still had contacts inside Havana, one of whom happened to be a cook at the Pekin Restaurant where Castro and his aides frequently dined. The CIA laboratory produced new poison capsules of synthetic botulism to be slipped into Castro's food. Varona was running an anti-Castro action group called Rescate, and he summoned a trusted member in place in Cuba to Miami. He gave this courier, Rodolfo Curbelo, the capsules as well as a letter with strict instructions on how and when to pass them to the Pekin cook. The CIA, Varona stressed, wanted to time the poisoning with the invasion, so it was critical that the attempt not be made until the word was passed by telephone. When Varona handed over the capsules and letter to Curbelo, a landing date had not yet been set.

After the date was set, Howard Hunt's paranoia took over. He had been in charge of shepherding six Cuban exile leaders selected by the Agency to form a provisional government that would be flown to the beachhead as soon as it was secured. Although he trusted Varona, who was designated minister of war, the reactionary Hunt distrusted Manuel Ray, whom he saw as a "Fidelism without Fidel" liberal who had been foisted on him by the Kennedy administration, and could envision Ray "informing the enemy" of the impending invasion. So Hunt decided to seal off his charges from the outside world. Four days before D-Day, he summoned them to the Lexington Hotel in New York and placed them under CIA guard. One day before the invasion, they were flown on an Agency plane with taped-over windows to the Opa-Locka Airfield outside Miami, where they were held incommunicado in a clapboard house on its fringe. As Varona paced back and forth, wondering where he was and what was going on, the CIA case officer in charge of the assassination plan gave Robert Maheu the word for Varona to activate his man in Havana. Maheau in turn phoned Trafficante, who frantically tried to reach Varona. Only Varona knew Curbelo's name and number in the Cuban capital, and the capo couldn't find him. When Brigade 2506 hit the beach, a healthy Castro was on his way there to take command. The action was over within less than 72 hours, leaving 200 of the brigade dead and 1,197 captured. Even as Trafficante sought desperately to reach Varona, Lansky lieutenant Joe Rivers stood by in the Bahamas with a satchel stuffed with gold for the word to rush in and take charge of the darkened casinos. Off the north Cuban coast, four Mafiosi, accompanied by a CIA agent, bobbed in a boat waiting to rush in and dig up $750,000 they had buried before fleeing Havana two years earlier. CIA insiders who had bought sugar futures took a drubbing after the failure of the Bay of Pigs invasion.

John and Bobby Kennedy, who knew nothing about the failed provocation and assassination plot, took the defeat as a family humiliation and vowed to get even. After an inquest cleared the decks, they ordered the CIA to organize Operation Mongoose, smaller in scale than Operation Pluto but more intense. The invasion had been too visible, the president ruled, and the new push should consist of covert actions that were "plausibly deniable," as typified by the *Rex* attack. The tactics would include economic sabotage, raids on military targets, infiltrations, black propaganda to encourage domestic opposition, and the creation of an underground force, with the eventual goal of overthrowing Castro. Brigade 2506 survivor A. L. Estrada recalled that after he and several comrades secretly testified at the inquest, they were taken to the White House to meet the president. Rip Robertson and Grayston Lynch, the CIA paramilitaries, were also present, as was Bobby Kennedy. "RFK asked if I wanted to work against Castro again," Estrada said. RFK would be the new action officer.

Thus began what was, when we began research in 1973 for *The Fish Is Red*, the most arcane period of the secret war. Richard Helms, a deputy director of the CIA at the time, testified to the Senate Intelligence Committee in 1975 that "it was made abundantly clear to everybody involved in the (Mongoose) operation that the desire was to get rid of the Castro regime and get rid of Castro . . . the point was that no limitations were put on this injunction." Helms, who was habitually flexible with the English language, viewed this as a loophole to continue the CIA-Mafia plots, since assassination was not specifically forbidden. But in May 1962, Bobby Kennedy was tipped off about the devil's pact, and he hauled Agency General Counsel Lawrence Houston on the carpet. "If you have seen Mr. Kennedy's eyes get steely and his voice get low and precise," Houston reminisced, "you get a definite feeling of unhappiness." But to Houston's surprise, RFK's rage was limited to the fact that he had been left in the dark; he instructed only that in the future he be informed if the Agency took up with the mob again.

The attorney general obviously assumed that the alliance was in the past. But a declassified CIA internal report reveals that the assassination plots not only were going on at the time RFK confronted Houston, but they continued to go on without him being notified. The report was prepared by the Agency's inspector general on April 27, 1967, after Johnny Roselli's attorney planted a self-serving item with columnist Jack Anderson that the Mafioso had tried to kill Castro with Kennedy's authorization. Roselli of course would have had no way of knowing from what level the authorization ultimately came. But of late it has become fashionable to accuse the Kennedy brothers of not only being witting about the assassination plots but of ordering them. For instance, Seymour Hersh in his relentlessly critical *The Dark Side of Camelot* quoted retired CIA official Samuel Halpern, who detested the brothers, as saying, "Kennedy asked [CIA deputy director Richard] Bissell to create a capacity for political assassination." But this may have been an anachronism. The inspector general reported that William K. Harvey was the CIA officer tasked with developing an executive action capability, meaning assassination. Harvey told the inspector general that very early in the Kennedy administration, before the Bay of Pigs, Bissell called him in on the subject, saying, "The White House has twice urged me to create such a capability." Possibly the deputy director was assuming an authority he didn't have in order to calm any reservations Harvey might have. More likely, he was alluding to the Eisenhower White House, under which the CIA-Mafia assassination compact had been formed in 1960, intimating a carry-over authorization. In this case it would have been Richard Nixon, the White House action officer, to whom he was referring. As the Watergate tapes reflect, Nixon expressed deep anxiety to his aide, Robert Haldeman, that the break-in might "blow the whole Bay of Pigs thing, which we think would be very unfortunate—both for the CIA and for the country . . . the problem is it tracks back to the Bay of Pigs." In fact, the inspector general's report, which breaks down the assassination plots into Phase One, which antedated the assignment to Harvey, and Phase Two, which followed, tends to exonerate RFK. It asserts that it was Phase One on which Houston briefed him, but "this was not done with respect to Phase Two, which was already well under way at the time Kennedy was briefed."

As I drove around what showed on the map as the south campus of the University of Miami in 1974, there was the feel of an aviation-age Stonehenge about the place. I was looking for artifacts of the CIA's Miami station, known gibberishly as JM/WAVE, which had flourished as virtually a city within a city after the Kennedys commissioned Operation Mongoose a dozen years earlier. During World War II the site had been the Richmond Naval Air Station, home base for blimps hunting German submarines in the Straits of Florida. The huge hangers had been destroyed by a hurricane, leaving bare foundations and jutting girders. The navy had deeded it to the university for future use, of which the CIA had an immediate need. The only structure left standing was a colonnaded, white-frame edifice in run-down condition that the navy had designated Building 25. From what the superannuated secret war soldiers told me, Building 25 was the "home office" of Zenith Technical Enterprises, which posed as an electronics firm but was actually the nerve center of the operations against Cuba. Salesmen paying cold calls on Zenith were directed by a notice on the door to various departments, all of which were dead ends. Should they venture into the lobby, they would notice business licenses and a certificate of award from the United Givers Fund.

JM/WAVE functioned on a budget of more than $500 million annually, had over six hundred personnel, and leased a fleet of over one hundred vehicles. The station chief, Ted Shackley, a Boston Brahmin dubbed the Blonde Ghost because his past was largely a blank, drove a Cadillac, as did Gordon Campbell, Shackley's deputy, who was in charge of the maritime arm. Those lower in the pecking order drove Chevys. There was a paramilitary supermarket where case officers planning a mission—they controlled some three thousand Cuban agents and subagents—could order weapons from a fifty-four-page catalogue showing Czech snub-nosed machine guns used by Castro's militia, mortars, rockets, and practically every military rifle and carbine in the world. Each item had a stock number but no price. To provide cover employment and commercial disguises, the Agency formed fifty-five dummy companies, ranging from Caribbean Research & Marketing on Okeechobee Road to boat repair shops, fishing companies, travel agencies and real estate brokerages. Inside the CIA, Eastern Airlines' midday Electra flight from Washington became known as the Miami Milk Run because as many as half the passengers were Langley types. The local real estate market picked up as the agents sought housing for their families. For security reasons, the agents were encouraged to socialize only with each other, and among the watering holes on their select list were the Stuft Shirt Lounge at the Holiday Inn on Brickell and the 27 Birds, where no one seemed to notice the clusters of Rolex watches with red, white and blue bezels.

For the most part, the Miami press corps displayed little curiosity over what was going on. But one columnist checked out the address of Ace Marine Survey, the owner of record of a suspected Agency sea raider, and found it smack in the middle of the Miami River. The columnist dialed Ace's listed numbers and inquired of the secretary who answered where they were located.

"I don't know," she replied.

"Does anyone there know?" the columnist persisted.

"Just a minute, I'll check." Following a long pause, she advised, "No one here knows."

"How do you get to work?" the columnist asked.

"Somebody brings me," she answered.

Frank Sturgis's role in Operation Mongoose was to fly hazardous "study flights" probing Cuba's electronic defenses so that boat missions could evade them. Sturgis was one of the oral-contract paramilitaries who no piece of paper would ever tie to the Agency. His case officer was Joaquin Sanjenis, whose brother, a police official in Havana, had warned Sturgis that Cuban security knew he was a double agent. Sanjenis, who met his contacts at the Anthony Abrams Chevrolet dealership in Little Havana, was the chief of Operation 40, which was notorious even in exile circles. The insiders I interviewed in 1974 were still talking in hushed tones about the supersecret outfit. It was assembled for the Bay of Pigs invasion and had been named after the number of original members (which subsequently expanded to sixty-five), many of whom were thugs and assassins. Operation 40 was supposed to follow in the wake of Brigade 2506 as it drove for Havana, liquidating ranking officials loyal to Castro by any means necessary. In particular, it was to thwart any postinvasion role for Manuel Ray, the liberal favored by the Kennedys. During Mongoose, Operation 40 did double duty, spying on Cuban exiles to ensure political correctness (its dossier system rivaled that of the Miami FBI) and running sabotage raids facilitated by the study flights. When a flight was scheduled, Sanjenis called Sturgis at his unlisted home number. Sturgis would take off in a light plane and bank south toward Cuba on a prescribed course. As he entered Cuban airspace, the electronic defenses would be alerted by the drone of his engine and a blip on the radar screen. The Cubans would talk excitedly over the radio, start up tracking devices, and ready night-fighting MiGs. A rocket crew would fix Sturgis's position on a target display board. On the sea off Cuba, the U.S.S. *Pocono*, an electronic spy ship bristling with antennas, would intercept the signals from the frenzied activity, and the next mission would know where the holes in the defenses were. For playing sitting duck, Sturgis was paid $600 a flight, and double that for his wife Jan should he be shot down. The paychecks were drawn on the Burdine department store, one of the many Miami establishments providing cover for JM/WAVE.

Another secret war commuter was Eugenio Martinez, the prolific *practico* (boatman). In keeping with the CIA's camouflage, Martinez and the other ace *practicos* who knew the Cuban coastline like the back of their hands were based at 6312 Riviera Drive, a palm-fringed street in Coral Gables lined with expensive homes. The attraction of this address was that it had a boat slip in back on a waterway that fed into Biscayne Bay and the open sea. Pleasure boaters passing by had no reason to look twice at the powerboat moored in the slip, which was actually a souped-up, armed raider. In December 1961, Martinez went on a typical mission when he landed a commando unit on a ten-day foray inside the island. The commandos blew up a railroad bridge and, in a scene out of *The Bridge Over the River Kwai*, watched as a train tumbled off the severed tracks. Then, on October 22, 1962, Martinez was sitting off the Pinar del Rio coast waiting for a commando party to return when he tuned to a Miami radio station. JFK was addressing the nation, declaring a blockade of Cuba. The missile crisis was on. Martinez was jubilant—surely the U.S. would invade now. But there was no invasion. The exiles viewed Kennedy's peaceful settlement with Khrushchev as a failure of will and were seethingly resentful.

The hostile actions mounted by JM/WAVE were tantamount to a massive crime spree. Every time a boat left for Cuba or a plane dumped firebombs, the Neutrality Act was broken. Every time a false flight plan was filed or aircraft registration numbers taped over, FAA regulations were violated. The transportation of explosives on the highways transgressed Florida law. The possession of illegal explosives and war materiel contravened the Munitions Act, and the procurement of automatic weapons defied the Firearms Act. Incorporation papers filed with the Florida secretary of state for the dummy companies contained false information. Tax returns filed with the IRS gave bogus sources of income. The Agency quietly arranged for nonenforcement. An elaborate recognition system was devised, and police, sheriffs, Customs, Immigration, Treasury and the FBI all looked the other way. Boat crews were given the password of the day for use if challenged by the Coast Guard. The only crackdowns under the missile crisis agreement were on action groups not on a CIA leash.

Bobby Kennedy, disappointed with the barely tangible success of Operation Mongoose, sidetracked it in favor of a Cuban Coordinating Committee that would step up the covert actions. As General Edward G. Lansdale, who had installed the puppet Diem regime in Vietnam and now was in overall command of the Cuba Project, put it, "Bobby wanted more boom and bang on the island." The previous caution had been dictated by the fact that over one thousand Brigade 2506 members remained in prisons in Cuba, but in December 1962 they were exchanged for food and medicine. At this juncture, I heard, the secret war entered a new phase: a second invasion was on the agenda. It would be staged from host countries to technically dodge the agreement with the Soviets. But the organization, training and coordination would take place in the United States. Nearly half of recuperated Brigade 2506 enlisted in the U.S. Army under special arrangements and were shipped to Fort Jackson, South Carolina. Three hundred were considered officer material and sent to Fort Benning, Georgia. To preserve the security and secrecy of the second invasion, the Cuban recruits were segregated from the regular troops.

Sturgis mentioned to me that another member of the Watergate team, who had been in on the earlier burglary of Daniel Ellsberg's psychiatrist's office in Los Angeles, might know something about the second invasion. Felipe de Diego had been, at age 23, the youngest bank president in Cuba before fleeing Castro, and his warrior instincts were aroused when his brother-in-law spun into the sea while providing air cover at the Bay of Pigs. I got to de Diego through his attorney, to whom I furnished an affidavit that I had carried out illegal break-ins for the FBI (de Diego subsequently got off). The darkly handsome de Diego preferred to talk while, on March 6, 1974, we cruised the streets of Little Havana in his long black Lincoln, since the Cuban cafes were known to have ears. He had been an intelligence officer in Operation 40 but disclaimed any knowledge of its sordid background. The experience gave him the resume to go to the Fort Benning command school. He was destined for assignment to Manuel Artime's MRR in Nicaragua, which had quartered Brigade 2506 before the first invasion. But he professed to be short on details of the second invasion plans.

In January 1963, Manuel Artime, known as the CIA's "Golden Boy," was skiing down the gentle slope of a New Hampshire resort as the guest of Bobby and Ethel Kennedy. Captured at the Bay of Pigs (as his MRR provocation near Guantánamo was aborted), the Desi Arnez look-alike was only a few weeks out of a tropical prison, but the talk that weekend wasn't about the fine powder; it concerned ways and means of getting rid of "that guy with the beard," as Bobby referred to Castro. The upshot was that Artime was put on a CIA retainer of $1,500 a month, and his revived MRR, based in Nicaragua, was slated to receive $250,000 a month to launch a "Second Naval Guerrilla" aimed initially at Cuban shipping. It became like old times in Little Havana. The MRR battle flag, a gold trident on a blue field, hung outside a newly opened recruiting station. General Lansdale flew down for a personal inspection. A group holding maneuvers in a field proudly told quizzical Miami police that they were training for the next invasion of Cuba. But I wanted to talk with Artime himself about that elusive second invasion. He was in Nicaragua, however, having become wealthy importing meat and machinery in partnership with the ruling Somoza family.

But there was a buzz in exile circles about another Brigade veteran who was Bobby Kennedy's personal favorite and was ticketed to lead his own amphibious force from the Dominican Republic in the east at the same time Artime and the MRR stormed the southside beaches. I met Enrique "Harry" Ruiz-Williams, who had been severely wounded in the first invasion, through Haynes Johnson of the *Washington Evening Star*, who had done a book on the Bay of Pigs. The interview took place on November 28, 1973, in Williams's Floralina Exploration Company office on the Federal Highway in Fort Lauderdale. Burly, round-faced, handsome, he combined the geniality of a Lions Club toastmaster with a manifest singleness of purpose. I asked him why he would abandon the security of his profession—he was a geologist—to "risk getting your ass shot off." "But I also had the red ass—I was mad at Castro," he retorted. "And I also had the guilty complex." In Cuba he had remained passive, resigned to the debauchery of the Batista regime. It was easy to see why Williams had been handpicked by Bobby Kennedy. Tough and progressive, he was at the same time fiercely anticommunist.

He recalled being summoned to Washington after an early release by Castro because of his injuries to meet with the attorney general. "I was really nervous to see him, the number two man in the country," Williams said. "And when I walked into that office, here was this young man without a coat and his sleeves rolled up and tie unknotted." The two hit it off immediately. Bobby was purging the exile leadership of such scalawag old-liners as Tony Varona so that if his plan to topple Castro succeeded, the new rulers wouldn't be an embarrassment. So flattered was Williams to be chosen by RFK that he remembered Bobby's exact words: "We've selected you to be, let's say, the man we trust the most in the exiles, but at the same time I want to make it clear that we're going to be calling the shots." When Williams proposed "to physically eliminate Castro," Kennedy digressed, saying that the interests of the United States and those of the exiles might not always be identical, but the goal of bringing democracy to Cuba was. When the president determined that it was the right moment, they would strike. But not to worry, Bobby said, "We're going to go."

Kennedy arranged for Williams to deal directly with Cyrus Vance, the undersecretary of the army, in working out the details for the induction of volunteers from the Brigade to be drilled at Forts Jackson and Benning. "We had at least three or four big meetings at Bobby's office," Williams disclosed, "with leaders of the Brigade and Vance and two or three others. Joe Califano, who was working with [Secretary of Defense Robert] McNamara, was there too." For its part, the CIA had to accept Williams even if they didn't control him. "I had the backing of Bobby," he said, "and they listened to me whether they liked it or not. And they liked it enough. I told my things to Bobby. And Bobby was the one who made this thing go."

The CIA agents assigned as liaison to Williams were Howard Hunt and James McCord, the future Watergaters. Hunt became Williams's link to Langley, McCord to the Fort Jackson contingent. There were numerous meetings, mostly in Washington, and countless phone calls. Usually Hunt or McCord would take him to lunch or come by his room at the Ebbitt Hotel, an Agency lodging of choice near the White House, late at night. "It's funny how these professional intelligence people work," Williams observed of Hunt. "He never opened up to me. He knew I liked my martinis, and he'd have a martini with me. But I never trusted him, and he never trusted me." Hunt, no fan of the Kennedys, might have been reticent to say much because he was aware that Williams was having a martini or two with Bobby and Ethel Kennedy at their Hickory Hill estate in Virginia.

Williams pointed out to me the location of his base in the Dominican Republic, thrusting a beefy finger on a wall map at Montecristi in the isolated northwestern part of the country. From there his expeditionary force would shove off for Oriente Province in easternmost Cuba, which, because of its mountainous terrain, paucity of highways, and long distance from Havana, would be the most difficult area for Castro to defend.

As Williams sensed, Bobby Kennedy was hands-on with the new plan to topple Castro. Captain Bradley E. Ayers, an Army Ranger on detached duty to train exiles in unconventional warfare, recounted in his book *The War That Never Was* how he encountered RFK at a CIA base deep in the Everglades in early November 1963. A sign read WALOOS GLADES HUNTING CLUB, which Ayers had reached by airboat. Squatting in a clearing were two helicopters, one a military Bell H-13 with its registration numbers taped over, the other a civilian model with the name of a West Palm Beach air service on its tail boom. Two men emerged from a Quonset hut illuminated by Coleman lanterns, and Ayers recognized both. One was Gordon Campbell, the JM/WAVE deputy chief who had sent the *Rex* on its ill-fated mission only weeks before. The other was the attorney general of the United States, who boarded the civilian copter and was whisked off. They had just pored over maps and charts, and RFK had given the go-ahead for Ayers's underwater demolition teams to blow up ships in Cuban harbors. Earlier, Kennedy was conducting an inspection of the JM/WAVE war room. Also in the room was William Harvey, who had devised the CIA's assassination capability. When Kennedy noticed an item on the teletype that linked JM/WAVE with Langley, he considered it a security breach and ripped it out. "Hey, where do you think you're going with that?" Harvey snarled, snatching it from the AG's hand. Kennedy shot him a burn-in-hell look and later ordered him transferred to Rome. At the same time, John Kennedy was trying to keep the political fences mended. At a reception at a Fort Lauderdale hotel arranged by George Smathers, he was introduced to Carlos Prio by Frank Sturgis. "Mr. President, meet Mr. President," Sturgis smiled.

Although no one outside his closest aides knew it, JFK was engaged in a clandestine operation of his own aimed at a rapprochement with Cuba that would have derailed the highballing secret war train. Why he embarked on this second track is uncertain, but his attitude toward socialist countries was moderating, as evidenced by his conciliatory "we breathe the same air as the Russians" American University speech in April 1963. Around that time McGeorge Bundy, the national security advisor, offered a possible new "direction of a gradual development of some form of accommodation with Castro." There the matter rested through the summer as the second invasion plan heated up. Then in September William Attwood, a JFK special advisor at the United Nations and trusted friend, heard unverified reports that Castro was dissatisfied with Cuba's status as a Soviet satellite and was looking for a way out. The president, perhaps pushed by trepidation that another *Rex* incident could infamously boomerang, approved of Attwood's conferring with Dr. Carlos Lechuga, the Cuban chief of mission at the U.N. As Attwood told it in his *The Reds and the Blacks*, ABC's Lisa Howard, who had interviewed Castro the previous May and was trusted by him, was brought in as an intermediary. Howard carried on long-distance phone conversations with Dr. Rene Vallejo, Castro's personal aide and confidant. The talks progressed so smoothly that on November 18 Attwood, on JFK's instructions, called Vallejo to propose that negotiations be held at U.N. headquarters after an agenda was worked out, and Vallejo agreed. On November 21 Bundy told Attwood that the president wanted to see him about the next move "after a brief trip to Dallas."

By this time, advance infiltrations for the Williams-Artime landings, which had been given the CIA cryptonym AM/TRUNK, had been fixed for December 1. A subplot had been added: Plan Judas, in which one of Castro's most faithful "disciples," a high-ranking officer who had been with him from the start, would spring a coup in return for a generous deposit in a foreign bank. On November 22, Williams told me, he participated in the penultimate meeting on the second invasion, held in a CIA safe house in northwest Washington. Attending were Deputy Director Richard Helms, Howard Hunt and several other CIA officers. As Williams put it, "It was the most important meeting I ever had on the problem of Cuba." He would mobilize his troops, and Artime was "ready with his thing in Central America." They were ready "to do a whole thing together." Williams and the Agency contingent were about to go out for a late lunch when they heard the news from Dallas. Williams retreated to his room at the Ebbitt Hotel, where Haynes Johnson, who had been chosen by RFK to scribe the Bay of Pigs story, was finishing up his research. The phone rang. Williams picked it up and recognized the voice of Bobby Kennedy, who asked to speak with Johnson. "One of your guys did it," he said, sounding flat and unemotional.

The assassination of JFK brought both the war and peace projects to a skidding halt. Not long afterwards, Howard Hunt told Williams, "Lyndon Johnson says he doesn't want to hear another thing about those goddam Cubans." The new president was pulling the plug on any project bearing the imprimatur of Bobby Kennedy, whom he despised. LBJ turned his attention to Vietnam, where he would soon find a pretext for committing land forces. JM/WAVE station chief Ted Shackley was transferred to Saigon, where he participated in the notorious Operation Phoenix. The huge JM/WAVE complex was gradually dismantled, its assets shuffled and transferred, and agents sent into deep cover.

The CIA treated Williams, who bore the Bobby stigma, like a parolee, and he went back to his geology career. But the Agency continued to throw money and logistical support at its Golden Boy, Artime, enabling him to carry on with the Second Naval Guerrilla. At first, the foraging for "enemy" targets was unrewarding. Then, on the night of September 13, 1964, the opportunity for the big score came—or so the MRR thought. Its attack vessel, the *Santa Maria*, was creeping through the Windward Passage between Cuba and Haiti, bent on shooting up a shore installation, when a large moving blip appeared on the radar screen. The *Santa Maria* launched a small boat to identify the vessel. Training a searchlight on its fantail and spotting the word "Sierra," the crew reported by radio that it was the *Sierra Maestra*, the pride of Cuba's merchant fleet. A second small boat was dispatched, and the two of them poured a stream of fire from 57-mm. recoilless rifles and .50-caliber machine guns at the quarry, leaving it dead in the water and blazing fiercely. The crew abandoned ship. A jubilant Artime was ready to announce a glorious victory at sea when he received an urgent message from the Somerset Corporation, a CIA proprietary in Panama that coordinated the Second Naval Guerrilla (scuttlebutt had it that Somerset was named after old Joe Kennedy's liquor-importing firm). Intelligence data placed the *Sierra Maestra* in waters far from the action. The MRR small boats took a closer look at the fantail of the deserted ship and read, "*Sierra Aranzazu*, Bilbao." A ghastly mistake. The *Sierra Aranzazu* was a smaller Spanish motor vessel carrying a cargo of cork, garlic and toys to Havana. Artime flew to Madrid to personally deny to Generalissimo Francisco Franco that his MRR was culpable, offering that it was a Castro trick to discredit the MRR. Reportedly, Franco didn't believe a word of it.

But the CIA wasn't finished with its tarnished Golden Boy, as the 1975 Church Committee found out. The Agency needed a cutout to deal with Rolando Cubela, the quirky agent in place known as AM/LASH, who was being passed a poison pen by Desmond FitzGerald's man in Paris even as JFK was being shot in Dallas. In late 1964, Cubela, who had vaulting ambitions for a major post in Cuba, requested the Agency to furnish him a silencer for a Belgian FAL rifle and a suitcase bomb with which to assassinate Castro. But FitzGerald didn't have full confidence in Cubela and was leery that the plot might backfire. So he brought in Artime to act as a facilitator, and Howard Hunt, temporarily sheepdipped as a "contract agent," to handle the CIA's end. The trio met at the Torre de Madrid apartments in the Spanish capital, where Cubela held a minor Cuban government posting. After several meetings, Cubela left for Havana with a CIA-crafted silencer and explosives as well as a promise from Artime that within forty-eight hours of Cubela pulling off his coup an MRR force of 750 men would be landed to back him up. But with the stage set, nothing was heard from AM/LASH. Then, on February 28, 1966, Cubela and six confederates were arrested for plotting to kill Castro. A Cuban double agent named Juan Felifel had gotten wind of the plot from his brother Anis, who chanced to be chief of intelligence for the MRR. It was not news to Cuban counterintelligence, who knew everything Artime was up to. General Escalante told me that his ace wireman, Colonel Arturo Rodriguez, infiltrated MRR headquarters at Monkey Point, Nicaragua, and bugged it so thoroughly that it held no secrets. In a dramatic trial, Cubela and his codefendants were convicted and sentenced to twenty-five years in prison. Castro, who knew Cubela from their student days, sent him books to read. But the trial had captured worldwide attention, and the CIA was on the spot. When LBJ's secretary of state, Dean Rusk, read about it in *The New York Times*, he braced Richard Helms, who responded with a whopper. "The Agency was not involved with Cubela in a plot to assassinate Fidel Castro," Helms wrote, "nor did it ever encourage him to attempt such an act."

Under the presidency of Richard Nixon, who had started it all, the secret war became more inventive. During 1969 and 1970, the CIA deployed weather modification to ravage Cuba's sugar crop and undermine the economy. I found out about this on September 27, 1975, when, after giving a lecture ("The FBI, the CIA and the Spy State") at a community college in Ridgecrest, California, I was approached by a man who displayed a civilian employee badge of the nearby China Lake Naval Weapons Center. Beckoning me to a corner of the auditorium where we could speak in private, he described the cloud-seeding technology developed at the center as a weapon of war. He said that planes from China Lake overflew Cuba and precipitated torrential rains over nonagricultural areas, leaving the cane fields arid and unleashing killer flash floods elsewhere.

Biological warfare against the Cuban swine herd was also on the agenda. According to *Newsday*, January 6, 1977, citing a CIA source, a U.S. intelligence officer passed a vial of African swine fever virus to an anti-Castro terrorist group. The vial was taken by fishing trawler to Navessa Island off Puerto Rico, often used by the Agency as an advance base, and smuggled into Cuba. Six weeks later, the country suffered the first outbreak of swine fever in the Western Hemisphere, decimating the pig population and causing a severe shortage of pork, the dietary staple in Cuba. The United Nations Food and Agricultural Organization called it the "most alarming event" of the year and futilely tried to track down "how the disease had been transmitted." The CIA declined comment.

Nor was a triple-assassination scheme in October 1971 exactly an off-the-shelf operation. It happened while Castro was the guest of President Salvador Allende in Chile. The thinking was that *el lider maximo* would be more vulnerable away from his home island and efficient ring of security. According to what Gerry Hemming told me—he claimed that some of his Interpen people were involved—Castro was to be shot during ceremonies upon his arrival in Santiago with a TV camera-gun fabricated by the CIA laboratory. Alpha 66 leader Antonio Veciana said that the attempt was abandoned when the trigger man sustained an appendicitis attack and his accomplice had to rush him to a hospital. A backup plan to blow up Castro's vehicle with a 400-pound charge of dynamite when he visited a copper mine near Antofagasta went awry because the electric detonator malfunctioned. The third brainstorm, Hemming said, was to nail Castro on his way home from Chile. It was set for the moment he appeared in the doorway of his Ilyushin jet after landing at the Lima Airport for a state dinner with Peruvian President Juan Velasco Alvarado. A Beechcraft Baron with a 20-mm. cannon behind its door was positioned on an apron where it could blast Castro's plane, then make a quick getaway. But the Ilyushin unexpectedly pulled into a special security area and was blocked from view.

A few months earlier, in April 1971, the produce stands and sidewalk cantinas along Flagler Street in Little Havana were abuzz with word that Howard Hunt was back in town, which surely meant the campaign against Castro was about to take a new turn. Hunt, "retired" from the CIA, was now chief spook of the Nixon White House's Special Investigative Unit, also known as The Plumbers, and was recruiting secret-war veterans for what he portrayed as a national security mission under a "superstructure" organization "above both the FBI and CIA." His enlistees numbered Sturgis, Martinez, Gonzales and Barker, the Miami Four. They were told that if they helped, there would be future reciprocation "in the liberation of Cuba." In the predawn hours of June 17, 1972, the quartet, led by James McCord, breached the Democratic National Committee offices in the Watergate complex. They were to photograph specific documents and to plant bugs. "We didn't question it," Sturgis explained to me. "We had been told that the money was coming from communist countries, including Cuba." As they went about their business, the door burst open, and they were arrested at gunpoint by a police undercover unit so shaggy in appearance that Sturgis at first thought they also were burglars. As he sat in jail, Sturgis had ample time to think about it. Had it been a setup, a tour de force by a CIA cabal to not only discredit Nixon but weaken the office of the presidency? "No president or dictator controls his own intelligence service," Sturgis ruminated. "It's the other way around." Nixon might have been thinking in the same tail-wagging-the-dog vein. On the White House tapes, he was heard mumbling about how much Howard Hunt knew and repeatedly alluding to the Bay of Pigs. "It all traces back to the Bay of Pigs," he lamented. He had given the Agency a license to kill, and now it was coming back to haunt him.

The secret war left a legacy of violence, treachery, corruption, narcoterrorism and murder that endures to this day. Mafia types who figured in the kill-Castro endeavors were themselves killed. In 1975, a matter of days before he was to appear before the Church Committee, Sam Giancana was shot point-blank in the back of the head in his Chicago home with a gun police traced to Miami. A year later, the body of Johnny Roselli, the hit-squad leader, was found stuffed into a barrel in Dumbfoundling Bay near Miami. The Church Committee had just released its report, which included Roselli's testimony about the Mafia-CIA assassination plots.

Operation 40 went on to coordinate the 1967 hunt for Che Guevara in the jungles of South America, where he was trying to instigate an insurrectional movement. But Che and his band moved only at night, so high-flying U-2 spy planes out of Panama were unable to spot them. At this juncture, a breakthrough technology was developed at a University of Michigan lab that used "infrared optical imaging" to detect heat pockets. In Che's case, heat was emitted from the tightly spaced bodies of his men was they moved through the cool jungle night as well as the Dien Bien Phu ovens they used for cooking. Under a cloak of strict secrecy, the CIA co-opted Mark Hurd Aerial Surveys, Inc., which was mapping the region for highway construction with twin Beech airplanes, to fly nighttime grid patterns with the planes' cameras loaded with the special infrared film. The film was rushed daily to a Mark Hurd hanger at the Santa Barbara, California, airport, where the "heat print" blowups, mounted on a screened-off wall, tracked Che's progress. It was here that the project's security broke down. Jim Rose, the ex-CIA pilot, happened to be hanger flying (recounting aerial exploits) with a Mark Hurd pilot who couldn't resist boasting of how he had helped trap Che. The trap was sprung on October 8, 1967, when Agency-trained Bolivian Rangers, guided by the heat-print mosaic, ambushed Che and his band in a canyon. Che was held overnight in a schoolhouse, then machine-gunned to death. Standing by was CIA agent Felix I. Rodriguez, who had orchestrated the hunt. An old hand in the secret war, Rodriguez had tried to assassinate Castro with a presighted rifle prior to the Bay of Pigs and had been Artime's MRR communications officer in Nicaragua afterward. By his own account, Rodriguez's proudest moment was lifting off in a helicopter with Che's body lashed to the right skid like a trophy animal. "On my wrist was his steel Rolex GMT Master with its red-and-blue bezel," he wrote in his memoirs. "In my breast pocket, wrapped in paper from my loose-leaf notebook, was the partially smoked tobacco from his last pipe." On April 20, 1976, Rodriguez retired from the CIA in a brief ceremony in which he was awarded the Intelligence Star for Valor. He had refused to accept it from CIA Director George Bush at Langley because he considered Bush a political appointee ignorant of covert actions (which Bush lived vicariously, signing off internal memos as "Chief Spook"). But as vice president under Reagan, Bush became personally close to Rodriguez, who had emerged from retirement to join Oliver North's operation resupplying the Nicaraguan Contras. When the scandal broke over the diversion of funds from the sale of arms to Iran to the Contras, Rodriguez was subpoenaed to testify by the investigating independent counsel. On the stand, he denied briefing Bush on the weapons smuggling and touchily rejected allegations that he had solicited millions of dollars in drug money to finance the Contras. For his part, Bush stuck by the unlikely story that he was "out of the loop."

What was left of Operation 40 degenerated into a narcotics-trafficking enterprise. In 1970, an Operation 40 plane with several kilos of cocaine and heroin aboard crashed in southern California. Shortly thereafter, Juan Restoy, who belonged to Operation 40, was caught with Bay of Pigs veteran Alonso Pujol in a federal drug sweep in Miami. The adverse publicity prompted the CIA to shut down Operation 40 in 1972, and its chief, Joaquin Sanjenis, retired with a secret medal. But Operation 40 was only part of a much larger network. In 1974 a joint federal-state task force reported that four Cuban noncoms in the secret war were tied in with the smuggling operations of Mafia panjandrum Santos Trafficante. "The CIA not only taught these individuals how to use weapons," the task force report stated, "but made them experts in smuggling men and material from place to place under Castro's nose. This training seems to be applied here." One frustrated investigator complained that the Agency had given the Cubans vital Latin America contacts and familiarized them with "every port and inlet into this country."

In 1968, as the CIA scaled back its Cuba campaign, Orlando Bosch's MIRR morphed into Cuban Power, a terrorist faction that, like the religious lunatic on the train in *On the Twentieth Century*, stuck trademark red, white and blue stickers at the scene of the crime. On May 31, a Japanese freighter docked at Tampa and a British merchantman under way off Key West were racked by explosions. The following day, in Miami, a man calling himself Ernesto staged a press conference condemning countries doing business with Cuba and warned that "other ships are going to explode." Although Ernesto wore a sack over his head in the manner of a Mafia defector before a Senate hearing, he was easily identified as Bosch. That summer Cuban Power terrorism spread to Los Angeles, where an Air France office, the Mexico Tourist Department and the British consulate were bombed, and Manhattan, where the diplomatic and tourist agencies of six countries with normal relations with Cuba were hit, and a time bomb was found in the Air France facility in Rockefeller Center. For good measure, two bars frequented by pro-Castro Cubans were bombed, and the audience attending a play, *The Cuban Thing*, at the Henry Miller Theater off Times Square were driven crying into the street by tear gas devices. But on September 16, 1968, Bosch was caught red-handed by FBI agents tipped off by an informant inside Cuban Power as he fired on the Polish motorship *Polancia* at dock in Miami. Convicted of terrorism, he was incarcerated at the Marion Federal Penitentiary, where he played gin rummy with Rolando Masferrer, locked up for violating the Neutrality Act.

When Bosch was released from prison in the fall of 1972 through the intercession of Florida politicians eyeing the exile-bloc vote, Republican Governor Claude Kirk rhapsodized, "When I think of free men seeking a homeland, I must necessarily think of Dr. Bosch." As it turned out, the mad bomber was free to resume his old ways, this time promising "an internationalization of the war." By early 1975 he was in Chile, where General Augusto Pinochet, whose junta had bloodily overthrown Allende, put him up in a government guest house while he conferred with Pinochet's secret police, the brutal DINA (National Intelligence Directorate), which was responsible for hundreds of *desaparecidos* during the dictatorship. "Bosch had a book on the life of Yasir Arafat with him," reported a Miami newsman who interviewed him there, "and an impressive stack of cash on the table." On September 21, 1976, Allende's ambassador, Orlando Letelier, an effective opponent of the Pinochet regime, was driving along Washington's Embassy Row when a radio-triggered bomb under his car exploded, killing him and a companion. As CIA director, George Bush was in the loop on this one: within a week the Agency knew that DINA and several CIA-connected Cubans were responsible. But it leaked an item to *Newsweek* reading, "The CIA has concluded that the Chilean secret police was not involved." The lie was put to that when DINA agent Michael V. Townley was arrested and convicted. Townley implicated two journeymen in Bosch's network, Guillermo Novo and Alvin Ross Diaz, who were tried and convicted, then acquitted at a retrial (when arrested in Miami, the pair was in possession of a pound of cocaine, a terrorist currency). And in 1993, after democracy returned to Chile, Manuel Contreras, the head of DINA at the time, was convicted of masterminding the Letelier murder. In a recent clemency petition, Contreras deposed that Pinochet approved and supervised all major DINA operations.

In early 1976, an informant tipped Miami Police Lieutenant Thomas Lynch that Bosch was planning the bombing assassination of Secretary of State Henry Kissinger, who had committed the mortal sin of making overtures to improve relations with Castro when he visited Costa Rica that March. Costa Rican authorities were notified, and four days before Kissinger's arrival Bosch, who had entered the country with a bogus passport, was jailed. Back in Miami, bombings were so rampant—four federal buildings, a bank, a police locker room and a county building were targeted—that the police sent an urgent dispatch to CIA headquarters seeking a list of all exiles trained in bomb making, as well as, if possible, an accounting of C-3 and C-4 plastic explosives left behind when the Agency closed shop. There was no answer.

In the most egregious terrorist act, Cubana Airlines flight 455 was blasted from the sky between Barbados and Havana on October 6, 1976, killing all seventy-three people on board. Two men who had deplaned in Barbados, Freddy Lugo and Ricardo Losano, were interrogated after joking about the bombing in a taxicab. In turn, they pointed fingers at Bosch and ex-Operation 40 member Luis Posada Carriles, in Venezuela, where Bosch had entered on a forged Costa Rican passport three weeks earlier. The pair, Lugo and Losano confessed, had supplied them with the two bombs they planted on the airliner. Murder charges were filed in Venezuela against Bosch and Posada but were eventually dropped for "lack of evidence."

In 1989, his foreign peregrinations at an end, Bosch illegally reentered the United States at Miami and was jailed on a parole violation warrant stemming from the *Polancia* incident. Coming to the aid of Dr. Death, as wags dubbed him, were Ileana Ros-Lehtinen, a Republican candidate for Congress from Miami, and her campaign manager, Jeb Bush, the president's son, who is now governor of Florida. The two were outraged that the Justice Department, citing an FBI report that Bosch "repeatedly expressed and demonstrated a willingness to cause indiscriminate injury and death," had ruled that Bosch should be deported. On July 17, 1990, however, Ros-Lehtinen and Jeb Bush got their way: George Bush's Justice Department reversed its position. Upon his release, an unrepentant Bosch called a press conference to denounce the terms of his liberty, which included the renunciation of terrorism. "They purchased the chain, but they don't have the monkey," he growled.

Bosch's accused accomplice in the Cubana airline bombing, Luis Posada, escaped from a Venezuelan jail in 1985 and materialized at the Ilopango Air Base in El Salvador, where he joined his old Operation 40 comrade, Felix Rodriguez, in the Nicaraguan resupply venture. The base has been cited in congressional hearings as the southern terminus for a "guns down, drugs up" trade. On October 5, 1986, one of the cargo planes, registered in Miami to the CIA proprietary Southern Air Transport, which had been set up to assist in Bay of Pigs logistics, was shot down. A surviving crewman, Eugene Hasenfus, talked, uncorking the Iran-Contra scandal. Among other things, he said that Posada and Rodriguez were "U.S. agents" who bragged of being friends of George Bush.

Posada personifies the meld between "respectable" domestic politics and terrorism through his connection to the Cuban-American National Foundation (CANF), which purports to represent 1.5 million Americans of Cuban descent. CANF was founded in 1981 by Jorge Mas Canosa, whose service in the secret war dated back to the Bay of Pigs when, according to Gerry Hemming, he was on board the *Santa Ana* during its aborted diversionary strike. Mas's rubric was that the most effective way to subvert Castro was by lobbying in Washington. A combative millionaire, he was feted at the White House by Presidents Ronald Reagan, George Bush and Bill Clinton. He harbored an ambition to become president himself—of Cuba after Castro was vanquished (some close observers thought he would have been a neo-Batista). He died in 1997, just as Miami-Dade County began investigating irregularities and possible overcharges in a $58-million contract awarded to the Mas family business (the probe remains pending). After his death, the carefully crafted image of CANF fell apart. On October 27, 1997, a cabin cruiser belonging to CANF executive board member Francisco "Pepe" Hernandez, a Bay of Pigs survivor, was stopped by the Coast Guard off Puerto Rico. When the four exiles on board gave a patently false story of being on a fishing excursion, a search turned up a secret compartment housing a small arsenal, including two high-powered sniper rifles with nightscopes. One of the exiles blurted out, "They are weapons for the purpose of assassinating Fidel Castro." The Coast Guard found that the boat's navigational coordinates were set for Margarita Island off Venezuela, where Castro was due to meet with other Latin American leaders in a summit. According to Cuba's General Escalante,

Mas had been looking for opportunities to assassinate Castro since 1966, when he infiltrated a gunslinger named Herminio Diaz into the vicinity of the Hotel Comodoro in Havana to shoot the Cuban president (Diaz died in a shootout with militia on May 29 of that year).

In an interview in *The New York Times* on July 11, 1998, Luis Posada professed that his terrorist activities had been discreetly subsidized by the tax-exempt CANF for years. "Jorge [Mas] controlled everything," he told reporters Ann Louise Bardach and Larry Rohter. "Whenever I needed money, he said to give me $5,000, give me $10,000, give me $15,000, and they sent it to me." Posada calculated that CANF paid him some $200,000 in total; all Mas asked was to be spared the details of what the money paid for. One action it apparently financed was a 1998 rash of bombings in Cuba in hotels, restaurants and discotheques in which an Italian tourist was killed. Posada admitted to the *Times* that he directed the bombings, which he defended as acts of war designed to cripple the regime by depriving it of foreign tourism and investment and by encouraging internal opposition. His manifesto: he still intended to kill Castro, and violence was the best way to end communism in Cuba.

In November 2000 Posada and several members of his brotherhood of violence were arrested by Panamanian authorities for intending to assassinate Castro when he arrived for the tenth summit of Latin American and European leaders. Posada entered Panama on a false passport, posing as a painter, apparently in imitation of his mentor, Dr. Bosch, who had become an aspiring Rembrandt in Little Havana. When seized, Posada was in possession of a cache of C-4 plastic explosives and a map of the University of Panama, where the summit was scheduled.

At Thanksgiving time 1999, when six-year-old Elian Gonzalez was rescued off Miami and delivered into the hands of Little Havana relatives, he became an instant propaganda pawn in the bitter fight against Castro. Ileana Ros-Lehtinen, the fan of Dr. Death who is now a member of Congress, showed up to play with Elian for the benefit of television cameras. The relatives showered him with playthings, a Nintendo, a trip to Disney World, and a toy gun, and did everything possible to convince him that life in America was better than in Cuba (but presumably left out Miami's disparate crime rate). When the Immigration and Naturalization Service followed protocol and awarded permanent custody to Elian's father, Little Havana and its politicians bellowed in protest, while the relatives conducted sham negotiations to stall turning the child over to his father. After Attorney General Janet Reno, tired of the relatives' repeated broken promises, sent an armed INS special team into their Little Havana house to take custody of Elian, there was an outcry that it was too heavy-handed, with the Cuban mayor of Miami, Joe Carollo, hyperventilating, "What they did was a crime. These are atheists. They don't believe in God." But what the INS did was only prudent. They knew they had to be surgical because Little Havana is an armed camp that would warm the heart of a Charlton Heston. They knew that in the protective ring around the house were ex-cons packing weapons and three Alpha 66 commandos not long returned from a raid on Cuba. Given the violence of the secret war, it might have been suicidal to politely ring the doorbell.

The Elian incident provided a snapshot of Little Havana today. One Cuban woman, angered that Elian had been restored to his father, shouted at the telvision cameras, "I feel ashamed of being an American." Swarms of protesters took to the streets, burning an American flag and pelting police with rocks and bottles. The hate has been passed down from generation to generation, perpetuating an insular society driven by the specter of Castro, out of step with the rest of America. It is like an alien country, so much so that counterprotesters spoofed it as the "Banana Republic." Its culture is so twisted that it regards the deadly Dr. Bosch as "a pillar of the community." Nowhere else in America are serial terrorists given a place of honor.

So the secret war augurs to march on, in one form or another, into the indefinite future. Blood dries fast.

11

THE UNTIMELY DEATH OF RFK

When I ran for U.S. Congress from San Francisco in the 1968 Democratic primary, my principal plank was to reopen the investigation into the assassination of John F. Kennedy. "To do less not only is indecent," my campaign literature highlighted, "but might cost us the life of a future President of John Kennedy's instincts." On June 5, shortly after midnight, this hortatory line seemed excruciatingly prescient. A senator from New York, Robert Kennedy had run in the same California primary, albeit for president, handily defeating his main opponent, Senator Eugene McCarthy of Minnesota, also a dove on the Vietnam War. At the end of his victory speech on stage at the Ambassador Hotel in Los Angeles, he flashed the V-sign and gave the war cry, "On to Chicago! Let's win there!" Chicago was the site of the Democratic National Convention that year, and many pundits viewed California as the last major hurdle to Bobby's wresting the nomination from Vice President Hubert Humphrey and going on to beat Richard Nixon in November. But as he traversed the kitchen pantry en route to a press conference, there was a volley of gunfire. RFK was mortally wounded.

As details came in, it didn't seem like prescience at all, but more like a colossal coincidence. Scores of witnesses in the crowded pantry saw RFK, with maitre d' Karl Uecker leading the way, shake hands with a kitchen worker. They saw a young man standing by the tray stacker spring forward at Kennedy, firing two rapid shots from a handgun. They saw the candidate reel backwards, throwing his right arm in front of his face for protection as his aides pounced on the gunman and, after a struggle during which more shots were fired, disarm him. RFK landed on his back, his arms splayed outward, a halo of blood widening about his head. Within inches of his right hand was a clip-on bow tie he had apparently snatched from someone close by as he sagged from the impact of three bullets in his torso and head.

On the face of it, it was an open and shut case. The gunman, identified as Sirhan Bishara Sirhan, a Jordanian immigrant, was caught with the smoking gun in front of a gallery of witnesses. At a press conference, Los Angeles Mayor Sam Yorty, a relentless red-baiter, supplied the missing motive: Sirhan was a communist because a "reliable police informant" reported that a car traceable to him had been seen several times parked in front of the W. E. B. DuBois Clubs, a leftist youth group (it turned out that Yorty had shot from the lips: the parking space in question was also in front of an Arab nightclub in which Sirhan's brother played in the band).

Yet I was troubled by the timing of the shooting, moments after RFK became an imminent threat to the continuing conduct of the Vietnam War. Vietnam was the lurking issue. Lyndon Johnson had defaulted as a candidate for reelection because of the mighty surge of antiwar sentiment in the country. Humphrey dutifully supported the conflict, and Nixon promised a "peace with honor" resolution (after gaining the White House, he dragged it on for four more years). There was also the nagging reaction of Edward Kennedy, as reported by NBC television correspondent Sander Vanocur, who had covered the RFK campaign and was on the plane bringing his body back from Los Angeles. As he came down the ramp in New York, Vanocur, facing his own network's cameras, told how during the flight Kennedy had remonstrated bitterly about the "faceless men" charged in the slayings of both his brothers and Dr. Martin Luther King, Jr., who had been shot by a sniper in Memphis two months earlier. First Lee Harvey Oswald, then James Earl Ray, and now Sirhan Sirhan, all with no evident motive. "There has to be more to it," Ted Kennedy was quoted by Vanocur. But Kennedy's words, uttered in an unguarded moment and never to be repeated in public, were lost in the rush of rhetoric about how America's violent society had spawned another deranged assassin. It was a person on my congressional campaign team who would ultimately turn in the lead that there was more to it.

The opportunity to run for Congress presented itself to me in early 1968, after a former ABC-TV assignments editor in San Francisco who reveled in chasing white-collar crooks introduced himself to me following my appearance on a broadcast on the Warren Report. The stocky, bearded man gave his name as Jonn Christian, and he shared the view that Dealey Plaza had not been a lone-nut event. From his media position, he had acquired the contacts to do something about it. Christian arranged a "ways and means" meeting at the Pacific Heights mansion of Fremont Bodine "Peter" Hitchcock, Jr., a millionaire member of the polo-playing Hitchcock family, which moved in the most select of social circles. He was hardly a Kennedy partisan—during the 1964 Republican National Convention in San Francisco, the Barry Goldwaters stayed at his Pacific Heights home—but he had gone to Harvard with JFK and admired him. This sentiment survived the fact that, before their marriage, his wife, Joan, carried on an affair with Kennedy that was arranged by Peter Lawford (Joan Hitchcock went public with her memoirs in 1975 when Kennedy's extracurricular romances were being dragged through the media).

Peter Hitchcock invited to the meeting Amory J. "Jack" Cooke, a vice president of the Hearst Corporation married to Phoebe Hearst; local ABC newscaster Harv Morgan; and Hitchcock attorney George T. Davis. Cooke thought the Hearst press might be open-minded, but Christian and I were skeptical. The editors possessed an unshakable faith in the institutions of government, whether it concerned the Vietnam War or the Warren Report, and Hearst feature writers Jim Bishop and Bob Considine had endorsed the Report before its ink was dry. When someone suggested that the issue belonged in the hands of Congress, a political campaign was born, and I was the candidate. For the first time in his life, Peter Hitchcock contributed to a Democrat, at least to the extent of paying the filing fee.

I thought I could win even though my opponent in the Democratic primary was a decent, colorless man named Phil Drath, who also was against the war, had run twice before, and possessed a legion of loyal followers. If I got past him, the incumbent Republican was John Maillard, a Brahmin known as The Admiral for his rank in the naval reserve and his support for the war in a city largely against it.

THE ASSASSINATION OF PRESIDENT KENNEDY
BROUGHT IMMEDIATE AND DRASTIC CHANGES IN THE
FOREIGN AND DOMESTIC POLICIES OF THIS COUNTRY

was the header on my campaign brochure. Jonn Christian served as campaign manager, and Harv Morgan took a leave of absence from his radio station to act as public relations advisor. We kicked off the campaign with a packed rally in Brown's Hall in Mill Valley, where jazz great Vince Guaraldi was the draw. After Guaraldi warmed up the audience, I gave my speech. In the middle of it there was a loud clap from backstage, and Blanche Dunphy, wife of the mayor of Sausalito, gasped audibly, thinking someone was shooting at me. It was only one of Guaraldi's side men dropping his instrument case as he packed up.

We were still struggling to get organized when Dr. King was shot. The following morning George Davis, Hitchcock's lawyer, called Christian and me to come to his office. With flowing silver hair and a staccato delivery, Davis was widely known as a criminal defense attorney, having defended Caryl Chessman, known as the Red Light Bandit, who was executed in 1960. After some discussion about the King case, Davis pointed to his bookshelf and remarked, "You know, I am the leading authority on hypnosis and the law."

Then he dropped a bombshell.

The lawyers for Clay Shaw, awaiting trial in New Orleans, had asked him to associate in the case. "The main witness against Shaw was hypnotized by the prosecution to help him recall details," Davis explained, alluding to Perry Russo. Knowing that I was close to Jim Garrison, he had a proposition for me. Introduce him to Garrison for a private meeting in which the DA would lay out his entire case against Shaw. "If I can be more convinced than I am now about Garrison's case," he said, "I might be of a mind to move into the case and, you know, help him out." I could hardly believe my ears. The only way Davis could help Garrison by joining the Shaw team would be to feed back information, which would be an egregious breach of ethics. Whatever he had in mind, it didn't sound right, so I let it pass. Davis capped the meeting by offering to become my campaign chairman, since he thought he could raise enough money to tide me over the primary. He never raised a cent.

"Money is the mother's milk of politics," observed Jesse Unruh, the Big Daddy of California politics, and it quickly became evident that I was in for a difficult weaning. Although it was before the era of million-dollar campaigns to pay for television blitzes, my late start, my lack of a political base and the overriding public interest in the Kennedy-versus-McCarthy contest resulted in a cash dribble. It was perhaps emblematic of how eclectic the campaign became that my largest single contributor was the legendary San Francisco madam, Sally Stanford, who had catered to the city's power elite. Bright and savvy, she knew instinctively that the Warren Report was a fable. After I gave her a presentation on the subject in her Pine Street mansion, Sally announced, "Bill, I want to contribute to your campaign, but first I have to go to my vault." With that, she reached down into her ample cleavage and pulled out five $100 bills. I immediately named her "vice chairlady" of the campaign.

In San Francisco, a tight union town, labor endorsements were vital. Harry Bridges, boss of the longshoremen, had already committed to Drath—a hangover, I was told, from previous years. As for the AFL-CIO, I was able to muster enough support to hold off Drath and obtain a "no endorsement." The Teamsters, however, grateful that I had helped

Jimmy Hoffa and written the article on farm labor, readily endorsed me. But memories were long, and the Teamsters did not endorse Bobby Kennedy even though by this time he had transformed himself from a hard-line hawk to a compassionate champion of the poor, hoisting the banner of Chavez's United Farm Workers.

With a virtually empty war chest, I had to forgo paid ads and create my own media spots. Harve Morgan booked me on a couple of radio talk shows in which the candidacy was mentioned, but on each occasion a Drath staffer called in demanding equal time. The Hearsts' *San Francisco Examiner* steered clear of the subject, but on the languid Sunday of May 5, I seized an opportunity at its rival, the *San Francisco Chronicle*. A reporter friend, Charlie Howe, was sitting in on the city editor's desk. I dropped in and took him across the alley to the M & M Bar, a newsman's hangout, for a quick drink, laying out some photographs on the bar.

Howe knew he was eyeing a grabby story. The photographs, taken by a press photographer in Dealey Plaza within minutes of the JFK assassination, showed three men being led away by shotgun-toting Dallas cops. They had been picked up behind the grassy knoll, but there was no record of who they were or why they were detained. The scowling man leading the trio had a thin face, jutting jaw, squinty eyes, and triangular nose. In juxtaposition I placed an artist's sketch of the suspect in the King murder. The sketch bore no resemblance to James Earl Ray, then being sought by the FBI as the "lone gunman." But it was strikingly similar to the Dealey Plaza suspect. "I'll run it," Howe said. "Should be able to give it good play." He did indeed.

When the *Chronicle* hit the streets that evening, its headline read, "STARTLING THEORY: KING KILLER DOUBLE." The two pictures bore the caption "Strange Parallel." The story said, "A former FBI agent yesterday raised the specter of a link between the assassinations of President Kennedy and Dr. Martin Luther King" with evidence strong enough to "warrant a Congressional investigation." I pointed out, the story elaborated, that in both assassinations a rifle with telescopic sight "was conveniently left at the crime scene," and that in both there was an abundance of similar physical evidence, including city maps with significant sites circled. "As you know," I was quoted, "the police use modus operandi files in any crime. Criminals tend to repeat certain things, have certain habits."

The story, which mentioned my candidacy, was a shot in the arm for the campaign. For days, the city buzzed with "strange parallels" talk. But in the end, the press coup turned out to be a final lunge. I had raised only $2,200, and it was gone. Drath conducted a poll that showed us running neck and neck, so he doubled his previous expenditure of $17,000, buying ads in the media and on buses and trolleys and festooning the town with signs. When the votes were tallied on the night of June 4, Drath had 41,000 to my 32,000. Not a bad showing, all things considered. The assassination issue had obviously resonated, but I had not been able to reach enough people in such a short time with so little money. Jesse Unruh was right.

Throughout the primary, Bobby Kennedy was asked by audiences whether he would reopen the investigation of his brother's death if elected. He hedged, saying he would not reopen the Warren Report, but remained silent on the question of whether he would take action on his own. RFK was a pragmatist, if anything, knowing that he had to control the Justice Department to launch a new probe. Privately, he gave every indication he would go for it. In 1967, he reportedly sent his former press secretary, Edwin O. Guthman, then a *Los Angeles Times* editor, to New Orleans to confer with Jim Garrison. In 1968, he left his campaign train in Oxnard, California, to personally check on a report that a telephone call originated there on the morning of November 22, 1963, warning of the impending assassination. Richard Lubic, an official in his California campaign, reached me at Garrison's office in April 1968 with news that the candidate intended to reopen the case after attaining the White House.

When RFK was cut down in the Ambassador Hotel, the murder of a candidate for federal office was not yet a federal crime. So primary jurisdiction was vested in the Los Angeles Police Department, with the FBI playing a secondary role under the civil rights statute. Due to the importance of the case, the LAPD assembled an elite squad, called Special Unit Senator (SUS), to control the probe. Then on July 1, only a few weeks after the shooting, George Davis called Christian, sounding excited. "I've cracked the case wide open," he declared, "and I need your help and Bill's." We rushed over to his office. He wanted Christian to deal with the media, and me to evaluate the story of a southern California preacher whom he had known for a long time, who was cloistered in a conference room. The preacher, Davis said, claimed to have encountered Sirhan Sirhan the day before the assassination under mysterious circumstances that smacked of accomplices. Upon recognizing Sirhan's photo in the newspaper the next day, the preacher had reported the encounter to the LAPD, which evinced little interest. Fearful that he knew too much, he fled north to the sanctuary of Davis's ranch. It was Davis's belief that the best life insurance his client could buy would be to go public with his story.

So Christian arranged to give his ex-colleagues at ABC an exclusive. The preacher would appear before their cameras at 10:30 the following morning, in plenty of time to meet the deadline for the evening news, which originated in New York. The floodlights were on when Davis, without the preacher, walked out to announce that the interview was canceled. He had finally reached the California attorney general, Tom Lynch, who had personally phoned LAPD Chief Tom Reddin. The police were on their way to interview the preacher; they had warned Davis that a judge had imposed a gag order prohibiting witnesses from making public statements.

As Christian and the ABC crew angrily trooped out the door, Davis beckoned to me. "Bill, see what you make of all this." He led the way to the conference room where, standing at the end of the table, was the object of all the fuss. "Bill, meet Jerry Owen." At fifty-five, Owen still exuded the physical strength of his boxing days. He stood well over six feet tall and weighed close to 250 pounds, a beefy, florid man with a roundish face dominated by a bulbous nose and darting blue eyes. His hair was dark and kinky, which had given rise to the nickname "Curly." He was outfitted in a brown business suit and wing-tip oxfords. His hands were like hams, his handshake crushing. He had his own church, he said, and was self-ordained.

I asked Owen to tell his story on tape, and he complied. Clutching the microphone with both hands, his eyebrows knitted in concentration, he launched into his narrative in a mesmeric voice. On the day before the assassination, he had left his Santa Ana ranch in his old Chevy pickup truck with a conspicuous chrome horse ornament on the hood. He was dressed in cowboy clothes. He was on his way to Oxnard, sixty miles up the coast from Los Angeles, where a friend boarded horses for him. He had a buyer for one and was going to bring it back. While stopped at a red light on Wilshire Boulevard in Los Angeles—he was taking the city route to buy boxing paraphernalia for a professional heavyweight—he picked up a young hitchhiker he would afterward recognize as Sirhan. The hood ornament prompted a conversation about horses. Sirhan said "he was an exercise boy at a race track, and talked about how he loved horses." Sirhan mentioned that he wanted to buy a lead pony for the track, and Owen offered that he had "a dandy up in Oxnard." As they drew near to the Ambassador Hotel, Sirhan asked, "Would it be all right if we stopped? I have a friend in the kitchen." Owen swung left on Catalina and pulled into a cul-de-sac at the rear of the hotel. When they resumed the trip, Sirhan told Owen that "if I could meet him at eleven o'clock on Sunset Boulevard, he would be able to purchase this horse for the sum of three hundred dollars."

At eleven that night, Owen pulled up at the designated location—a bowling alley—and Sirhan was there. Also present were a young man and woman Owen recognized as being with Sirhan on the street corner when he thumbed a ride earlier that day; they looked a bit like hippies to Owen. Sirhan handed Owen a $100 bill and apologized that he couldn't have the balance until the following morning. Owen put up at a hotel overnight. In the morning, which was election day, he was contacted by a different man in a flashy suit with another $100 installment and the message that he was to show up with the horse that night at eleven in the cul-de-sac at the rear of the Ambassador Hotel, at which time he would be paid the final $100. Owen told the man he couldn't make it because he had a preaching engagement at the Calvary Baptist Church in Oxnard that evening. He handed the man his calling card, telling him that when they had the money he would deliver the horse anywhere.

Owen capped his account by saying he spent the night in Oxnard after preaching, then heard about the RFK shooting on television when he stopped for lunch at a Los Angeles restaurant on his way home. He recognized newspaper photos of Sirhan as the hitchhiker and reported his experiences of the past two days to the LAPD. That was the basic hitchhiker story, which implied that Sirhan had accomplices and that Owen was to play some unwitting role by positioning his pickup and horse trailer at the rear of the Ambassador on election night. But the story was riddled with internal contradictions, and it didn't make much sense. Why would conspirators planning to shoot RFK if he won the primary lure Owen and his horse rig to the hotel? It was not the most likely of getaway vehicles. But that may have been the point. And the long-unemployed Sirhan had four $100 bills in his pocket when arrested.

"George, how long have you known Owen?" I asked Davis in a private moment.

"I've known him thirty years," the attorney replied, "and I'm inclined to believe what he says."

The following morning the LAPD arrived in the persons of Lieutenant Manuel Pena and Sergeant Enrique "Hank" Hernandez, who were ramrodding the SUS investigation. I ushered them up on the elevator to Davis's office. Both were bulky and glowering. They questioned Owen for two hours, trying to break down his story, but he stuck to it. Then they took Owen over to the San Francisco Police Department, where Hernandez, a qualified operator, questioned him on the polygraph. Hernandez phoned Davis to inform him that his client had abused the truth so badly that he "blew the box." Owen had concocted the story, he said, and that was it as far as the police were concerned. It was nothing more than a cheap publicity stunt.

I agreed with the LAPD that the story was largely fiction, but I disagreed entirely with dismissing it as a publicity ploy. Owen had not sought media attention and in fact had ducked it until Davis swayed him that he would be safer by getting the story out. My feeling was that the preacher spun his jeremiad to put an innocent face on a preexisting relationship with the accused assassin and included enough factual elements to make it convincing.

Christian and I decided to fire up our own probe, scraping together a modest slush fund. The first question was, Who is Jerry Owen? His true name was Oliver Brindley Owen, and he billed himself "The Walking Bible" because of his ability to recite from memory 31,173 verses from Scripture. He traded horses on the side and owned a piece of a club fighter named "Irish Rip" O'Reilly. In the 1930s he had been a sparring partner of heavyweight champion Max Baer and a Hollywood bit actor before a flash of divine inspiration sent him on the evangelical circuit. Owen sported a rap sheet, FBI number 4-261-906, which suggested that he was good with matches. On March 22, 1964, a warrant was issued in Tuscon, Arizona, for first-degree arson with the intent to defraud an insurance company in the burning of his own church building. Although he alibied that he was elsewhere at the time, a witness, Samuel Butler, testified that the preacher offered him $1,000 to light the fire. Owen was convicted of arson conspiracy and sentenced to eight to nineteen years in prison (the conviction was reversed in 1966 when Butler recanted his testimony in a death-bed statement). Los Angeles Police records listed similar torchings in Castro Valley, California, in 1939; Crystal Lake Park, Oregon, in 1945; Dallas, Texas, in 1947; Mount Washington, Kentucky, in 1947; and Ellicott City, Maryland, in 1951. Owen collected insurance settlements in several of the fires, but in the Maryland blaze his $16,000 claim was rejected on grounds of insurance fraud. "A witness observed Owen moving personal effects out of the house prior to the fire and then return them," the police reported. But the persistent preacher appealed and eventually was awarded $6,500.

Jim Rose, the repentant CIA flyboy who a year earlier had made the approach to the Russians in Mexico City, was the ideal candidate to make some inquiries since he was clean-cut and disarming. Posing as a recently discharged serviceman with strong anticommunist convictions, he talked with the pastor of the Calvary Baptist Church in Oxnard, one Reverend Medcalf, to determine if Owen had in fact preached there on election night. Medcalf stated he had taken over the church in mid-July after it had been shuttered for six months because the previous pastor had failed financially. No, he didn't know the Reverend Jerry Owen. In Hollywood, Rose learned that the bowling alley on Sunset where Owen said he had been met by Sirhan's friends the night before the election had long been closed and was now a broadcasting studio. But a registration card of the St. Moritz Hotel across the street verified that a J. C. Owen, giving the preacher's correct home address in Santa Ana, checked in at midnight. So we knew that Owen had stayed in Los Angeles that night, just as he told me, but lied about preaching in Oxnard on election night. So where was he when Kennedy was shot?

That poser was resolved when Christian talked with the Reverend Jonothan Perkins, an elderly minister that Owen told me had accompanied him to LAPD headquarters shortly after the assassination. Perkins was a long-standing friend of Owen, and for over twenty years he had been the personal secretary of Gerald L. K. Smith, a virulent anti-Semite who founded the Christian Nationalist Crusade. Perkins recounted that on election day Owen dropped by to see him, mentioning that a former exercise boy at a race track whom he had met hitchhiking was going to buy one of his horses for $400. The only reason he was hanging around Los Angeles, Owen said, was to complete the sale. He had the horse in a trailer and was to meet with the hitchhiker and some of his friends that night at the Ambassador Hotel.

The following morning Owen showed up again, this time in a dither. According to Perkins, Owen asserted that on election night he "went down there to meet him and pick up his other three hundred dollars — that was the night of the assassination. He waited around there, and when Sirhan didn't show up he went to a hotel here." Owen thought that Sirhan was really interested in buying the horse and would recontact him at the hotel. But now he recognized suspect Sirhan as the prospective buyer. "I waited for him," Owen told Perkins. "Man alive, they was just going to use me as a getaway, as a scapegoat. They would have gone four or five miles and shot me in a vacant lot." So *before* the assassination Owen had told his old friend about picking up the suspect. And he went on to claim he was at the rear entrance to the Ambassador with a horse on election night, later falsely telling me he was in Oxnard. Clearly, Owen was a fabulist of the first order.

But the SUS had slammed shut the book on Owen. When LAPD records were released to the State Archives a decade ago, there was an interview report by a police desk sergeant that a female private detective "has the name, mug shot, etc. of a young man who says he was with Sirhan when he attempted to purchase a horse from preacher." The report, dated July 13, 1968, a week after Pena and Hernandez returned from grilling Owen in San Francisco, was routed to Pena as the SUS point man. A line was drawn through the words "says he was," and the qualifier "may have been" substituted. With the same pen, Pena ordered, "No further invst. Sirhan not with Owen on 6/3/68 or any other time."

Upon delving into the backgrounds of the SUS pair, we found CIA connections. On November 13, 1967, more than six months before the RFK shooting, Fernando Faura of the *San Fernando Valley Times* covered a rollicking retirement party for Manny Pena at the Sportsmen's Lodge in Burbank. "Pena retired from the police force to advance his career," Faura wrote. "He has accepted a position with the Agency for International Development Office of the State Department. As a public safety advisor, he will train and advise foreign police forces in investigative and administrative matters." It is an open secret that the Office of Public Safety of the Agency for International Development (AID) has long served as a cover for the CIA's program of supplying advisors and instructors to national police and intelligence services in Latin America and Southeast Asia engaged in anticommunist operations; the curriculum included assassination techniques. FBI senior agent Roger

LaJeunesse, Jr., whom I had known in the Bureau, confided that Pena had left the LAPD for a "special training unit" at a CIA base in Virginia. In fact, Pena, with whom LaJeunesse often worked, had gone on tours of detached duty with the CIA under AID cover for over a decade. Only five months after the "retirement" shindig, Fernando Faura was walking down a corridor at LAPD headquarters when he spotted a familiar figure. As the reporter told it to me, the square face and fireplug frame seemed to belong to Manny Pena, but now he sported an expensive dark blue suit, handlebar mustache and heavy horn-rim glasses. "Manny?" Faura probed. "Hey, Manny, I damn near didn't recognize you with that disguise!" Pena sheepishly explained that the AID job was not quite what he expected, so he quit and resumed his duties with the LAPD.

We found out later that Hank Hernandez also went on detached duty as a CIA instructor. After retiring, he distributed an employment resume boasting that in 1963 he played a key role in "Unified Police Command" training for the Agency in Latin America. He functioned under AID cover, and was awarded a medal by the Venezuelan government, then concerned with Fidel Castro's "exportation" of the revolution. The CIA links of Pena and Hernandez raised the question of whether Langley was pushing buttons in the RFK investigation.

The CIA seems to have borrowed heavily from Los Angeles law enforcement. In 1964, I met one of their on-tap agents, although I didn't know it at the time. All I knew was that a former hospital patient of my wife, a nurse, introduced me to his brother, Hugh C. McDonald, a division commander in the Los Angeles County Sheriff's Department. McDonald, who was on temporary duty as Barry Goldwater's chief of security for the 1964 campaign, asked me if I wanted to join the team (I didn't). In 1965 he flew me in a sheriff's helicopter over the still-smoldering Watts section of Los Angeles after the riots. By 1968, when I was in Los Angeles authenticating the Zapruder film, he had retired from the sheriff's department and was selling Hughes helicopters to law enforcement. I called him to say I had the film; he had a projector in his office and invited me over. But to my surprise, he claimed that the backward head snap was not caused by a gunshot from the front but from a "jet propulsion" effect. He took me to dinner that night, spinning a story of how he had solved the JFK case. Acting on a tip, he had tracked down a professional hit man named Saul to a hotel in Madrid, Spain, where Saul confessed he had been the trigger man in Dealey Plaza. I asked McDonald what he was going to do about it, not really buying the story since it seemed so farfetched. He was going to pursue it in his own way, he replied rather cryptically. In 1975 he published a paperback book, *Appointment in Dallas,* which purported to be the "final solution" to the JFK murder, and it became a brisk seller. To my amazement, he confessed in the book that he had first met Saul at Langley and was, in fact, a CIA operative himself, having carried out a number of assignments in Europe. But when he killed Kennedy, McDonald wrote, Saul was not hired by the Agency but by a mysterious private cabal that paid him $50,000. It was a classic limited hangout, which conceded a CIA tie to the assassin but put him on someone else's payroll for the big hit. And it was, I knew, pure fiction. In 1968, McDonald told me he already had confronted Saul, at a Madrid hotel. In *Appointment in Dallas,* the confrontation took place in 1972 in a London hotel.

It was also the account of Sandy Serrano, a youthful RFK volunteer at the Ambassador on election night, that Pena and Hernandez strove mightily to discredit. Interviewed by Sander Vanocur on NBC within minutes of the shooting, Serrano described how she was sitting on the stairs of an emergency exit to escape the stifling heat of the Embassy Room, where a packed house awaited RFK's victory speech, when a young woman with a "funny nose," wearing a dress with polka dots, brushed past her and slipped through the door. She was accompanied by two short, swarthy young men. A short time later, after what sounded like backfires, the same woman and one of the men scurried back down the stairs, shouting, "We shot him! We shot him! We killed Kennedy!" The missing man, Serrano would say, was a dead ringer for Sirhan.

In his book *Special Unit Senator,* LAPD Chief of Detectives Robert Houghton recalled the dilemma the witness posed: "Manny Pena knew that as long as Miss Serrano stuck to her story, no amount of independent evidence would, in itself, serve to dispel the polka-dot-dress girl fever, which by now, in the press and in the public mind, reached a high point on the thermometer of intrigue." So Serrano was singled out for special treatment. First, Hernandez took Serrano out for an SUS-bought dinner. When wining and dining failed, he took her down to police headquarters and put her on the polygraph. The burly detective demanded to know when her "pack of mistruths" had gotten out of hand. The harsh intimidation got results. Sobbing, Serrano conceded that she had heard other witnesses talking at the police station after the shooting, and "maybe that's what I'm supposed to have seen." She was conceding the impossible, since she had described the incident on NBC before she and other witnesses were bundled off to the police station.

But the SUS wrote her off, and now only Vincent DiPierro remained to be dealt with. DiPierro, a waiter who had been in the pantry when the shooting broke out, gave police a statement that dovetailed with Serrano's. He said he noticed Sirhan lurking by a tray stacker only because "there was a very good-looking girl next to him." She had an odd nose and wore a "kind of lousy" polka-dot dress. "Together they were both smiling," DiPierro related. "As he got down he was smiling. In fact, the minute the first two shots were fired, he still had a very sick-looking smile on his face." Hernandez proferred DiPierro a carrot, suggesting that it was mistaken identity. In fact, the detective had someone in mind who had worn a polka-dot dress. She was a pretty co-ed named Valerie Schulte, who had presented herself to the police on just that possibility. But Schulte conspicuously had a broken leg covered by an ankle-to-waist cast, and at the moment Sirhan opened fire from the front, she was tagging along well in back of Kennedy. But DiPierro went along with the suggestion. "There was so much confusion that night," he explained. With that, Chief Houghton declared, "SUS closed the vexing case of the polka-dot-dress girl."

Not quite. On April 20, 1969, Vincent DiPierro, evidently regretting his turnabout, wrote KHJ radio reporter Art Kevin, whom I knew from his coverage of the Jim Garrison investigation, congratulating him on a series on the unanswered questions in the RFK case, including the Jerry Owen and polka-dot-dress girl angles. DiPierro stated that the segment on the polka-dot-dress girl was the "first real, true report" on the subject, and offered to help on "this controversial issue." It was several days before Kevin could drive out to the DiPierro residence. The doorbell was answered by his father, Angelo DiPierro, a maitre d' at the Ambassador, as Vincent stood in the background. DiPierro *père* said the FBI had come by and described how painstakingly agents and police had reconstructed events in the pantry. Almost pleadingly, he told Kevin to forget it, his son's life might be in danger. When Kevin pressed on, he yelled, "I know who you are. You run with those kooks, Bill Turner and Mark Lane." He shoved the door shut.

In early 1969, Sirhan Sirhan was put on trial for first-degree murder. His lead attorney, Grant Cooper, spurned our offer of help on the grounds that a conspiracy defense would make his client look like a contract killer. The prosecution's case was damningly simple: Sirhan had been caught in the act, and premeditation was demonstrated by the hand-scrawled entries in his notebooks (recovered from his home by the LAPD), such as "Robert F. Kennedy must be assassinated before 5 June '68." Cooper tried to spare Sirhan the death penalty by proving "diminished capacity." His star witness was Dr. Bernard Diamond, an expert from the University of California at Berkeley, who testified that the defendant was so susceptible to hypnotic suggestion that he could be made to climb the bars of his cell like a monkey. But in keeping with the no-conspiracy defense, Diamond did not propose that there was a hypnoprogrammer on the loose. Instead, he theorized that Sirhan was in a self-induced trance triggered by the hotel's lights and mirrors when he shot Kennedy, noting that he was "subject to bizarre, disassociated trances, in some of which he programmed himself to be the instrument of assassination." In fact, I thought, witnesses in the pantry reported to the press that Sirhan had exhibited symptoms of being in a trance state (dilated eyes, superhuman strength in resisting being overpowered), but the idea that it was self-induced seemed to be gratuitous. His background yielded no motive for him to want to hypnotize himself to kill the senator.

After a quiet trial, Sirhan was convicted. A sentence of death had hardly been pronounced when an independent ballistics examination found that two bullets fired in the pantry came from different guns. The criminalist who discovered this was William W. Harper, whose impeccable credentials derived from having testified at some three hundred trials around the country. A slight, sandy-haired man with a soft-spoken passion for justice, Harper had acquired a healthy skepticism about the work of the LAPD's crime lab chief, DeWayne Wolfer. As a public service, he studied Wolfer's findings in major cases, and in late 1970, after Sirhan's appeals were exhausted, gained access to two relatively unmutilated bullets that Wolfer had sworn were fired from Sirhan's revolver "to the exclusion of all other weapons in the world." The bullets, removed from Kennedy and injured newsman William Weisel, should have had identical distinctive markings. But Harper concluded that he could "find no individual characteristics in common between these two bullets." There was perforce a second gun.

The news stunned Los Angeles authorities. DA Joseph P. Busch announced that he would look into the matter. One of the first things DA investigators did was question Thane Eugene Cesar, an armed security guard who had been to the immediate right rear of Kennedy when the shooting erupted (in fact it was Cesar's clip-on bow tie that RFK grabbed in his right hand as he was shot). An employee of Lockheed Aircraft's "Skunk Works," which developed the CIA U-2 spy plane, Cesar was moonlighting for newly-founded Ace Security, which was hired by the hotel for crowd control. Cesar, it turned out, was a Cuban American who registered to vote with George Wallace's archconservative American Independent Party. Minutes after the shooting, Donald Schulman, a runner for CBS News who was in the pantry, went on the air: "A Caucasian gentleman [Sirhan] stepped out and fired three times; the security guard hit Kennedy all three times." Moments later, he modified this to say that Sirhan fired three times at Kennedy, hitting him all three times, and that the security guard fired back. The LAPD rejected Schulman's testimony as mistaken. But garbled as it was, which is not unusual for someone witnessing an unexpected and traumatic event, Schulman was consistent in his observation that the security guard fired a weapon. And the autopsy report of Coroner Thomas Naguchi corroborated that Kennedy was struck by three .22-caliber bullets, all in the back of his body. In fact, Naguchi concluded that, based on the powder tattooing, the fatal shot to the right rear of the head was fired point-blank from only one to three inches away. Since Sirhan stepped out in front of Kennedy, and, according to witnesses, never got his gun closer than one to three feet, simple geometry dictated that he could not have squeezed off the three shots that hit the senator. The second gun had to belong to someone very close to Kennedy at his right rear.

"Did you ever fire a shot?" DA investigators asked Cesar. "No," he replied, saying he drew his gun but got knocked down after the first shot and didn't see anything. He claimed he was carrying a .38 revolver but let slip that he might have shown another gun, his .22 revolver, to a police sergeant after the shooting. This contradicted an earlier statement that he had sold the weapon three months earlier. The investigators picked up on this discrepancy, but, as the transcript clearly reflected, their primary concern was whether any outsiders knew about it. We did, and on October 13, 1972, Christian called the man who had bought the gun from Cesar. His name was Jim Yoder, and he had worked with Cesar at Lockheed before retiring to Arkansas. Yoder disclosed that he purchased the gun on September 6, 1968—three months *after* the assassination—which was documented by a receipt Cesar gave him. Yes, Yoder said, the LAPD had called him, and he had given them the same information. Asked if he still had the gun, Yoder said no, it had been taken in a burglary about the time of the police call.

I recently talked with a man whose camera contained, in his words, "the only photographs of record of the assassination." At the time, Scott Enyart was a high school RFK enthusiast who was trailing along after his hero, snapping picture after picture. In the pantry, he was slightly behind the senator to his left, and when the shooting began, he snapped as fast as he could. As he left the pantry, two LAPD officers accosted him at gunpoint and seized his film. Later, he was told by Detective Dudley Varney of the SUS that his film would be developed and was needed as evidence in the Sirhan trial. The photos were not used at the trial, but Varney informed Enyart that the court had ordered all evidential materials sealed for twenty years. After the twenty years, Enyart formally requested that his photos be returned. First he was told that the State Archives couldn't find them, then that they had been burned. So Enyart filed a lawsuit, which finally came to trial in 1996; a jury awarded him $450,000. Curiously, during the trial the Los Angeles city attorney defending the suit announced that the photos had been found, misfiled, in Sacramento. But the courier retained by the State Archives to bring them to the Los Angeles courthouse claimed his briefcase containing the photos was stolen from the car he rented at the airport. Thus vanished the RFK version of the Zapruder film, which might have shown who shot him from behind.

But the presence of a second gunman became indisputable in 1974 after union official Paul Schrade, who was wounded in the pantry, filed a civil action to discover if a person or persons other than Sirhan were responsible for his injuries. Judge Robert A. Wenke ordered a panel of experts to refire Sirhan's weapon and compare the test bullets with those recovered from the victims. I was skeptical that a match would be made because .22-caliber bullets are not as susceptible to distinctive marks as larger caliber ones, which was why Mafia hit men favored them. As it turned out, all the panel could determine from the lands and grooves was that the pantry bullets came from the same model of gun as Sirhan's, rather than his particular one. The panel's report led off with a confusing statement that there was "no substantive or demonstrable evidence to indicate that more than one gun was used." Although it went on to say there was no evidence that there wasn't a second gun either, the press jumped the gun with such headlines as "PANEL SAYS ONLY ONE GUN."

At this point, one of Schrade's attorneys, Vincent Bugliosi, reduced the complexities to simple arithmetic. The famed prosecutor of the murderous Manson Family and author of *Helter Skelter*, Bugliosi took note of how the LAPD crime lab had accounted for eight bullets, which was the capacity of Sirhan's revolver. Seven were recovered from the victims after they had been taken to hospitals, and the eighth had been lost in the ceiling interspace. But Bugliosi remembered seeing an Associated Press wirephoto showing two policemen inspecting a hole in a door frame just outside the pantry. A ninth bullet? The attorney made the rounds of the precinct stations and learned that the policemen were Sergeants Robert Rozzi and Charles Wright. Rossi signed a statement for Bugliosi in which he said that the object in the hole "appeared to be a small-caliber bullet." Over the phone, Wright was positive it was a bullet, but before Bugliosi could get it in writing, the LAPD stepped in and muzzled him. Undaunted, Bugliosi secured statements from Coroner Naguchi and hotel personnel that they had observed two bullet holes in the center post of the pantry's swinging doors, through which Kennedy had passed, raising the count to eleven. The LAPD countered that the holes actually were dents caused by serving carts, but Bugliosi put the lie to that by determining that the carts were two feet too low and had no protrusions.

If there was even a sliver of doubt that the LAPD was engaged in a cover-up, it was dispelled in late 1976 when Bugliosi was on a lecture tour. He was approached by a college police science professor, William A. Bailey, who was an FBI agent at the time of the shooting. On June 5, 1968, Bailey said, he was assigned to lead a three-man team of agents to carefully examine the crime scene. He verified FBI photos that had been recently released. One of them showed two circled holes in the center post. "I noted at least two (2) small-caliber bullet holes in the center post of the two doors leading from the preparation room (pantry)," he deposed. "There was no question in any of our minds as to the fact that they were bullet holes and were not caused by food carts." Other FBI photos revealed two additional circled holes in the wall to the left of the doors, which brought the bullet tally to thirteen. As Bugliosi told the media, "The time has come for us to start looking for the members of the firing squad that night."

Yet Chief of Police Daryl Gates kept insisting that there was nothing new in the case. To snuff out this pretention, in 1982 we were able to finance an acoustical analysis of the sounds in the pantry that night as captured by three media tapes: one by radio reporter Andrew West of the Mutual Broadcasting System, who had followed Kennedy into the pantry; another from an ABC open mike on the nearby stage where RFK had given his victory speech; and a third by radio reporter Jeff Brant. The idea was to distinguish the sounds of gunshots from all other noises. The analysis was conducted by Dr. Michael H. L. Hecker, a top forensic acoustics expert who had analyzed the gaps in the Nixon tapes. On a target range, I fired a .22-caliber revolver as my own tape rolled, then handed the tape to Hecker at the prestigious Stanford Research Institute laboratory in Menlo Park, California, as a gunfire exemplar. Bugliosi and I watched, fascinated, as the printout from Hecker's instruments identified shot after shot, well surpassing eight. Hecker furnished an affidavit stating, "On the basis of auditory, oscillographic and spectrographic analysis of these recordings, it is my opinion, to a reasonable degree of scientific certainty, that no fewer than 10 (ten) gunshots are ascertainable following the conclusion of the Senator's victory speech until after the time Sirhan was disarmed."

By this time Jerry Owen had come back on stage as at least a material witness. It happened by sheer chance shortly after the Sirhan trial when the SUS inadvertently released a classified report along with an unclassified document. On New Year's Eve 1968, Los Angeles County sheriff's deputies arrested seventeen-year-old John Chris Weatherly, who tried to barter his way out of an auto theft charge by supplying a tip on the RFK assassination. According to the deputies' report, the youth had been told by a Santa Ana stable owner named Bill Powers and another cowboy that a preacher and Sirhan Sirhan had borrowed Powers's pickup truck "to take a horse to Los Angeles for sale the day of Kennedy's murder; that when the preacher returned, Sirhan was not with him, but he still had the horse, said he couldn't sell it in L.A." The report quoted Weatherly as saying that the preacher wanted Senator Kennedy killed because if the war was stopped, "the Vietnamese would come to this country via Honolulu or Hawaii, and God would get angry and cause a tidal wave."

The preacher was no doubt Jerry Owen, whose ranch was a short distance down the dry bed of the Santa Ana River from Powers's stables. Christian talked with Powers, who was a cowboy straight out of the Marlboro ads: rawboned, laconic and thoroughly believable. He said that Owen often bought bundles of hay for his horses from him. The preacher also had bought an old pickup truck of his, but, being short of cash, still owed $300 on it. A day of two before the election, Powers went on, Owen drove up to the stables in a luxurious Lincoln Continental and pulled out a fat roll of $1,000 bills. "I'll pay you for that truck," Owen announced, peeling off one of the bills. The preacher was in an expansive mood, Powers related, and introduced him to two passengers: a huge black man, who talked about his days as a boxer, and a diminutive young man in the back seat who said nothing. On a previous occasion, Powers had seen the young man riding a horse on the riverbed with the preacher. When he saw Sirhan's picture in the newspapers a few days later, Powers thought he recognized him as the backseat passenger. But the cowboy didn't want to report the sighting because he feared the preacher. "He can have you bumped off," Powers said. "He wouldn't just think about it—he'd do it. And then he'd say a little prayer."

There the matter rested until 1975, when a civil trial began in Department 32 of the Los Angeles Superior Court. The plaintiff was Jerry Owen, who had sued KCOP-TV for breach of contract and defamation of character after it canceled his new televangelical program "The Walking Bible." The cancellation came after Christian, seeking to trace large amounts of money Owen was spending on the show, called the station's attention to his curious background in the RFK case. As the trial loomed, we urged KCOP to retain Vincent Bugliosi, who had become absorbed with our investigative file while representing Paul Schrade, to put on an affirmative defense; that is, to prove that Owen was in fact involved in the RFK assassination. Bugliosi tried to subpoena John Chris Weatherly and another witness at Powers's stables, but they had skipped town out of fear for their lives after someone shot at Weatherly in the driveway of his residence. But the attorney managed to persuade a balky Bill Powers to take the stand. The cowboy testified about the preacher's arrival at the stables shortly before the election in a newly acquired luxury car, about his flashing a thick roll of $1,000 bills—"It was no Montana bankroll," Powers insisted, referring to the con-artist trick of wrapping a large banknote around small ones—and about the quiet man in the back seat he believed was Sirhan.

I was intrigued with the identity of a character witness Owen proposed to call. Her name was Gail Aiken, and she was one of the most devoted members of the preacher's flock. A year earlier I had researched an article on the May 15, 1972, shooting of Governor George Wallace at a Maryland shopping mall by Arthur Bremer, another "loner." The research raised so many unanswered questions—for instance, Bremer's finances and links with "Jesus People"—that I hoped the case would be reopened (the article was about to be published in an anthology, *Government by Gunplay*). As in the RFK shooting, the timing was exquisite: Wallace was taken out of the presidential race when the polls reflected that if he ran as an independent that November, he would siphon off sufficient votes from Richard Nixon to pull the Democratic nominee dead even. According to White House counsel Charles Colson, Nixon became agitated at news of the shooting and "voiced immediate concern that the assassin [sic] might have ties to the Republican Party, or even worse, the President's re-election committee." Nixon was plainly concerned about the exposure of dirty deeds the committee had sponsored, which would happen three weeks later when its Watergate team was caught. Was it more than coincidence that Gail Aiken was Bremer's older sibling, which I had learned when I talked with their father? On cross-examination, Bugliosi braced Owen, "Do you know Arthur Bremer's sister?" The preacher seemed startled that the cat was out of the bag. He hemmed and hawed, then gudgingly admitted he knew a Gail Aiken. Not surprisingly, Aiken was spirited back to Miami before Bugliosi could call her as a hostile witness and pry into whether there was a relationship between Owen and her brother.

The trial reached its climax when Owen's attorney tried to discredit Powers's identification of Sirhan as the silent man in the rear seat of the Lincoln. For some reason, he didn't use the hulking, black ex-boxer named Johnny Gray who also was a passenger that day at the stables. Instead, he brought on Gray's mulatto son, Jackie Gray, to testify that it was he, not Sirhan, who was in the rear seat (later his sister, Brenda, would tell us that Owen had dyed Jackie's sandy hair jet-black to match that of Sirhan). But Bugliosi elicited from young Gray that he was only thirteen at the time—Sirhan was twenty-three—and that his sole visit to the stables had occurred months earlier. Bugliosi noticed that he was of limited mental capacity but at the same time, in his simplicity, incapable of invention, and questioned him gently.

Yes, Jackie Gray said, his father had frequently mentioned Sirhan.

"He told you that he knows Sirhan very well, is that correct?" Bugliosi queried.

Yes, Gray responded.

"Where did he tell you he first met him?"

Without hesitation, Gray answered, "Through Mr. Owen."

Owen's attorney shot to his feet, frantically trying to impeach his own witness. But Judge Jack A. Crickard orally tested young Gray and found him competent.

"Did you hear Reverend Owen talk about Sirhan many times?" Bugliosi continued.

Yes, Gray acknowledged, Owen mentioned buying Sirhan clothes and giving him money.

The attorney remembered that the SUS chart of Sirhan's whereabouts in the period preceding the assassination had a two-month gap. Since there seemed to have been some kind of custodial relationship, Bugliosi flashed onto something he had seen in our investigative file— the possibility that Sirhan was a real-life Manchurian Candidate.

"Did you ever hear your father or Reverend Owen say anything about Sirhan being in a trance?" Bugliosi asked.

Young Gray replied, "This is in a room to hisself [sic], in a room that he always been in, in a room that some of the things he is doing is wrong."

This prompted Bugliosi to recall that Dr. Diamond had testified that incriminating passages in Sirhan's notebook, such as "RFK must die," had been scrawled while in a trance.

"Did you ever hear them say that sometimes Sirhan would do things and not know that he did them?" Bugliosi probed.

"Right," Jackie Gray replied matter-of-factly.

Judge Crickard was obviously annoyed that a surmounting criminal case had been brought into a civil courtroom and awarded Owen an amount barely sufficient to pay his lawyers' fees. The jurist was correct: the RFK case belonged in the hands of a special prosecutor and grand jury. But the Los Angeles criminal justice establishment had made its decision with injudicious haste and was not about to reconsider. The one hope had lain at the state level, with Chief Deputy Attorney General Charles A. O'Brien. The attorney general is charged with taking over a case when local law enforcement has failed, and we had thoroughly briefed O'Brien on what we had found out. In 1970 the pugnacious Irishman had urged his boss, Tom Lynch, to step in, saying, "Tom, I think we should go for a special prosecutor to investigate the Kennedy case." Lynch, who was about to retire, responded, "Charlie, you can do anything you want after you're elected." O'Brien, a Democrat, ran for attorney general that year against Republican Evelle Younger, an ex-FBI agent. He lost in a photo finish, and the case stayed closed.

But the Manchurian Candidate file remained open. Richard Condon's chilling novel of that name, made into a motion picture starring Frank Sinatra, was based on Soviet and CIA experimentation carried out during the Korean War in hypnoprogramming a subject to kill. There was, in fact, an authentic case history: in Denmark in 1952 an ex-convict named Bjorn Nielsen hypnoprogrammed a pliable former cellmate to rob banks and shoot anyone who resisted. To override his partner's natural reluctance to kill, Nielsen implanted in his mind a high moral purpose: the money was to be used to unify all Scandinavia.

When the partner was finally apprehended after fatally shooting a teller, he could remember nothing. Nielsen had induced an amnesiac block. It took a prison psychiatrist nineteen months to unlock his mind and unmask Nielsen. The partner was freed, and Nielsen was convicted of robbery and murder.

On September 10, 1972, I visited Sirhan in San Quentin Prison as an investigator for Roger Hansen, his attorney at the time, who was drawing up an appeal based on the ballistics evidence that the fatal bullet could not be matched to Sirhan's gun. His eyes were soft and doelike, set under bushy, arched eyebrows. He was bright and personable, not at all the plastic figure that had emerged from the news coverage. He had come to the United States to continue college studies in political science but somehow got the idea that he wanted to be a jockey. Horses could have been the nexus with Jerry Owen, but he couldn't remember a preacher of that name or a horse deal. When I asked him about election night at the Ambassador Hotel, his face took on a vague look. He recalled going to the hotel, but not necessarily because Kennedy would be there. The night was a jumble of images. There was a girl in a polka-dot dress at a silver coffee urn. "I met the girl and had coffee with her," he told me. "She wanted heavy on the cream and sugar. After that I don't remember a thing until they pounced on me in that pantry."

Sirhan could have picked up the polka-dot-dress girl imagery from news reports, and his claim of amnesia was self-serving. But the indications mounted that he was a hypnoprogrammed decoy. On August 14, 1975, I interviewed Dr. Eduard Simson-Kallas at his home in Monterey, California, where he was in private practice after being chief of San Quentin Prison's psychological-testing program. On the walls of his study were diplomas from Heidelberg University, Stanford and other prestigious schools, as well as professional honors plaques, including fellowships in the British Royal Society of Health and the American Society for Clinical Hypnosis. After Sirhan entered San Quentin in 1969, Simson examined him for a total of thirty-five hours. Due to his European training, Simson was well aware of the criminal potential of hypnosis, and the more he probed the inmate's mind, the more he became convinced he had been hypnoprogrammed to shoot RFK. The high moral purpose implanted to motivate Sirhan, the doctor thought, was the righteousness of the Arab side in the conflict with Israel. Sirhan had recited for Simson the same story he gave me: after meeting the polka-dot-dress girl who wanted coffee "heavy on the cream and sugar," he blanked out until being wrestled into submission. Simson pointed out that if Sirhan was hypnoprogrammed, the girl could have been, by prearrangement, the triggering mechanism—the Queen of Hearts in *The Manchurian Candidate*. "You can be programmed that if you meet a certain person or see something specific, then you go into a trance," he elucidated. What about Dr. Diamond's trial testimony that Sirhan was easily programmable but induced himself at the hotel? "That was the psychiatric blunder of the century," Simson scoffed. He insisted that it is utterly impossible for a person to place himself in such a deep trance that he sustains an amnesiac block. Can he be deprogrammed? I asked. Simson said that the secret could be unlocked once rapport had been established, followed by numerous hypnotic sessions. In fact, he felt he had made substantial progress with Sirhan. "If I had been allowed to spend as much time with him as necessary," Simson declared, "I would have found out something." But Associate Warden James W. L. Park cut him off on the curious ground that he "appears to be making a career out of Sirhan." Simson, who had worked at the prison for six years without being restricted before, handed in his resignation. "A medical doctor spends as much time with a patient as the disease demands," Simson remonstrated. "So does a psychologist."

All doubt about the legitimacy of the Manchurian Candidate hypothesis was eliminated in a dramatically graphic way on March 17, 1976, when I visited Dr. Herbert Spiegel in his uptown Manhattan office. A professor at Columbia University Medical School, Spiegel ranks in the top echelon of American psychiatry and is a preeminent authority on hypnosis. I was attracted to Spiegel because he had pioneered the Hypnotic Induction Profile, which graded the susceptibility of a person from 0 to 5 by recognizing a "clinically identifiable configuration of personality traits." He had studied the psychiatric reports on Sirhan, emphatically rejecting Dr. Diamond's theory of automatic induction and designating him a Grade 5, which placed him in the 5 to 10 percent of the general population most susceptible to hypnosis. The doctor screened for me a videotape he had made, which showed the hypnoprogramming process live and unrehearsed. It had been taped in 1967 for NBC television, narrated by anchorman Frank McGee as part of the network's smear of Jim Garrison by demonstrating that he used hypnosis to plant a conspiracy fiction in the mind of Perry Russo, the star witness against Clay Shaw. But it proved nothing of the kind and was cut from the program.

What the videotape really showed was the making of a Manchurian Candidate. The subject was a forty-year-old New York businessman Spiegel had rated a Grade 5, who held liberal political views and had once marched in a civil rights parade. After a brief warm-up session, Spiegel achieves a quick induction. "Try to open your eyes; you can't," he tells the subject, whose eyelids quiver but remain shut. The doctor confides that there is a communist plot aimed at controlling television and paving the way for a takeover. "You will alert the networks to it," he instructs. Then he shifts the subject from the formal or deep trance to the posthypnotic state, where his eyes are open and he appears normal. At this point, Spiegel explains to McGee that the subject is in the grip of the "compulsive triad": he has no memory of having been under hypnosis; he experiences a compulsive need to conform to the signal given under hypnosis; and he resorts to rationalization to conform to the instructions of this signal.

Glaring accusingly at McGee, the subject launches into an "exposé" of the communist threat to the networks. He talks about dupes in the media and how they are brainwashing the entire nation. "I have a friend in the media," he says, "but friendship should stop when the nation is in peril." The rationalization has set in. Spiegel snaps his fingers one, two, three, reinstating the formal trance. With his eyes closed, the subject persists in the same argument about communist penetration of the media, giving an adopted name as the ringleader. McGee argues forcefully against the subject, and as the pressure builds, the subject slips into deepening paranoiac depression. Spiegel snaps him out of the trance. The subject can't remember a thing. When the videotape is played back for him, his face mirrors incredulity as he spouts Birch Society rhetoric.

"I can't conceive of myself saying those things," he protests, "because I don't think that way."

I asked Spiegel, after he had switched on the lights, "If you had stuck a gun in the subject's hand and instructed him to shoot McGee, what would he have done?"

"Ah, the ultimate question," Spiegel responded. "I'm afraid he might have shot him."

It was Dr. Spiegel who pointed us in the direction of a possible suspect as Sirhan's hypnoprogrammer. Anything mentioned in the presence of a subject under hypnosis is automatically etched into his mind, Spiegel advised, especially if it comes from the hypnotist. And it might flow out at any time. This brought us back to Sirhan's notebooks containing his "automatic writing," the ones from which his prosecutors had excerpted "Robert F. Kennedy must be assassinated before 5 June '68" as proof of premeditation. But the notebooks also had entries such as "please pay to the order of Sirhan" that implied money had been proferred and references to a Corona horse-breeding ranch and its part owner, actor Desi Arnaz, where he had once been a hand, and whose boss was a member of the New Jersey Mafia.

But the one that stuck out was "Salvo Di Di Salvo Die S Salvo." It obviously alluded to the notorious Boston Strangler, Albert Di Salvo. When I had talked with Sirhan in San Quentin, he insisted that he had no idea who Di Salvo was. If that was true—the Boston Strangler case was some years earlier—it stood to reason he had heard the name while in a trance. It so happened that the Di Salvo murders had been cracked by the use of hypnosis, and the hypnotist was a Dr. William Joseph Bryan, Jr., who had an office on the Sunset Strip of Los Angeles. An imposing man with a wrestler's girth, Bryan billed himself as "probably the leading expert in the world" on the use of hypnosis in criminal law, and boasted about being called into baffling cases by law enforcement agencies, including the LAPD. The Boston Strangler was his tour de force, and he mentioned it at every opportunity.

But there was a flip side to Bryan. During the Korean War he put his hypnosis skills to use as, in his words, "chief of all medical survival training for the United States Air Force, which meant the brainwashing section." After the war he reportedly became a CIA consultant in their experimentation with mind control and behavior modification, called the MK-ULTRA program. In 1969, the California Board of Medical Examiners found him guilty of sexually assaulting women patients who submitted under hypnosis, and he was placed on probation for five years. Although a libertine, Bryan was a Bible-thumping fundamentalist preacher who traveled the same southern California church circuit as Jerry Owen. He claimed to be a descendent of the fiery orator William Jennings Bryan, who opposed the teaching of evolution in the landmark 1920s Scopes "monkey trial" in Tennessee.

It was Bryan's voracious eroticism that brought him into sharper focus as Sirhan's programmer. Following his sudden death in Las Vegas in the spring of 1977, two Beverly Hills call girls got in touch with us through an intermediary, saying they had been "servicing" Bryan an average of twice a week for four years and knew quite a bit about him. As an FBI agent, I had interviewed a number of prostitutes and found them to be as credible as other members of society. The girls, who gave their names as Janice and Diane, were usually together at the sessions with Bryan, who they called "Doc." At the outset of their relationship, Doc instructed them to dial an unlisted number at his office. If someone else answered, they were to say they were with "the Company" and they would be put through to him. He repeatedly confided that not only was he a CIA agent but that he was involved in "top-secret projects." During the last year of his life, Janice and Diane continued, Doc became deeply depressed because his paramour had run off with another man and was strung out on drugs. To relieve his depression, they frequently stroked his enormous ego by getting him to "talk about all the famous people you've hypnotized." As if by rote, Doc would begin with his feat of deprogramming Albert Di Salvo for attorney F. Lee Bailey, then brag that he had hypnotized Sirhan Sirhan. Janice and Diane didn't attach much significance to the Sirhan angle because Doc had told them many times that he "worked with the LAPD" on murder cases. What they didn't know was that Bryan had absolutely no contact with Sirhan *after* the assassination.

By this time I felt we had put together a convincing storyboard for conspiracy. The number of bullets fired eclipsed the capacity of Sirhan's revolver, and he had had no opportunity to reload. Geometrically, it was impossible for Sirhan to have fired the lethal shot, which was point-blank from the rear. The portraiture of Sirhan as a Manchurian Candidate was sharp. And Jerry Owen's relationship with Sirhan prefigured the assassination, as did Bryan's. But the public retained the original holograph of Sirhan caught dead to rights in the pantry with a smoking gun in his hand, and, unlike the JFK affair, no spate of literature had presented the case for conspiracy. Not one solid book. The void seemed to fill when Random House commissioned Jonn Christian and me to produce a book unsubtly titled *The Assassination of Robert F. Kennedy: The Conspiracy and Coverup*. It was the personal project of the firm's editorial director, Jason Epstein, who was impressed with Vincent Bugliosi's involvement. When I completed the manuscript, it was closely vetted for libel by Random House lawyers, and I spent countless hours documenting a defense in truth. "I know this is a pain, but it will be worth it when we're sitting in a courtroom a year from now," Epstein consoled. He was delighted with the literary content of the book. "I hope you're as pleased as we are with the way it turned out," he wrote Bugliosi shortly before publication in October 1978. "The jacket looks great, but more important is the tough case that is made between the covers." There was a first printing of 20,000, an unusually high number. Random House took out ads, the reviews were generally favorable, and I went on "The Merv Griffin Show" to thump the book. Bugliosi called from New York to say that the book was on prominent display in all the bookstores and that all signs pointed to lively sales. He should know, I thought; his *Helter-Skelter* was a runaway best-seller.

But after this initial burst of enthusiasm, Random House fell silent. Calls to Jason Epstein went unanswered. Bookstore shelves went unfilled. Anyone trying to order copies from the publisher were told the book was "forced out of stock." As for paperback rights, Random House at first contended the rights were unsold because there was no interest, then admitted that they had embargoed the rights—an egregious breach of contract—because a man linked to organized crime threatened a lawsuit. His name was Harold Jameson, and he possessed a long rap sheet under FBI Number 799 431. He had been interviewed by the House Select Committee on Assassinations, which was not looking into the RFK case, due to what Chief Counsel G. Robert Blakey termed "a troubling Dallas-Los Angeles parallel." We had reported that parallel: Jameson had been detained by sheriff's deputies at Dealey Plaza moments after John Kennedy was shot, and he was also at a Los Angeles hotel not far from the Ambassador when Robert Kennedy was shot. In fact, he had been questioned by the LAPD following the RFK shooting, which was recounted by Chief Robert Houghton in *Special Unit Senator*, also published by Random House. "In addition to his Mafia and oil contacts," Houghton stated, "he was friendly with 'far-right' industrialists and political leaders of the [Texas] area." What we had added was information from Roger LaJeunesse, who supervised the FBI's investigation, that linked Jameson with Owen through one of those oil contacts. I had gone over all of this with the Random House law trust, and Jameson's threat had been anticipated. I could not imagine that a mighty publishing house with an ironclad defense in truth would cave in to a mobster, but whatever power had supervened, it was over Epstein's head. "I don't want to talk about it," he told Betsy Langman, the writer friend who had called his attention to our literary project to begin with. Random House continued to ignore our entreaties. On December 15, 1984, Bugliosi wrote the firm's then-president, Robert Bernstein, seeking his intervention in view of "the ongoing inability and/or unwillingness of other Random House officials to properly address this matter," emphasizing the question of suppression in "withdrawing the Turner-Christian book from circulation." No response.

After *The Assassination of Robert F. Kennedy* disappeared from the book-stores, those copies that had already been purchased became much sought after. Library shelves were pilfered, and an underground churned out photocopies. The demand reached the point that a copy in mint condition resold for as much as $250.

In May 1983, there was a second opportunity to bring the case to national attention. ABC's highly rated documentary television program "20-20" became interested, based on *The Assassination of Robert F. Kennedy* and Dr. Hecker's audiotape analysis that no fewer than ten shots were fired. ABC flew Bugliosi and me to New York for two days of sifting and sorting the evidence with producer Ab Westin. Satisfied, Westin was set to go. But ABC Vice President David Burke, an old Kennedy family retainer, and another VP blackballed the project, and it was abandoned.

So RFK remains the forgotten assassination. That may change if Sirhan's current attorney, Lawrence Teeter, succeeds in his quest for an evidentiary hearing on grounds that too many bullets were fired and his client was a Manchurian Candidate. On his witness list is Dr. Herbert Spiegel, the hypnoprogramming expert. To paraphrase Vincent Bugliosi, the time is overdue to look for the members of the firing squad that night. And to find out who paid for the bullets.

12

ESCAPE FROM THE CIA

On August 18, 1971, at 6:35 P.M. a helicopter swooped down from the misty sky over Santa Marta Acatitla Prison outside Mexico City. Its skids barely touched the ground in an interior courtyard as two inmates hurriedly climbed aboard. Then it lifted over the thirty-foot wall in plain sight of the tower guards who, seeing that it was painted in the colors of the attorney general of Mexico, didn't fire a shot. The following morning Warren Hinckle, the quondam editor of *Ramparts*, called me, an edge of excitement in his voice.

"Bill, Joel's escaped. He made it out by helicopter. Judy will let us know when he makes it across the border and we can meet with him."

Joel was Joel David Kaplan, a nephew of Jacob M. "Jack" Kaplan, the New York sugar baron, whose Kaplan Fund had been exposed in 1965 as a CIA conduit. Judy was his sister, Judy Kaplan Dowis, an heiress to the Kaplan family fortune, from whom he was estranged. She had been trying to spring Joel from prison ever since he had been convicted of the 1961 murder of a business associate in Mexico. As newspaper banners proclaimed it "The Jailbreak of the Century," we anxiously awaited the "go" call from Judy, with whom we had been in touch on previous escape schemes. Her determination was fueled by a belief that Uncle Jack (the "old skinflint") was in some fashion responsible for Joel's plight. All Warren and I knew was that, after foraging through the dense jungle of the Kaplan case for four years, we had sufficient bits and pieces to suspect that Joel had been framed and that the CIA and Cuba were among the players. But we needed Joel to fill in the details.

From the start, as might be expected with intelligence matters, it was a wilderness of mirrors. The story began during the course of my clandestine meeting in Grand Central Station in 1967 with Jack Kaplan's accountant, Albert Arbor, when he mentioned, almost as a social note, that there was a black-sheep nephew doing time in a Mexico City penitentiary for killing a partner. In view of the intrigue that swirled around Jack Kaplan, I doubted that this was your basic axe murder, and I flew down to the Aztecan capital. At the time, Joel was lodged in Lecumberri Prison, which rose like a medieval castle in the heart of a slum district, pending his appeal to the country's highest court. Posing as a Kaplan relative, I was admitted uncritically by a warden more fixed on my comely female companion than my credentials. As I memoed Hinckle:

> Inside the prison . . . a mariachi band strolled aimlessly while prisoners proudly displayed arts and crafts they had produced for outside sale. Joel was brought in . . . we had fifteen minutes, with a guard sitting a few feet away in apparent disinterest. Joel was pale and gaunt, with a saffron tinge resulting from a case of hepatitis. His handshake was limp and clammy, and he seemed to possess the edginess of a man waiting for the other shoe to fall. His remarks were cryptic, to say the least. He just looked blank when I asked him if he were a CIA agent. He claimed his partner wasn't really dead. He kept mentioning Havana, saying I'd get some answers there. He said he'd been framed, but seemed reluctant to say who framed him. "Somebody else's money was involved," he kept repeating. I asked whose money. The guard shrugged a halt to the interview, and Joel was led away.

Admittedly, he didn't want to say anything that might jeopardize his appeal.

So Hinckle and I delved into the background of the Kaplan affair. The family had been making money in the Caribbean for a long time through their ownership of Southwestern Sugar & Molasses, which had operations throughout the region. In the late 1920s, Joel's father, A. I. Kaplan, who founded the company, had a bitter falling out with his brother, Jack Kaplan, over running their lucrative Cuban molasses business. The family feud left A. I. broke and Jack in control of Southwestern and the Kaplan Fund. In 1957, as A. I. lay dying, Jack sealed his coup by reducing young Joel to a figurehead vice president of the firm, no more than a salaried employee. The battle line was drawn.

In truth, the wizened Jack and the spindly Joel looked at the company and the world through vastly different filters. Jack was a sugar king who thrived in a cutthroat business, where success hinged on fractions of a cent a pound. He was proud of his philanthropies on behalf of Brandeis University and the New School and his support of such liberal politicians as Hubert Humphrey and Chester Bowles. By the time that Castro came to power, however, Jack and his Kaplan Fund were in deep trouble. The IRS alleged that Jack used the fund as his "alter ego," manipulating stocks under its shelter for personal gain, and recommended that a large sum of back taxes be levied and the foundation's tax-exempt status be revoked.

At this bleak juncture, the CIA came to Jack's rescue, dropping the "national security" curtain over the fund in reciprocation for services rendered. Not only had Jack allowed the Agency to use the fund as a conduit, he had gone on a mission for which he was uniquely qualified. In late 1959, Cuba had begun shipping a large tonnage of sugar to Russia, which threatened to lead to economic dependence. So it sent Jack as an envoy to Havana with a proposal to monopolize Cuban sugar exports at a price so sweet only a communist would turn it down. Had Castro accepted, it would have been a signal that he was "safe" to deal with. But he didn't. Jack returned with a sharply critical report that contributed to the CIA's growing conviction that Castro was traveling irreversibly down a socialist path. He agreed with the U.S. decision to end all dealing with the "untrustworthy" Castro even though it meant the loss of his Cuban sugar facilities, at least temporarily. Confident that before long the Castro government would collapse or be overthrown, Jack transplanted the operations to an interim location in the Dominican Republic. It was no coincidence that the Dominican Republic was the recipient of the lion's share of CIA monies piped through the Kaplan Fund to build "democratic left" bulwarks against communist and rudely anti-American power groups.

As for Joel, his beliefs drifted skittishly towards the left. He had joined Southwestern Sugar & Molasses as a fuzz-cheeked youth shortly after World War II, hedgehopping around Central and South America overseeing the family business. It was the plight of the workers toiling in the company sugar fields and mills that aroused his progressive leanings. Then he met a politically opposite but fellow playboy. Half Cuban and half Puerto Rican, he was a darkly handsome conniver named Luis Vidal, Jr., who happened to be the godson of Generalissimo Rafael Trujillo, the sadistic dictator of the Dominican Republic. Vidal's father moved in select circles in Washington, being Trujillo's personal business agent in the United States. Joel would later recall, "The old man had clear access to the White House—all the way up to Ike himself." Vain to the core, Vidal *fils* liked to boast that he was related, alternatively, to Jacqueline Bouvier (Kennedy), author and playright Gore Vidal, and the wealthy Gore political family from Tennessee.

He presided over a recondite entity called the Paint Company of America, which, despite its pretentious name, could not be found in the standard business directories. It appears to have served as a front for its proprietor's legal and illegal activities. As would emerge later, the introverted Joel was tied in with the gregarious Vidal on both the entrepreneurial and social levels in the late 1950s. One of Vidal's principal enterprises was gunrunning. Ethically flexible, he would deal with anyone who had enough money, regardless of their political beliefs. He knew all the dealers who had access to weapons, from B-24 bombers from World War II to vintage Enfield rifles. He would fly to a key contact city—Dallas, Miami, New Orleans—and write orders from

Latin American revolutionaries in the afternoon and counterrevolutionaries at night.

In 1959, Vidal began freelancing for the CIA, which used him as a cutout to deliver arms to groups it preferred not to negotiate with directly. In 1960, he set up Afratronics, Inc., whose stated purpose was to exploit industrial development in emerging African nations. Vidal appointed Joel a director as well as Robert A. Vogeler, a former executive of International Telephone & Telegraph (ITT). It may say something about Afratronics's true mission that Vogeler was subsequently imprisoned for seventeen months in Hungary, charged with being a CIA spy.

Then Luis Vidal disappeared. On November 18, 1961, police patrolling the Mexico City–Cuernavaca highway spotted bloodied clothes in a ditch. In the jacket pockets were a key to room 908 of the Continental Hilton Hotel, 603 pesos ($48), and six checks drawn on the account of the Paint Company of America endorsed by Vidal. Four days later, in the same vicinity, a bullet-riddled body was found in a shallow grave. By law the police needed two persons to identify the body as that of Vidal to open a murder case. A maid at the hotel swore that this was the same man she had observed in room 908 ten days earlier, even though she became hysterical when she saw the body at a distance on a slab and ran from the morgue. A voluptuous dancer from New York, who purported to be Vidal's wife, identified the body as her husband, even though it had blue eyes and Vidal's were brown (when later challenged, the dancer proposed that "someone has changed his eyeballs"). There were more glaring discrepancies. Morgue attendants noted that the deceased was between fifty-five and sixty years old; Vidal was thirty-eight. He was so much more Turkish than Latin in appearance that they nicknamed him El Turco. He appeared far larger than the bloody clothes, yet the police never tried them on him. Nor did they send for Vidal's dental charts from New York or take fingerprints. So dubious was the police "identification" that health authorities refused to issue a death certificate.

At the time the body was found, Joel was in Peru negotiating the purchase of two warehouses to store molasses. Six days later, still in

Peru, he took a call from a Southwestern secretary in New York, who informed him that his partner had been found murdered near Mexico City; it was in one of the local newspapers. Joel calmed himself with the idea that if you swim with the sharks like Vidal did, you risk being eaten. But Joel was swimming with the sharks as well. He recalled that on Tuesday, November 7, when he had been in San Antonio arranging the sale of molasses tanks, Vidal called from New York saying he was in deep trouble and might have to "disappear for a while." He asked that their scheduled meeting in Mexico City be held as soon as possible, and he sounded pleased when Joel said he could be there two days later. Joel and Southwestern's representative in Mexico, Luis deGaray Jaimes, met Vidal at the airport and dropped him off at the Continental Hilton. He seemed his usual self and alluded only in generalities to being in trouble. If he really were in a bind, Joel thought it odd that he used his real name going through immigration at the airport and registering at the hotel. In fact, he gave every indication of drawing attention to himself.

Hinckle and I found out that on November 24, the day Joel received the news of his partner's death, a man using the name Luis Vidal, Jr., crossed the border from Mexico into Guatemala. His description matched that of Vidal, the passport photo looked like him, and the passport number, 2938J2, was issued to him by the U.S. State Department. From there on, Vidal vanished, never to surface again under that identity. Given the dark alleys he prowled, it was not surprising. Plying both sides of the street in arms trafficking is a dangerous game, and so is espionage.

And then there was the Dominican connection. President Kennedy had been trying to oust his godfather, Rafael Trujillo, who was viewed as a despot so fiendish as to invite a socialist takeover. Under the code name Operation EMOTH, the CIA supplied an internal opposition group with weapons to assassinate the dictator. When Kennedy learned of it, he ordered the Agency to pull out of the conspiracy because "the U.S. as a matter of general policy cannot condone assassination." Too late. The following day, May 30, 1961, Trujillo was ambushed in his car on a coastal highway and killed. His son, playboy Ramfis Trujillo, ran the conspirators to ground and exacted ghastly revenge. It was quite possible that Vidal's urgent need to disappear six months later was dictated by some role he played in the Trujillo assassination.

The Mexican police hauled in Luis deGaray, the hapless Southwestern factotum, for two weeks of interrogation, which featured immersing his head in ice water until he almost drowned. He ultimately capitulated, giving a statement that on the night Vidal disappeared from the Continental Hotel he loaned a 1953 Buick to Joel, which was returned hours later with a broken window and blood on the upholstery and the left rear wheel. DeGaray quoted Kaplan as being incredulous about the bloodstains: "It is not possible. I did myself wash them off." This rather absurd scenario was contradicted by the duty watchman at the Southwestern office, where deGaray said he awaited the return of the vehicle, who testified that absolutely no one went in or out of the office that night. That didn't bother the police, who began searching for Joel.

After finishing his business in Peru, Joel had returned to New York, only to find that Uncle Jack had removed his name from the office door and declined to speak with him. On the advice of an attorney, Joel took off for Europe to see how the situation played out. On a spring day in 1962 he walked out of his hotel and into the arms of Spanish police. Not to worry, he was told by Luis Pozo, the Spanish chief of Interpol, Spain had no extradition treaty with Mexico. A few days later, however, Pozo shifted into reverse. "Orders have come down from the highest sphere of the Spanish government," he apologized. Without the formality of a hearing, Joel was whisked onto an airliner bound for Mexico City. Clearly, a powerful hand had intervened with the Spanish strongman, General Francisco Franco.

The corrupt workings of the Mexican justice system soon started in motion. A judge, citing lack of evidence, reduced the charge from murder to being an accessory, but before Joel could write out a bail check the federal district attorney stepped in and removed the judge for "incompetence." Joel retained one of the country's most distinguished constitutional attorneys, Victor Velasquez, who in the end threw up his hands with the comment, "Obviously, something other than the law is keeping Mr. Kaplan in jail, because there are no legal grounds for him being there at all." Six prominent judges refused to hold trial because the evidence was so questionable, but a seventh, whom Velasquez called "politically compromised," tried Joel, found him guilty, and sentenced him to twenty-eight years in prison.

In December 1967, only months after my frustrating visit to Joel in Lecumberri Prison, the Mexican Supreme Court upheld his conviction, and he was transferred to the modern, high-security Santa Marta Acatitla Penitentiary on the outskirts of the capital. I counseled Judy Dowis, who was living on a hillside estate in Sausalito, that it was time to get an American attorney, one who could shield Joel once he was out and could deal firmly with Uncle Jack to recoup Joel's share of the family trust (the elder Kaplan had rewritten the trust to exclude Joel unless he was "freely established in a state of the United States," which he didn't figure would happen for many years). The name of the game was power, I told Judy, and the attorney should be high-powered. The one I had in mind was Melvin Belli, the flamboyant San Francisco "King of Torts," whose courtroom melodramatics were legendary. He was a nonconformist, who once likened being dropped by the American Bar Association to getting kicked out of the Book-of-the-Month Club. I had met him when he hosted a reception for Jim Garrison in his Russian Hill penthouse, inviting the San Francisco rainmakers who contributed to the investigation. Although Belli had defended Jack Ruby in Dallas (unsuccessfully) and had publicly debated Mark Lane, taking the Warren Commission's side, he felt that Garrison deserved a fair hearing. Judy, a New Age type with a Hopi Indian blanket slung over her shoulder, found instant kinship with Belli, whose flowing silver mane was offset by a crimson-lined cape.

In Santa Marta, Joel kept himself mentally busy conjuring up escape strategies. It was not that he didn't have creature comforts. As he wrote Judy, he and other "distinguished prisoners" in fact "have two servants who prepare our meals, clean our cells, do the laundry, etc.

We pay them ten pesos a week. Other necessities like whiskey, women, etc., are taken care of through obliging guards." Despite the amenities, Joel didn't want to squander a large chunk of his life in detention. And there was a question of his safety. While in Lecumberri, a guard confessed that he had been bribed by two Americans to kill him by knife, poison or any method that could be made to look like suicide. The Americans even supplied the guard with a suicide note printed in a hand strikingly similar to Joel's, admitting he had murdered Vidal and saying he was too depressed to go on. Joel's New York lawyer, Edward Bobick, told him that this was part of a CIA setup called Project Halliburton. But Bobick didn't say how he knew this or what Halliburton was all about.

Joel's determination to abscond was sharpened by visits from people who promised to obtain his freedom but didn't deliver. The first, in 1963, was from a U.S. foreign service officer in Mexico City, Goodwin Shapiro, who, despite Ambassador Fulton Freeman's refusal to intervene, took an interest in the case. Shapiro became suspicious of a frame-up when the hotel maid who had identified the body in the morgue as that of Vidal presented herself at the American embassy to confess, with Catholic remorse, that she had been coerced into the identification by the authorities. Shapiro interviewed Joel in prison and vowed to explore the matter further. He had hardly begun, however, when he was unexpectedly transferred to South Korea.

The second, in 1965, was from de Lessups Morrison, who had served as JFK's ambassador to the Organization of American States (OAS) and had been mayor of New Orleans. Morrison told Joel he was interested in his quandary because the Kaplan sugar firm had facilities in Louisiana. But any hope from that quarter evaporated a few days later when Morrison's private plane crashed on his way back to New Orleans. It was a year later, in 1966, that I learned from Minutemen defector Jerry Brooks that Morrison's pilot, Hugh Ward, had been an investigator for Guy Banister and a fellow member of the Minutemen and the Anti-Communism League of the Caribbean, which was waging covert actions against Castro. Whether this was a coincidence or a connection I never was able to determine. All that could be verified was that Morrison, although a domestic liberal, was stridently anticommunist and as OAS ambassador had advocated preemptive action against Castro.

The third noteworthy visitor was Uncle Jack's eminent barrister, Louis Nizer, who dropped by in 1968 on his way to the Mexican Film Festival in Acapulco with Jack Valenti, the sycophantic Lyndon Johnson aide ("I sleep better knowing Lyndon Johnson is my president") whom Nizer had helped, through his clout in the film industry, become Hollywood's designated spokesman. Nizer at first talked vaguely, giving no legal exegesis, then promised, "I'll have you out of here shortly." But Joel was leery of anyone sent by his uncle, whom he suspected was paying to keep him in custody. Besides, Nizer had told Judy, "It won't hurt Joel to sit in jail for a while—he's been a very naughty boy." Joel considered Nizer's visit nothing more than an attempt to pacify him.

Joel's thoughts turned to escape. His first brainstorm was to bribe the prison ambulance driver to bundle him out the gates when he feigned an acute attack of appendicitis. But the driver, flush with a $5,000 down payment, went on a drinking binge to celebrate and was fired for reporting for work intoxicated. Then Joel hatched a plan with his brother Ezra in which $100,000 in bribes would be paid to several medics and health officials to declare him officially dead. He would then be taken from prison in a body bag and delivered to a bribed funeral home. There a dead body would be waiting, which would be buried as Joel David Kaplan, while the live Joel was on his way to Peru. Joel savored the irony of this charade, since it was similar to the one Mexican authorities had used to convict him. But when Ezra tried to get the $100,000 from Uncle Jack, who was the trustee of their inheritances, the answer was a flat no. Joel was convinced more than ever that his uncle wanted him out of circulation. The campaign to free him continued as a family affair when, in 1965, Joel married Irma Vasquez Calderon, an attractive Guatemalan whom he had met when she visited a fellow inmate. As Joel put it, "She would joke about it, saying I was a really good catch, for where else could she meet an American millionaire but in a Mexican prison."

Joel had heard about all the tunnel escapes during World War II and thought he could exit the same way. Irma recruited a young Mexican couple who set up a chicken farm within sight of the guards patrolling the Santa Marta walls. But what was filling its shed was not a population explosion of fowl but a huge pile of dirt from the tunnel digging. For six days the excavating went on splendidly, then disaster struck: a thick vein of lava rock blocked further progress. Irma, nearly in tears, took Joel a chicken dinner that night.

It would be Judy Dowis's persistence and checkbook that eventually freed Joel. I put her in touch with Jim Rose, whom I had recently dispatched to Mexico City to contact the Russians regarding the JFK assassination, and he drove down in Judy's Jaguar to case Santa Marta. The best he could come up with was a scheme to start a fire in the prison's linen storage room that would distract the guards while Joel was smuggled out in a linen supply truck driven by two Cuban exiles. But this didn't sound workable, so Judy turned to Rose's Miami colleague, Martin Casey, who was a kind of personnel manager for the anti-Castro paramilitaries. Casey drove right over to Nelli Hamilton's boardinghouse, a tan clapboard structure on Fourth Street near Little Havana. Nelli was a surrogate mother to the collection of paramilitaries staying with her, and her strictest injunction was no guns at the dinner table. They jocularly referred to themselves as the Soldiers of Misfortune, after their propensity for picking losing sides. How ironic, I thought, that Nelli's boys, who ached to do in The Beard, as they called Castro, were being recruited to liberate an inmate who, I suspected, had collaborated with the enemy.

In the end, the Soldiers of Misfortune failed to come up with a viable plan, try as they might. But one of their ranks, Jerry Porter, thought he knew the one man who could pull it off. Balding, nearing fifty, Porter was a wartime PT boat commander, former male model and occasional pillhead who claimed to have been in charge of CIA arms shipments out of New Orleans in preparation for the Bay of Pigs invasion ("I didn't want the job," Porter insisted, "but the CIA had enough on me to void my passport if I didn't cooperate"). People in this netherworld tend to have their own Who's Who, and Porter touted Vic Stadter, a master smuggler. The trouble was, he didn't know how to get in touch with Stadter other than through Burl Ives, the folk singer and movie actor. When Judy finally got Ives on the phone, he allowed as how his friend Vic lived in Glendora, not far east of Los Angeles.

Forty-eight years old when Judy phoned him, Victor E. Stadter had curly, reddish hair with a flaring mustache and wore cowboy outfits. A rugged individualist who disdained bureaucracy in all its forms, Vic was a straight shooter who exhibited old-fashioned chivalry, especially when it came to a woman in distress such as Judy. A hard drinker, he preferred, of course, Old Smuggler Scotch. He had a reputation as one of the hottest pilots for hire, a crap shooter who could flee up canyons and survive. Although he had done a stretch in prison for hauling marijuana, he contended he had been stung by an informant and actually confined his trafficking to nondrug contraband ranging from capuchin and spider monkeys to lobsters and linens. Cocky to the core, Vic was a bogeyman to U.S. Customs agents, who never were able to catch him in the act. He told me he didn't believe in national borders. They should be eliminated. "If that happened, Vic," I retorted, "you'd be out of business." When he heard Judy detail her brother's fix, money didn't matter. This was a job he could enjoy; a form of revenge, as it were, for a rank injustice. As he put it afterward, "Hell, I would have taken him out for nothing."

When Vic signed on, Joel was advancing an escape plan of his own. Citing frequent bouts of hepatitis, he would seek a transfer from Santa Marta to the cleaner mountain air of the penitentiary at Cuernavaca; security there was so lax an inmate could just walk away. Vic was pressed into service to tail the prison van and make sure that it wasn't ambushed on the way. The transfer was set for the night of January 16, 1971, facilitated by an $80,000 bribe. As it turned out, the bribed officials had been dismissed months earlier and had no authority to arrange anything. Vic, who was well acquainted with the *mordida*, wasn't surprised. "If you bribe a man to violate his responsibilities," the smuggler said, "he is no longer trustworthy to anyone." But that didn't deter Vic from putting out feelers in Mexico City about what cash ante in what high place might work. He was soon approached in the lobby of his hotel by a stranger who knew his name. "If you somehow succeed in this," the man proposed, "we'll give you fifty grand to throw him back into Mexico." Vic could hardly refrain from breaking the man's nose. He was obviously just a cutout, but for whom? A Mexican agency? The CIA? Uncle Jack? The incident persuaded Vic that Joel was no ordinary prisoner.

By now Joel was so depressed by one failure after another that he began swigging Bacardi rum in copious amounts. It was while he was out in the prison yard, his head spinning in the bright sun, that the revelation came to him. "I could fly out of here by helicopter," he thought out loud. When Vic heard of Joel's bright idea, he began ticking off in his mind "the thirty or forty things that could go wrong." But the irresistible tug was that it had never been done before and required no bribe. Vic wasted no time getting organized. He himself couldn't fly a helicopter, but he dragooned an old crop-duster buddy, Harvey Orville Dail, better known as Cotton, to fly it. It didn't matter that Cotton had never gripped the controls of a chopper either; Vic paid for a crash course. Next he had to procure a chopper. In an aviation journal he found a Wyoming millionaire advertising a Bell 47 fitted with a supercharger for flying in the Rocky Mountains, a feature that would be needed for the high altitude of Mexico City. The price was a bargain $65,000, in cash. The next hurdle was getting the craft into Mexico without arousing suspicion, which Vic jumped by setting up a faux company in Honduras called Milandra Mining, after his wife's maiden name. After Cotton lifted Joel out of the prison yard, he would make a beeline for a remote airstrip where Vic would be waiting in a Cessna 210, also registered to Milandra Mining, to fly the fugitive to the Texas border. Cotton, still skeptical, traveled to Mexico City to scout the prison. He returned a believer, figuring he could get the chopper in and out in less than forty seconds, which didn't give the tower guards much time to gather their wits and get off shots. "You don't shoot at guards; you wave at them," Vic reassured Cotton, promising that the guards would believe the chopper belonged to the attorney general. Irma had seen the attorney general's helicopter flying over Mexico City many times. "How do you know it's the attorney general's?" Vic had asked. "It's all blue," she replied. So Vic added two gallons of blue enamel to his shopping list.

Just as they were set to go, Cotton came down with a serious case of cold feet. "Vic, you know I don't rat out," he said, "but I just don't think I can handle it yet." Improvising, Vic put Cotton's helicopter instructor, Roger Hershner, on the payroll of Milandra Mining to fly the craft to the fictitious Honduras mine site. Cotton flew the Cessna south, while Vic tagged behind in a bronze Cadillac convertible with a woman wearing a blonde wig as his companion, for all appearances on a Mexican lark. It was not until they all gathered at a gravel airstrip near the village of Actopan, which Vic had chosen as an advance base, that Hershner learned the truth. "Okay, Vic, I'll do it," Hershner agreed after Vic had put the escape in terms of a mercy mission. But he had one question: what was Joel in for? "Murder," Vic admitted. Hershner, a military veteran, shook his head and mumbled, "Just like Vietnam."

The breakout itself went off without a hitch. As he skimmed over the prison walls and dropped into the courtyard, Hershner waved and the guards simply watched, expecting perhaps the attorney general himself to step out. Vic had instructed Hershner to stay on the ground only for a ten-second count, rotors spinning, then take off if Joel wasn't on board. But Joel, holding a newspaper for identification and pursued by a flock of inmates who realized what was happening, reached the chopper inside the ten seconds. With him was a cellmate in for passport forgery, Carlos Contreres Castro, who he insisted on bringing along over Vic's objection that the additional weight might be too much. Ever polite, Hershner introduced himself to his two passengers, then gunned the engine, and they shot up and out. The tower guards remained motionless, their rifles racked, not sure whether to shoot or salute.

In rain and falling darkness, Hershner found his way back to the advance base, where Vic waited with the Cessna 210. As the chopper floated down, Vic couldn't see whether Joel was on board. Just then there was a lightning bolt, and Joel was illuminated as if a flashbulb had gone off. Stage one had gone perfectly. Stage two: leaving Contreres to make his own way to his native Guatemala, Vic would hightail it with Joel in the Cessna to Brownsville, Texas, some two hours distant, and clear Customs and Immigration. It would have been much safer for Vic to sneak Joel into the United States as if he was another load of lobsters, but Uncle Jack had amended the trust to require Joel to be legally established in the country. When they landed at Brownsville, Vic crossed his fingers, knowing his reputation inevitably preceded him. "Well, well, if it isn't the great Mr. Stadter," the Immigration inspector taunted. "And to what do we owe the pleasure of your company?" The inspector paid scarce attention to the wonky-looking Joel, who meekly produced a crumpled Navy discharge as proof of citizenship, and searched Vic and his plane for contraband. Vic sweated out the lengthy searches, afraid that at any moment Mexican authorities would alert U.S. border posts about the jailbreak. But it didn't happen. The Mexico City police were interrogating Irma in her apartment, convinced that the helicopter had deposited Joel at a hideout within the sprawling metropolis. No one reported a helicopter landing at Actopan, dropping off two passengers, then heading off to the north with only the pilot aboard.

After the Mexican authorities learned that Joel had crossed the frontier, however, they requested the FBI to find him and kick him back. Actually, the Bureau was on shaky legal ground. Mel Belli researched the Mexican penal code and discovered that escaping was not a crime unless violence was employed or a bribe was offered, neither of which applied. But the FBI and Mexican police didn't always observe legal niceties in handing over wanted persons to each other. So Vic was not surprised to find out, when he phoned ahead to his wife Mary at their old mansion in Glendora, that FBI agents had come calling and taken up vigil on the grounds. Vic responded by flying unannounced into a little-used airstrip near Glendora and smuggling Joel into the mansion in the dead of night. As he peered through a slit in the curtains at the FBI pickets, Joel realized he was not yet free. But after a week the agents decamped, having detected no sign that Joel was there. Judy Dowis called Warren and me, and the three of us flew down to Ontario Airport, near Glendora. Vic picked us up and, with one eye glued to the rearview mirror for a tail, drove us to the mansion.

It had been four years since I saw Joel in Lecumberri, and he looked even more emaciated. A series of illnesses had taken their toll. But now, as he recuperated, he could tell his story. While a press posse beat the bushes looking for the "helifugitive," Warren and I signed him to a book contract, and Holt, Rinehart & Winston bought the publishing rights. With his share of the advance against royalties in pocket, Joel moved to a basement apartment in an old Victorian in San Francisco's Pacific Heights so that we could debrief him. He was soon joined by Irma and their daughter Aura, the recent product of a conjugal prison visit. Joel talked about his family background, his peregrinations as a businessman, how he was railroaded at the trial, life in prison, and the dramatic escape.

But I was salivating to hear about who he thought he escaped from. Recalling our Lecumberri conversation, in which he cryptically referred to "answers in Havana," I asked, "What was the Cuban connection?" Anguish wreathed Joel's face; it was obviously a touchy subject. In the 1950s, while traversing the island on Southwestern business, he witnessed how Cubans hated Batista. "I could feel the Cuban anger — a pathetic anger, since life seemed so hopeless. No one moved a finger to help them. The American companies made millions from Cuba and cared only about keeping things as they were, and Batista made millions in the process of obliging them." So Joel was disposed to exult when Fidel Castro took over on New Year's Day, 1959.

Since Joel wore his heart on his sleeve, it was not surprising that he was subtly recruited by Cuban intelligence. Six months after the revolutionary victory, two Cubans who styled themselves representatives of the government dropped in on the Southwestern office in Mexico City and asked to talk with him alone. Joel accompanied them across the street to a bar called the Tampico Club, where they discussed the sugar and molasses trade. Evidently Joel passed this initial screening, for the Cuban pair set up a series of meetings. Finally, they proposed that he deliver some diplomatic documents to Peru, ones they could no longer transmit through the usual channels because of adverse diplomatic conditions. Joel agreed, since he was going to Lima the following week anyway.

There in the Hotel Bolivar he received a call from a Daniel Carlos, who would be waiting in the hotel bar with two books on his table. Joel sat down, exchanged pleasantries, slid a brown, taped envelope across the table, and left. He made similar deliveries to Ecuador. On one mission he was instructed to sit on a park bench, holding a newspaper in hand as identification. "A man came limping along, sat down next to me, and gave me the prearranged signal: 'I have exceedingly tight new shoes,'" Joel recounted. "I got up, leaving the newspaper and envelope." It was straight out of a grade-B espionage film. "Joel Kaplan, courier," I laughed.

But the ongoing Mexico conversations with his Cuban handlers then took a turn that was not very comical. They knew that Joel was a sometime partner of Luis Vidal in arms smuggling, which he had undertaken to satisfy a need for adventure. "They wanted to know all about it: how big the transactions were, where the arms were sent, who was bringing them in from the States. They said that they were more interested in certain arms not falling into the hands of certain people than in our general business dealings. They appeared to know about all the groups operating in the Caribbean; their intelligence seemed excellent. They were particularly sensitive about what was going on in Guatemala, and asked me to tell them when Vidal planned to ship into there. I agreed."

At that time, Guatemala was a staging area for the impending Bay of Pigs invasion—Brigade 2506 was quartered there—of which Joel was unaware. The Cuban agents, who were, asked Joel to cut the Gordian knot by diverting arms shipments. The level of risk had escalated:

furnishing intelligence was one thing, but actively participating in clandestine operations was another. Joel hesitated, then assented, thinking he was "on the side of the angels." Before long he was in action. A load of M-1 rifles and ammunition was to be flown to an abandoned airstrip in southern Veracruz state, not far from the Guatemalan border, where it was to be picked up by an anti-Castro group. Joel diverted the shipment to a nearby sugar mill for temporary storage. The following night a twin-engine Beechcraft bumped down on the grass strip. Joel was waiting. He told the pilot there was no cargo that night. "Then I warned him to get out or he might get arrested or his plane confiscated," Joel said. "He just turned tail and flew off into the sunset." The next morning a pro-Castro outfit, sent by Cuban intelligence, hauled the load away. Several days later, back in Mexico City, Joel heard from an angry Vidal. Joel alibied that the shipment had been seized by the authorities and that the airstrip was too "hot" to be used any more. Vidal sounded skeptical and was cool to Joel as the Bay of Pigs invasion failed and the months leading up to his own disappearance that November fell off the calendar. "I think he may have had some idea of my relations with the Cubans," Joel surmised. "The CIA had its sources too. One could figure that they told Vidal if he didn't already suspect it himself."

As for the events of that November, Joel could sense early in the game, when he was in San Antonio and Vidal urgently requested his presence in Mexico City, that something other than business might be afoot. His suspicions were heightened when, shortly after hanging up on Vidal, a mutual acquaintance unexpectedly materialized in the Texas city, explaining that Vidal was "in terrible trouble" and wanted to rendezvous with them both. The man was Evsai Petrushansky, a murky character who let it be known that he had been in U.S. intelligence during World War II and afterward carried out counterintelligence assignments for the Israelis. It was not at all reassuring that Petrushansky brought with him not only forged passports but a companion with a withered right arm, whom he introduced as Harry Kopelsohn, "a great soldier of Israel" and an intelligence agent who once had hunted Nazis. In fact, Joel was so shaken by their sudden advent that he ducked out into the street, found a pay phone, and called the Cuban embassy in Mexico City. He asked for "Ruben in the Economics Department," the recognition code his Cuban handlers had given him in case of emergency. The Cubans, intensely interested in what Vidal was up to, suggested that Joel go with the flow and keep in close touch.

After the trio arrived in the Mexican capital and met with Vidal, Petrushansky announced that he was taking Vidal out for a while in a Buick Jaime deGaray had loaned them. Joel sat alone in the hotel bar, trying to make some sense of these odd goings-on until the wee hours of the morning. Finally, Petrushansky showed up, saying there was broken glass in one of the car's windows. "There was a disagreement and Vidal has suffered a little accident," Petrushansky said, indicating that he was returning the Buick to Joel. Alarmed, Joel phoned the Cuban embassy and after some delay was plugged into "Ruben." "You'd better disengage, and do it fast," Ruben instructed, after hearing Joel's account. "Otherwise, it might be too dangerous." The warning prompted Joel's early departure for Peru, where company business awaited.

Much later, while in Lecumberri, Joel heard bits and pieces of what supposedly had happened that puzzling night. "I'm told that Kopelsohn bought a corpse at the University of Mexico Medical School," he said. "They ran into some difficulty and ended up with a corpse that was far from a dead ringer for Vidal." Petrushansky and Kopelsohn dug a shallow grave at the side of the highway to Cuernavaca, pumped four bullets into the body, mutilated the facial features, and returned deGaray's Buick, with its incriminating broken window and bloodstains, to Joel. Meanwhile, Joel heard, Kopelsohn's contacts in the Israeli underground whisked Vidal away. But through their inquiries at the hotel, the Mexican police learned about Petrushansky and Kopelsohn and charged them as accomplices with Joel in the "murder." Kopelsohn was extradited from Germany, where he ran a bordello. His trial was a farce, with a panel of judges adopting the defense's claim that he was the wrong Kopelsohn. Petrushansky was located in a New York jail, charged with pornographic filmmaking, but fought extradition. He lost all his appeals, however, and was on the verge of being removed to Mexico when, on April 16, 1965, his attorney met with the uniquely accessible U.S. secretary of state, Dean Rusk. Rusk ordered Attorney General Nicholas Katzenbach to "take the necessary steps to terminate this litigation and to have Petrushansky released from custody." That left Joel as the odd man out. It was evident to him that the same power that freed Kopelsohn and Petrushansky was keeping him in confinement.

In our debriefing, Joel revealed that after he was informed of Vidal's "murder" while in Peru and after repairing to New York, he kept on going to Paris, where he checked in with the Cuban embassy. He was advised to proceed to Prague in the Eastern bloc, from which the Cubans would fly him to sanctuary in Havana. But he decided not to go underground and instead flew off to Madrid, where he was unceremoniously arrested and deported to Mexico. But the Cubans did not forget him. In the fall of 1962, Joel was visited in jail by a well-dressed European, who introduced himself simply as "a friend from the Czech embassy." The Czechs, Joel knew, often acted as surrogates for the Cubans, whose diplomatic ties with Mexico were rather delicate. What the Czech suggested was that Joel employ a certain local attorney said to be experienced in handling difficult cases. A few days later, the attorney showed up, displaying a handwritten note from Dr. Carlos Lechuga, the Cuban ambassador to Mexico, asking that "special interest be taken in the matter of Joel Kaplan" (a year later Lechuga was the Cuban ambassador to the United Nations in New York and carried on confidential negotiations with JFK's aide, William Attwood).

The attorney proposed that Joel feign a serious illness, and the attorney would supply a jeep to transport him to an outside medical facility. The jeep would drive by the Czechoslovakian embassy, where "a stranger" would be stationed to assist Joel inside. From this haven Joel could then be spirited to Cuba. At first everything went according to plan. When he faked severe headaches, he was sent out for treatment. And sure enough, awaiting him was a jeep, a driver, and an armed escort. But miles short of the Czech embassy, the jeep broke down. "My mind went racing with possibilities," Joel recalled. "Could I slip off into the crowds? The guard would neither shoot me nor find me." But he didn't have a peso on him, and he had made no preparations for being loose in the middle of the city. He decided his best bet was to reschedule the escape, and it was set for a few days later. This time he would have money in his pocket. "On that day," Joel said, "I was having lunch in the mess when two guards came, pulled me right out of there, and transferred me to Lecumberri."

So what was the bottom line to this tangled web of a story? "I believe Vidal, who had done some work for the CIA, arranged a disappearance for himself, which the CIA either set up or took advantage of to frame me," Joel theorized. My own scenario elaborated on this. It all devolved from the Bay of Pigs vortex. It stood to reason that the CIA wanted Joel out of the way for a long time, not only because he had been "a naughty boy," as Louis Nizer put it, by diverting arms consigned to the invasion brigade, but because he posed a threat to the renewed operations against Cuba under Operation Mongoose. At the same time, Vidal was in "terrible trouble," possibly due to his duplicitous arms trafficking, and needed to erase his identity. Staged disappearances are not unheard of in the shadow world of intelligence, as when Dr. Bosch announced that Jim Rose had gone down at sea, killing off his Carl Davis identity. In Joel's case, it was Vidal, probably directed by the CIA, who killed two birds with one stone by recruiting Petrushansky and Kopelsohn to enact his murder charade and implicate Joel. Despite their boasts of links to Israeli intelligence, the Mossad had no reason to become involved. Petrushansky was selected by Vidal because he was a mutual acquaintance of Joel's who could manipulate him, and Kopelsohn was brought in to assist. But the duo botched the "murder" job so badly that they entrapped themselves. Only the CIA, enjoying a cozy relationship with its Mexican counterpart, had the ability to keep the fix on in Joel's case while arranging the release of Petrushansky and Kopelsohn. The unusual intervention of Secretary of State Dean Rusk attested to that.

After snapping up hardcover rights, Holt, Rinehart & Winston set publication of *The 10-Second Jailbreak* for May 1973. In a trade journal ad, Holt promised "major national advertising" and a "national TV and radio promotion tour." The editors brought in well-known writer Eliot Asinof to structure the manuscript like a screenplay, and Columbia Pictures bought feature movie rights for $140,000, outbidding Paramount. Bantam Books purchased paperback rights for $25,000, planning a tie-in with the film when it was released. After the book hit the bookstores, the reviews were uniformly favorable and the first printing sold out. *Playboy* ran a condensation. International interest was such that French, Japanese, United Kingdom and Mexican editions were published. *The 10-Second Jailbreak* was off and flying.

The first hint of trouble came when Holt didn't order a second printing and reneged on the promise of a promotional tour, which would have featured the colorful Vic Stadter. We found out that Uncle Jack had flexed his muscles, instructing Louis Nizer to send a letter complaining that he had been inaccurately portrayed. To emphasize the point, he dispatched hirelings to pressure bookstores into removing the offending volume from prominent display. Then our film agent called with word that Columbia Pictures was not going to give us credits, as the contract stipulated. I phoned Irwin Winkler, the producer. "Irwin, I hear that Columbia is trying to divorce our book from the movie and not give us credits," I said. "If that happens, Columbia is going to be sued big time." Winkler confirmed that Nizer, who as counsel for United Artists and MGM was a Hollywood heavyweight, had coerced Columbia on behalf of Jack Kaplan. The studio caved in, taking the position that the film, which it titled *Breakout*, was "fictionalized" and not an adaptation of the book. This raised the eyebrows of *Publishers Weekly* columnist Paul Nathan, who noted in the issue of March 24, 1975, that "speculation regarding possible CIA involvement" was contained in the book. When Melvin Belli's law partner, Vasilios Choulos, who was handling Joel's affairs, leaned on Columbia, a studio attorney responded that representatives of Uncle Jack insisted his depiction "was inaccurate and should not be included in any motion picture photoplay," although the studio agreed that by contract the authors had to be credited.

But Columbia refused to cooperate with Bantam in its anticipated tie-in and withheld permission for its paperback edition to carry the film's title and the cover copy to name its stars, Charles Bronson and John Huston, so Bantam pulled out. No sooner had Holt sold the reprint rights to a small house, Manor Books, than the mail brought a letter from the law firm of Greenbaum, Wolff & Ernst warning that its client, Jack Kaplan, would sue should it consummate any paperback sale. It was paradoxical that the Greenbaum firm was trying to suppress publication, since it had a reputation as a sentinel guarding freedom of the press for such major publishers as Harper & Row and Random House. In fact, the Ernst in the firm was Morris L. Ernst, who served as general counsel for the American Civil Liberties Union. It was not until after his death in 1976 that it came out that he had an almost slavering relationship with J. Edgar Hoover, who in 1950 enlisted him to try to stop the presses on Max Lowenthal's critical work, *The Federal Bureau of Investigation*. As had Lowenthal's small publisher, Manor Books ignored the threat and produced the paperback. Jack Kaplan never sued; it is doubtful that he wanted to go through the discovery process, which would have stripped bare his affiliation with the CIA.

In *Breakout*, which was released in 1975, Charles Bronson played Vic Stadter, receiving a sum that made him Hollywood's first million-dollar man. His wife, Jill Ireland, portrayed Judy Dowis. Randy Quaid was Cotton Dail, and Robert Duvall, Joel. And the legendary actor-director John Huston played the part of Uncle Jack. But it was reduced to a cameo role, with all references to the CIA winding up on the cutting room floor. Since book authors have no artistic control, the finished product was strictly an action film devoid of the political intrigue that would have given it meaning. At the box office it grossed $13 million, not bad for a potboiler in those days, but far short of the attendance a significant film might have drawn. Joel, Vic, Hinckle and I had to settle for the modest advance Columbia gave us. The studio had contracted for 2½ percent of the producer's net in addition to the advance, but it was the era of Hollywood "creative accounting" that charged widespread expenses (a practice that was later challenged by actor Cliff Robertson and other Hollywood artists), and we wound up deep in red ink. Although *Breakout* still is shown as a late-night movie on television, it is doubtful we will ever get out of the hole.

Breakout was still in its theater run in June 1975 when there was a copycat escape from a Michigan prison in which an accomplice hijacked a helicopter and lifted out inmate Dale Remling. Although Remling was captured in a bar, the underground Irish Republican Army shortly thereafter airlifted a member out of a British penitentiary; the IRA sent Irish partisan Warren Hinckle a note reading, "Thanks for the idea." Liberation by airlift became a trend, a high-tech alternative to old-fashioned tunneling. One of the most recent escapes came on June 26, 1999, in France when, according to the Associated Press, a helicopter dangling ropes hovered over a Marseilles prison yard and "whisked away several prisoners in an escape worthy of an action-adventure film," an obvious allusion to *Breakout*.

But Joel remained in jeopardy. After the manuscript was in the hands of the Holt editors, he liked to sneak over to my home in Mill Valley for long philosophical talks lubricated by Jack Daniels. On one such night, he drove off in his little Toyota with Irma, and, as usual, I tailed him as far as the Golden Gate Bridge to make sure he was all right. He was weaving slightly, but I attributed that as much to night blindness from his decade in prison as to the bourbon, and peeled off. I was home in bed when, at 2:00 A.M., Irma called. Joel had been arrested by the police for drunk driving. "*Sus uniformes, azul o pardo?*" I asked. "*Pardo*," she answered.

I woke Vasilios Choulos at home. "Piss call, Choulos," I said. "Joel's been arrested by the CHP (California Highway Patrol) for drunk driving. His prints will be sent to the FBI in Washington. You have forty-eight hours." Choulos was equal to the task. He arranged to have Joel arraigned later that morning, telling the judge he was a rabbinical student who never had been in this kind of trouble before.

Released on his own recognizance, Joel fled to New Mexico, where his sister Judy had relocated. Before long, Choulos learned that Mexico, not wanting to risk further embarrassment, no longer sought Joel's extradition, which meant that the FBI had called off its search. But Joel didn't breathe that much easier, apprehensive that the forces which framed him in the first place might yet have it in for him. He, Irma and their daughter moved to Florida, where they lived quietly. In 1985 Joel David Kaplan, his body ravaged by diseases he had caught in prison, died. He had escaped from the CIA, only to become the victim of his false imprisonment.

13

LOOK OUT AHEAD

In his book on espionage, *The Secret War*, Sanche De Gramont summed up thirty years ago:

> Many Americans believe that only Hoover stands between them and Communism. As many others are convinced that he has personally wiped out organized crime in the United States. A relentless advertising campaign has created the image of an ideal and infallible FBI. While it is far from that it is no closer to the Soviet-style secret police. The FBI does not solve the problem of an effective police force in an open society. Rather, it is the product of a given society, dependent on its myths and failings. There is a wide breach between the FBI's public image and its reality.

The Hegelian mystique of the FBI that prevailed through the Hoover decades gradually diminished after he was gone. But the Bureau infrastructure and old-boy culture remain substantially intact, with change measured only in fractions. The push for radical reform that should have begun after Hoover's death was blunted by John Mohr, whose clique remained the power behind the throne through a succession of

new directors. In 1975, after I was appointed an investigative consultant to the National Wiretap Commmission, a congressional body mandated to explore the effectiveness of the 1968 electronic eavesdropping
law intended to curtail abuses, Mohrites reacted with fury and tried to
oust me. When he took office in 1981, Ronald Reagan, who was numb
to the concept of civil liberties, unshackled the FBI, and Hoover-era
abuses resumed. Agents investigated and surveilled more than a thousand individuals and groups opposed to Reagan's aid to the Nicaraguan Contras and the "death squad" regime in El Salvador. Those
targeted number the Maryknoll sisters, the United Auto Workers, and
the National Council of Churches.

The FBI remains plagued by a macho ethos that breeds racism and
sexual harassment. After the 1992 Ruby Ridge siege of militia militant
Randy Weaver's cabin, in which an FBI sniper took out three people,
including Weaver's wife with a babe in arms and his son, division chief
Michael Kahoe covered up by destroying a report critical of the deadly
force. He attempted to justify his action by saying he intended to protect the "best interests" of the FBI, an echo of the Hoover watchword
"Don't embarrass the Bureau," but a court decided that the best interests of the country would be served by eighteen months in prison. The
macho mentality dominated again during the 1993 standoff at the
Branch Davidian sect's compound in Waco, Texas. Six years later it
came to light that the Bureau had lied about the fact that it had pyrotechnic devices, which might have touched off the inferno in the flimsy
structure that claimed some eighty lives, including eighteen children.
Ignored in the pyrotechnic fuss was how the FBI intimidated Attorney
General Janet Reno into authorizing a tank assault in the first place.
After fifty-one days, the Bureau contended that its hostage-negotiating
team was exhausted and that there were no replacements. By 1999,
Reno was so incensed with the FBI's flimflam that she took the un-
precedented step of ordering U.S. marshals to seize the files from the
Bureau and bring them over to Justice for independent review.

For all his reputation for probity, FBI Director Louis Freeh seemed
unwilling to crack down on ethical violations in his own ranks. The

Bureau's internal probe of Ruby Ridge resulted in gentle taps on the wrist for the officials involved. In fact, in 1995 he promoted his old friend Larry Potts to be his Number Two man, but a Justice Department inquiry found allegations that Potts had been part of the cover-up. When Potts left the Bureau in 1997, his upward mobility stalled by the scandal, his cohorts flew into Washington for a farewell dinner. Although the affair was purely personal, they billed the government for "official business" in the form of a nonexistent "ethics seminar" at the FBI training academy. On the face of it, the offense merited termination if not criminal prosecution for fraud. But a board composed of neo-Mohrites, detested by the field agents as "the club," issued a mild censure for "inattention to detail," as Freeh sat on his hands. Nor was the Director proactive on ethics when it was discovered that New Haven agents signed false arrest warrants, an egregious violation. The senior agent on the arrest squad was handed a five-day suspension, but his pay was restored by an internal board. Gregory Dillon, the Connecticut state investigator who reported the bogus warrants, wrote Freeh, urging him to enforce his touted ethical "bright line," but there was no reply. The Bureau is so protectively entrenched that an outside board is sorely needed to review its conduct.

In contrast, Freeh had zero tolerance for President Bill Clinton's ethical lapses. No sooner did Independent Counsel Kenneth Starr leave office in 1999 than he was lavishly praised by the FBI Director for his investigation of Clinton, which was widely seen as slanted and prejudicial. Freeh commended Starr for his "persistence and uncompromising personal and professional integrity," going on to gush, in a pointed reference to the president, "You have always respected the truth and have never engaged in any misleading or evasive conduct or practice." And in what can only be construed as a nasty dig, he wrote that the "laboratory division scientists"—who matched Clinton's DNA to Monica Lewinsky's blue dress—joined in applauding. Commented a White House spokesman, "We've come a long way from J. Edgar Hoover to the Federal Bureau of Infatuation."

The backbiting rankled Clinton, who, in a moment of exasperation when a reporter asked about campaign finance irregularities, flared, "The FBI wants you to write about that rather than write about Waco." Freeh's emergence as a presidential ethics vigilante probably stemmed as much from political partisanship as moral certitude, as the "attaboy Starr" letter indicated. If his views differed that radically from Clinton's, and he could not suppress them, he should have gracefully resigned rather than become a loose cannon. Although politically restrained from firing him, Clinton had to wonder why he had appointed him in the first place. On paper he looked good: ex-altar boy, field FBI agent, federal prosecutor and judge. The land mine in that curriculum vitae was "FBI agent," which meant that he belonged to the uncompromising culture that protects its own at all cost and is politically rock conservative. At a time when many metropolitan police departments are becoming more progressive, the Bureau remains a bastion of reaction. To bring it into the new millennium, a director of more visionary virtues is needed, one perforce from the outside.

Since the end of the Cold War, there has been a search for new espionage enemies. The void seems to have been filled, at least in part, by an array of friendly and unfriendly nations, among them Russia, China and India, on the prowl for the economic, military and scientific secrets of the last superpower. The Clinton administration forged a plan, called CI-21, to create a national counterintelligence czar to ferret out spies. The plan was in response to a series of failures capped by the 1994 case of Aldrich Ames, who operated for years as a Soviet mole inside the CIA, and the current matter of Wen Ho Lee, a scientist at the Los Alamos nuclear lab. For years, the FBI was fixated, in what some see as racial profiling, on proving that Lee was a spy for China, but ended up without a scintilla of evidence. Meanwhile, congressional critics charged, the Bureau failed to widen its hunt for suspects, performing a superficial investigation. So Lee stood accused only of downloading classified files onto his own computer disks, the same violation ex-CIA Director John Deutch admitted to but was pardoned for by Clinton.

Appointing a czar is only a quick fix, not a remedy. Take the case of the recent Clinton-administration drug czar, General Barry McCaffrey, who found the task far more daunting than chasing a retreating Iraqi army in Operation Desert Storm. While the flow of hard drugs increased, his only "victory" was in cracking down on medical marijuana, leading to the conclusion that the war on drugs is too important to be left to generals. It is doubtful that a counterintelligence czar—Louis Freeh was named—would fare any better. The problem is fundamental: From its inception, the FBI recruited candidates more suited to criminal investigations than the subtleties and nuances of counterespionage, for which it is responsible domestically. As I wrote in *Hoover's FBI* three decades ago, "the type of man who would make the best counterspy would never pass FBI muster or flourish in its anti-intellectual environment. Hoover might look down his nose at the 'Harvard Yard liberals' and somewhat off-beat types employed by the CIA, but in the final analysis the machine-gun mentality didn't crack spy rings." Nothing has changed. Shifting counterespionage jurisdiction to the CIA, which already has that responsibility abroad, would make the most sense. So would shifting counterterrorism, a growing problem, which, from the standpoint of intelligence acquisition, goes hand in hand with counterespionage. But this might be difficult to do, since the Bureau under Freeh has staked out the turf, wangling a budget doubled in size since 1992 to $3 billion.

It is a crime for a citizen to lie to the FBI but not a crime for the FBI to lie to citizens. This gross inequity should be removed by stripping away the Bureau's security blanket, the doctrine of sovereign immunity, and making it accountable for its actions. The same applies to the CIA, whose motto "The truth shall set you free" is mocked by its stock in trade: deception, duplicity, dirty tricks and deadly deceits. It operates on a classified budget in the neighborhood of $27 billion a year that gets hidden in military accounts, unvouchered expenditures and the director's discretionary funds. It is a law unto itself, flouting control even by its own civilian directors, who are largely transients appointed by uninquisitive presidents. The insolence this breeds was exemplified in 1964 when Richard Helms, then deputy director in charge of all covert operations, lectured the Warren Commission that it "would have to take his word for the fact that Oswald had not been an agent of the CIA." The worthlessness of his word was revealed in 1975 when the Church Committee, probing intelligence abuses, concluded that Helms had kept secret from his own boss, Director John McCone, the existence of certain covert operations.

In reality, the Agency is accountable to no one, not even itself. This was brought home in the April 25, 1967, report, recently declassified, of the CIA inspector general, who was looking into the CIA-Mafia plots to assassinate Castro. When columnist Jack Anderson first broke the news that the devil's pact existed, there was tremendous angst inside the Agency that the entire off-channels operation would be exposed. "Can we plausibly deny that we plotted with gangster elements to assassinate Castro?" the inspector general asked. Labeling his report an "imperfect history," the inspector general advised, "Because of the extreme sensitivity of the operations being discussed or attempted, as a matter of principle no official records were kept of planning, of approvals, or of implementation." As a consequence, the inspector general had to rely on the "skeletal notes" and "foggy memories" of those agents who could be identified as participants. Nor did he push to find out which additional agents were involved on the grounds that it "would have risked making witting a number of employees who were previously unwitting," thus leaving the record imperfect rather than knowing who had the need to know.

Although there is an intelligence oversight committee in Congress, it can hardly be expected to succeed where even the inspector general failed. The impossibility of outside control, given the Agency's current structure, was bluntly exhibited by a high-ranking CIA officer in a 1978 conversation with Gaeton Fonzi, an investigator for the House Select Committee on Assassinations. The officer asserted that "the clandestine mentality that is drilled into CIA operatives until it is instinctual would permit most of them to commit perjury because, in their view, their secrecy oath supersedes any other." The officer braced Fonzi: "You represent the United States Congress. What is that to the CIA?"

Those defiantly alarming words should rouse Congress to action and bring the CIA fully under civilian control. This would help eliminate the corruption endemic to Agency operations. Jack Kaplan was protected in his violations of IRS codes because he allowed his fund to be used as a CIA operational conduit.

There was the ungodly alliance with the Mafia.

And the CIA has a drug habit. Alfred McCoy's classic study, *The Politics of Heroin in Southeast Asia*, detailed as early as 1972 how the CIA proprietary airline, Air America, hauled narcotics to market for the indigenous peoples of the Golden Triangle helping fight the Vietnam War. In 1998, Gary Webb's volume *Dark Alliance* told how the CIA shielded major drug traffickers who aided the Nicaraguan Contras, resulting in a flood of crack cocaine into United States cities. The same protective blanket was thrown over Honduran drug dealer Juan Matta Ballesteros, another CIA ally in the Contra affair. The CIA contracted with Matta's airline, SETCO, to fly supplies to the Contras, and then, in 1989 when the Justice Department inquired, lied that it had "no records of a SETCO Air." The House Intelligence Oversight Committee, which knew better, reported that there was no evidence CIA officers "ever concealed narcotics trafficking information or allegations involving the Contras." The deception might have been expected from a committee chaired and staffed by former CIA officers.

Since the advent of the Cold War, the engineers of United States foreign policy have been domineered by a compulsion to combat communism around the globe while holding their noses and propping up the unsavory allies who espouse the cause. In large measure, the instrument of this policy has been the CIA through its covert action repertoire of dirty tricks, assassinations, destabilization of governments, economic sabotage, paramilitary adventures, black propaganda, and weapons and drug trafficking.

There have been some "successes," notably the 1973 Chilean coup that toppled the democratically elected Salvador Allende and brought to power the military dictatorship of Augusto Pinochet. But the lengthy campaign against Cuba eventuated in a blown invasion, a skein of unsuccessful assassination attempts, and a legacy of terrorism and drug and arms running. In Guatemala in the early 1990s, a paid CIA agent, Colonel Julio Roberto Alpirez, was responsible for the killings of two people, one an American suspected of leftist sympathies. In the 1980s, the CIA intervened in Afghanistan after the Soviet invasion, arming the resistance, who Ronald Reagan called "freedom fighters," just as he did the Contras, with every conventional weapon from carbines to Stinger missiles. The aid worked; in 1992 the resistance dislodged the communist regime in Kabul.

The Agency should have had a clue, however, when the hard-line Islamic regime that took over refused to return the Stingers and they fell into the hands of terrorists, that it had been more than slightly shortsighted. Afghanistan became the world's biggest supplier of opium, and the world's most dangerous terrorist, Osama bin Laden, is harbored there. The principal beneficiary of the CIA's largess, Commander Gulbuddin Hekmatyar, who was fanatically anti-American, became the leader, trainer and inspiration to the terrorists and guerrillas of the Afghan international operation. Across the sea in New York, the zealots who truck-bombed the World Trade Center in 1993 turned out to be followers of a blind Egyptian prayer leader, Sheik Omar Abdel Rahman, a recent and honored visitor to Afghan training camps, whose U.S. visa had been cleared by the CIA. If the Agency was forced to close down its covert action branch, there would be no loss to national security, only the removal of the blowback threat as epitomized by the Bay of Pigs fallout and the Afghan contretemps. This would leave the CIA to concentrate on what it was originally chartered to do—gather and analyze foreign intelligence.

Whenever a proposal for a renewed federal inquest into the JFK murder is raised, Warren Commission loyalists point to the report of the House Select Committee on Assassinations as the final resolution. Not so. Although the HSCA probe began with a bang, it ended in a whimper. The committee was created in 1976 in response to broad public sentiment aroused by a wave of publications spelling out the defects of the Warren Report and disclosures of the Church Committee, which suggested that the CIA-mob compact to kill Castro had something to do with JFK's death. At the urging of Coretta King, the congressional black caucus pushed to reopen the Martin Luther King case as well. Left out was the Robert Kennedy assassination, which was widely viewed as an open-and-shut case.

Richard Sprague, a tough-minded Philadelphia prosecutor with an astronomical conviction rate, was named chief counsel. Sprague had hardly settled in before he ran into stonewalling by the intelligence agencies. According to his deputy counsel, Robert Tannenbaum, "The FBI and CIA looked upon the Committee as the enemy," and attempted to frustrate it at every turn. So did some members of Congress. Tannenbaum recalled that the investigation had hardly gotten underway when a quartet from Capitol Hill challenged Tannenbaum as to why it should go on, admitting they hadn't liked Kennedy. One of them, the troglodyte John Ashbrook of Ohio, added, "And we want to tell you this: We'll be damned if we're going to give a nickel for you to investigate that nigger, King."

But Sprague bored in, as his tiff with CIA official David Atlee Phillips illustrated. Sprague regarded Phillips as critically important as a suspect or material witness. A tall, suave ex-actor with a theatrical air about him, Phillips had teamed up with Howard Hunt to broadcast black propaganda during the 1954 CIA-orchestrated overthrow of the leftist Arbenz government in Guatemala, making the country safe for United Fruit. When Castro took over, Phillips was in deep cover in Havana, but emerged to link up again with Hunt for the Bay of Pigs planning (in preparation for which Phillips visited Guy Banister in his New Orleans office to discuss a propaganda telethon). After the invasion, Phillips became chief of covert action in Mexico City, focusing on Cuban operations. But he was hardly desk bound, jetting to the JM/WAVE station in Miami and to Langley, among other destinations. Before the HSCA, Phillips testified that there were no CIA photographs taken of Lee Harvey Oswald during his September 1963 trip to Mexico City because surveillance cameras were malfunctioning at the time, which turned out to be untrue. Sprague intended to charge Phillips with perjury and, in addition, to sue the CIA because it wouldn't release files unless he signed a secrecy oath. Sprague considered the demand absurd because the Agency was "the subject of the investigation."

When committee members realized that Sprague was taking direct aim at the CIA, they blanched. "Every member of the HSCA didn't want to even be there," Fonzi recounted. Sprague and Tannenbaum were dumped. Brought in as chief counsel was G. Robert Blakey, a Cornell University law professor who had served on Robert Kennedy's anti–organized crime staff. Blakey proved more flexible. He negotiated a "working arrangement" with the CIA requiring all HSCA personnel viewing files to sign a secrecy oath and stipulating that all interviews of agents past or present be cleared with and monitored by the Agency. This of course had the effect of permitting the CIA to disarm any potential smoking guns. To make matters worse, Blakey supplied the CIA with copies of his files. A committee researcher, Patricia Orr, spent two days on hands and knees on my living room floor inspecting my spread-out files on anti-Castro activities, copying those she thought relevant. Although I cooperated with the HSCA on the condition that my work was for its exclusive use, Blakey sent Orr's forty-page report on my research to the CIA, a dereliction that endangered my sources. The CIA then classified the report so that it could not be released.

Despite Blakey's sweetheart deal with the CIA, HSCA investigators were able to make some progress because they were in the field and out of reach. In Miami, Gaeton Fonzi and Al Gonzales were told by Alpha 66 leader Antonio Veciana that a CIA officer using the name Maurice Bishop had supervised the formation of the group in Havana in 1960, during the early days of the counterrevolution. His last mission for Bishop, Veciana said, was the 1971 camera-gun attempt on Castro's life in Chile. But it was an encounter in Texas in September 1963—when Alpha 66 rented the house on Harlandale in Dallas, where a police informant spotted Oswald—that linked Bishop to the assassination. As he had on previous occasions, Bishop instructed Veciana to meet him in Dallas at the Southland Center complex to go over Alpha 66 matters. When Veciana entered the lobby, he observed Bishop engaged in conversation with a young man who, after a few minutes, walked off with a wave. After the assassination, Veciana recognized the young man as Oswald. Subsequently, in a Miami contact, Bishop asked Veciana to offer his cousin, a Cuban intelligence officer in Mexico City, a large cash sum to say he and his wife had met with Oswald, a patent attempt to portray the accused assassin as a Castro agent. The CIA denied to the HSCA that it had employed anyone using the name Maurice Bishop—it has a "funnies" section that issues the noms de guerre—but an artist's drawing based on Veciana's description strikingly resembled David Phillips, even down to the dark spots below his eyes. Veciana, possibly out of fear, possibly in the hope of continuing to receive Agency funds, stopped one step short of fingering Phillips as Bishop. In a stroke of luck, however, Fonzi and Gonzales ran into a retired CIA officer in Miami who, on January 16, 1978, gave them an earful. The officer, Ross Crozier, divulged that circa 1963 he had known David Phillips as the propaganda coordinator for all Cuban exile groups being run by the Agency. Was Bishop a pseudonym used by Phillips? Yes, Crozier replied, giving the first name as Maurice without prompting.

But the committee never called Crozier as a witness on this crucial point. Instead, it permitted Phillips to disavow being Bishop or knowing Veciana by name. According to Fonzi in his abjectly named *The Last Investigation*, staff members urged Blakey to bring perjury charges against Phillips, but he refused. Two months later, Blakey terminated most of the investigative staff on the pretext of a budget crisis, truncating a probe that was mining highly promising territory. Former HSCA investigators I have talked with are convinced that from the start Blakey intended to cover just enough ground to write a final report that would satisfy the committee. Were it not for an eleventh-hour development, the report would have echoed the Warren Commission Report. But an acoustical analysis of police radio tapes indicated that more than three shots were fired, which meant that there had been at least two shooters. The final report adjudged, "President John F. Kennedy was probably assassinated as the result of a conspiracy." But Blakey absolved the intelligence agencies of any complicity while pointing accusingly—

and circumstantially—at Carlos Marcello and Santos Trafficante. The HSCA closed shop prematurely, recommending that the Department of Justice pick up where it left off. Of course, the department has done nothing—its investigative arm is the FBI.

The HSCA also left the King murder dangling, opining that James Earl Ray was the likely shooter, although part of a low-level conspiracy involving two St. Louis racists. From the start I doubted that Ray, a prison escapee, would cross the street to assassinate anyone out of racial bigotry. On the other hand, he would be an ideal candidate for the role of fall guy. So when Jim Rose was tracing the steps of Jerry Owen in Hollywood in 1968 after the RFK shooting, I had him drop by the nearby St. Francis Hotel, where Ray had stayed before he took off on the road to Memphis and the King slaying. Unlike the St. Moritz Hotel, where Owen was registered, the St. Francis had no phones in the rooms, only a public phone booth in the lobby. Rose photographed the scrawlings on its interior. One, in Ray's handwriting, turned out to be the direct phone number of a Robert Row at Litton Industries in Beverly Hills, a major defense contractor. Interesting, I thought, because Litton operated the shipyard at Pascagoula, Mississippi, which built aircraft carriers, and which Ray had listed as a former employer on a boarding-house application. I passed on this possible link to the military-industrial complex to the HSCA but heard nothing further.

Coretta King and son Dexter King would not buy into the HSCA's rednecks-only theory. But it was not until 1993 that cracks began to appear in the government's stand that there was nothing more to it. That year William Pepper, a London-based trial attorney who was Ray's latest legal representative, persuaded Thames Broadcasting to stage a moot trial of Ray—he had never had a trial—to be shown on Home Box Office television. It was presided over by a retired judge, with real jurors. The state's case was presented by a former Memphis prosecutor, and Pepper put on a defense that Ray was set up to take the tumble. I testified as to the FBI's propensity to engage in lawless law enforcement. The jury "acquitted" Ray.

The King family appealed to Attorney General Janet Reno to reopen the investigation into Martin Luther King's murder, and she agreed to a limited examination based on two new developments. One was the admission by Loyd Jowers, who owned a cafe across from the Lorraine Motel where King was shot, that he had been paid $100,000 by an intermediary to set up Ray. The other was the surfacing of an FBI agent who had searched Ray's car at the time and found a written reference to "Raoul," who Ray claimed had manipulated him. In the meantime, Pepper filed a civil suit against Jowers as a device for bringing the case to trial, which was held in December 1999. The verdict: there had been a conspiracy involving the FBI, the CIA, the Mafia, and the military. Juror David Morphy commented, "We can look back on it and say we did change history. But that's not why we did it. It was because there was an overwhelming amount of evidence and just too many odd coincidences."

Five months later, Reno's Justice Department announced that it could find no credible evidence of a conspiracy, which was incredibly insulting considering the wealth of evidence the civil trial had produced. Coretta King deserves the last word. "This is not about money," she told the jury. "We're concerned about the truth, having the truth come out in a court of law so that it can be documented for all. I've always felt that somehow the truth would be known, and I hoped that I would live to see it. It is important, I think, for the sake of healing so many people—my family, other people, the nation."

Dexter King marveled at how the media turned against the Kings when the specter of the government as perpetrator was raised. "It is amazing to me that as soon as this issue of potential involvement of the federal government came up, all of a sudden the media just went totally negative against the family." His mother reminded him, "Dexter, your dad and I have lived through this once already. You have to understand that when you take a stand against the establishment, first, you will be attacked. There is an attempt to discredit. Second, to try and character assassinate. And third, ultimately physical termination or assassination." Jim Garrison found out how swift and ruthless the character assassination could be.

There is a Greek chorus of the mainstream media that swells every time the assassination controversy heats up, no matter that their forensic knowledge of the case is at best sophomoric. Take CNBC News anchor Brian Williams, who on September 30, 1999, tried to yank the rug out from under Minnesota Governor Jesse Ventura when, in the course of a *Playboy* interview, he ventured that JFK was shot by assassins in the employ of the military-industrial complex. "I believe Kennedy was going to withdraw us from Vietnam, and there were factions that didn't want that," Ventura explained. Williams tried to wipe out that motivation by flatly declaring that JFK "planned a huge commitment of troops" to Vietnam. I have news for Williams. Only weeks before Dallas, on October 11, 1963, John Kennedy issued National Security Action Memorandum No. 263 directing that "no formal announcement be made of the implementation of plans to withdraw 1,000 U.S. military personnel by the end of 1963," and have them all out by 1965 in line with his intent to "Vietnamize" the conflict. That Williams felt compelled to slip in the rebuttal on a news program demonstrates how knee-jerk defending the Warren Report has become in the electronic media. The same can be said for the print media, whose bias might be less spontaneous. Years ago, when the first waves of doubt washed over the report, the CIA instituted a campaign called "Countering Criticism of the Warren Report," which was part of its Operation Nightingale, named for the bird that sings in the dark, to stifle the critics. Nightingale was a companion piece to the older Operation Mockingbird, which proselytized journalists, writers and broadcasters to act as covert assets manipulating public opinion. According to Agency document 1035-960, its key tactics were to "discuss the publicity problem with liaison and friendly elite contacts (especially politicians and editors)" and to "employ propaganda assets to answer and refute the attacks of the critics. Book reviews and feature articles are particularly appropriate for this purpose." Certainly Jim Garrison was a Nightingale target when Jim Phelan and Edward Jay Epstein penned their slanted articles. And Oliver Stone's film *JFK* provoked a media jihad. While not all of the attack was CIA-inspired, there was one book in reaction to *JFK* that had the imprimatur of Langley written all over it.

The volume was arrogantly titled *Case Closed*, as if it were the final solution. The author was Gerald Posner, a former Wall Street lawyer who had scribed three obscure books. Tendered a six-figure advance against royalties by Random House, a tidy sum ordinarily reserved for recognized authors, Posner churned out a manuscript that largely put a reverse spin on the known facts. He eliminated Guy Banister as a suspect by dismissing the testimony of his secretary, Delphine Roberts, who put her boss together with Oswald in a dangle operation, as that of a right-wing kook, even though her daughter confirmed the relationship between Oswald and Banister. He turned amateur psychologist to diagnose Oswald as a societal misfit seeking a perverse niche in history, a stretch even the Warren Commission was loath to make. Posner claimed he interviewed an autopsy doctor, J. Thornton Boswell, and Dealey Plaza witness James Tague, who was nicked by a bullet fragment; both denied to Dr. Gary Aguilar that they had even spoken with Posner, much less altered their original accounts. Random House pumped up sales of *Case Closed* with a whopping advertising campaign featuring full-page ads in the *New York Times*, while *Time*, *Newsweek* and *U.S. News and World Report* gave it rave reviews. Posner became the avatar of the "lone nut" buffs.

It was during Posner's promotional tour that the book's spooky background emerged. He appeared on the "Kevin McCarthy Show" in Dallas with Jim Marrs, the author of *Crossfire*, upon which the film *JFK* was partially based. Marrs recounted to me how it went. Off the air the folksy Marrs chatted with Posner, asking how long he had researched the case. "Three years," Posner replied. "Son, I have socks older than that," Marrs riposted, going on to inquire how he came to write the book. Posner elucidated that Random House editor Robert Loomis got in touch with him, dangling a promise of cooperation from the CIA. The Agency came through, affording him access to Yuri Nosenko, the KGB defector. Nosenko contended that there was no relationship between the Soviet agency and Oswald, which fit perfectly with the "lone nut" theory.

It was not surprising that Loomis was behind *Case Closed*, since he has uniformly defended the official versions of the JFK, RFK and Martin Luther King assassinations. In 1968, he commissioned *Special Unit Senator*, which hewed to the LAPD's line of no conspiracy while ignoring the CIA connections of the top investigators. A few years later he signed up Jim Phelan for his memoirs, which featured a screed against Jim Garrison. In 1978 he angrily demurred when Random House Editorial Director Jason Epstein brought out my and Jonn Christian's *The Assassination of Robert F. Kennedy* and happily concurred when it was subsequently suppressed. After Coretta and Dexter King called for a reopening of the Martin Luther King case on the basis of new ballistics evidence, Loomis trotted out Posner again to write *Killing the Dream*, which squelched the notion that the assassination was organized. "All the conspiracy theories have undermined the public's belief in government," Loomis told *Publishers Weekly* when Posner's JFK book was published. "They believe that everybody's in cahoots, that we have murderers in the CIA. That's what has been accepted, and that, to me, is a crime."

More than three decades after the JFK assassination, former Soviet Premier Mikhail Gorbachev saw it as a pivotal event in recent world history, whose solution remains an overarching issue. In October 1998, while visiting Dallas, Gorbachev declaimed that Kennedy's hallmark 1963 speech in which he stated "we breathe the same air as the Russians," marking a breakout from hostility to conciliation, is even more relevant today than then. "Thirty-five years ago he already saw what we have come to understand only now," Gorbachev said. "The best memory of this man would be to understand his deeds and thoughts and to translate them into policies and more importance in the life of nations. He looked far ahead and he wanted to change a great deal. Perhaps it is this that is the key to the mystery of the death of President John F. Kennedy."

Gorbachev's words mirror the wide perception abroad of the United States as a national security state whose ultimate authority is a secret government. William Pepper touched on the subject in his summation at the 2000 Memphis civil trial: "When Martin King opposed the war, when he rallied people to oppose the war, he was threatening the bottom lines of some of the largest defense contractors in this country." Pepper charged that government intelligence agencies, acting on behalf of that power elite, did away with King. Another example of the secret government in action came in the form of a secret plan drafted in 1984 by Marine Colonel Oliver North, then on detached duty with Ronald Reagan's National Security Council. North was trying to prevent exposure of the illegal sale of missiles to Iran to bankroll a Nicaraguan Contra force specifically denied funds by Congress. His plan called for the suspension of the Constitution and declaration of martial law in the event of an "emergency" such as significant internal dissent. The chief counsel for the Senate Iran-Contra committee that investigated the near-miss, Arthur Liman, placed North at the center of a "secret government within a government," with its own army, air force, diplomatic agents, and intelligence operations.

It was the threat posed by their own secret government that prompted Brazilian officials to hold an International JFK Seminar in August 1995, although I didn't know it when I agreed to participate. The invitation, extended to six other veteran American investigators by the Secretariat of Culture of the City of Rio de Janeiro, alluded cryptically to "parallel powers" being on the agenda. When our delegation arrived at the Rio airport, a bus belonging to the Superior Court of the State of Rio de Janeiro was waiting. On board were plainclothes military police as personal guards, a precaution taken, I was told, because as a former FBI agent I might be targeted by the U.S. intelligence units that operated with impunity in Brazil. As it turned out, the court was our host. Held in the auditorium of the Tribunal of Justice, the seminar opened with the chief justice and five sitting judges who would moderate the panel discussions stipulating that the Kennedy murder was a coup d'état carried out by an American secret government whose Brazilian counterpart is known as "parallel powers." The purpose of the seminar was to draw a detailed picture of the Dallas coup so that the features of an incipient Brazilian one might be recognized. The country was only six years out of the nightmare of a military dictatorship that had lasted for three decades. "We have a fragile democracy," Judge Tecio Lins e Silva asserted. "We need to know how to recognize the threat and protect against it."

The 2000 electoral coup of George W. Bush greatly emboldened American intelligence hawks. Right out of the box, on January 3, 2001, staunch Bush backer Congressman Bob Barr of Georgia introduced a "Terrorist Elimination Act" to nullify a string of presidential executive orders forbidding the government to engage in assassinations. Coupled with the move was Bush's appointment of career covert operative Richard Armitage as deputy secretary of state under General Colin Powell. A tall, balding power-lifter whom Powell once referred to as "my white son," Armitage is more of a Rambo than a diplomat. According to a fellow Special Forces Vietnam veteran, he liked to "sit ambush" on the trails in Laos and Cambodia. During the Reagan years he was an assistant secretary of defense for international security affairs; government stipulations in the Oliver North trial cited him as one of the Defense Department officials responsible, through CIA links, for the illegal transfers of weapons to both Iran and the Contras. In 1989, as a result of the scandal, he was denied a high state post. Despite his shady past, Bush appointed Armitage to a position in which he can craft a more brutish foreign policy. The immorality code justifying the license to kill was perhaps best articulated by the CIA's late spymaster supreme, James Jesus Angleton: "If intelligence-gathering agencies are as necessary as I believe them to be, then they must repay our blind trust and acknowledge that there may always be moments in all secret organizations when tyranny manages to slip its leash."

As Oliver Stone put it, "despite the relative lack of happy endings in Turner's pieces, the reader comes away empowered, with renewed understanding that history and politics belong not to some select few but to all of us." I hope that *Rearview Mirror* has contributed in some measure to that empowerment by shedding light on the dark parapolitics of the FBI, CIA and private intelligence triad.

Index